JOHN WALKER
U.S.AGENT
AMERICAN ZEALOT

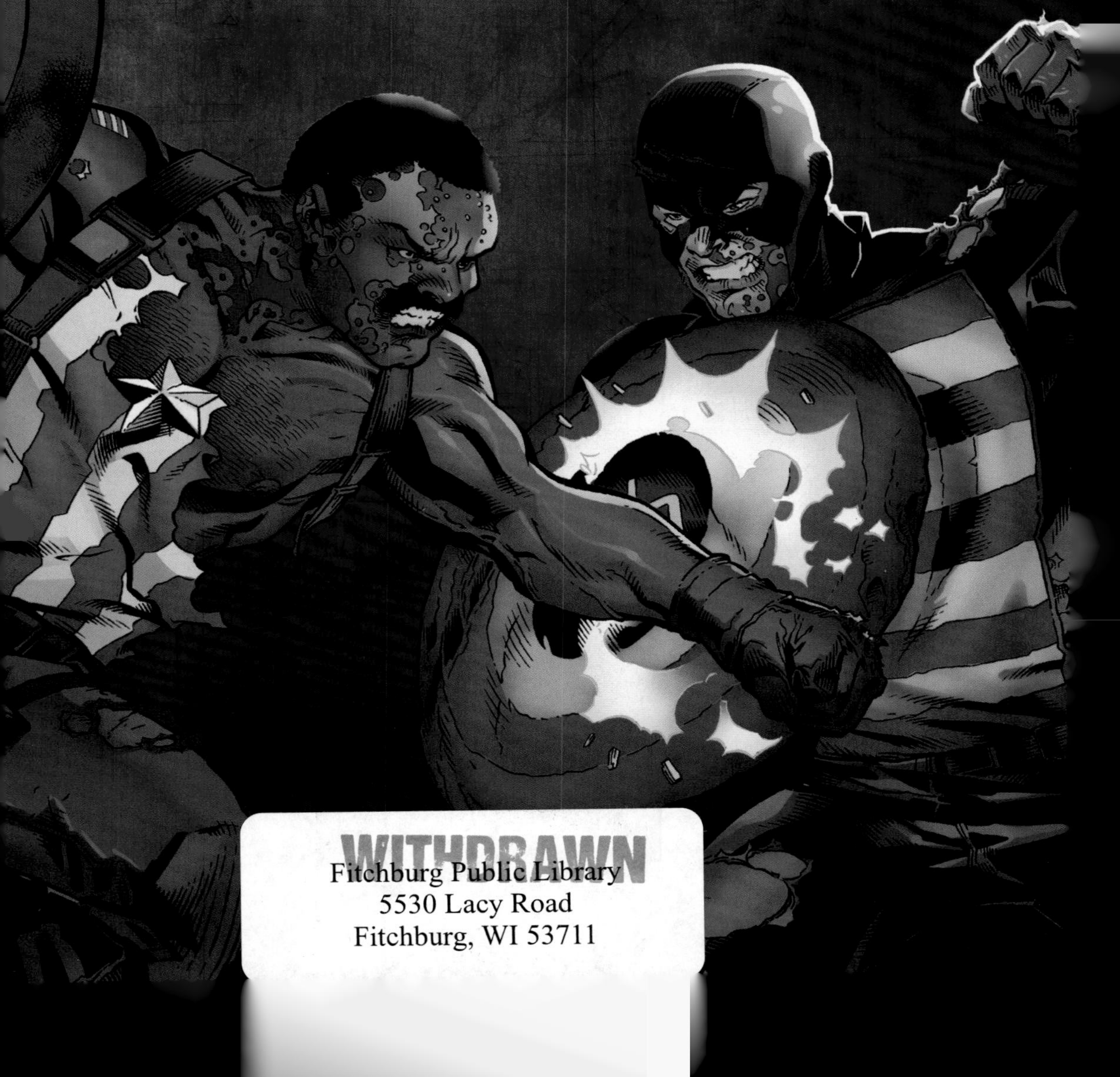

THE FIERCELY PATRIOTIC JOHN WALKER USES HIS SUPERHUMAN STRENGTH, AGILITY AND ENDURANCE—AND HIS SHIELD—TO DEFEND AMERICAN VALUES. ONCE, HE WAS CAPTAIN AMERICA. NOW, HE IS...

JOHN WALKER U.S.AGENT
AMERICAN ZEALOT

WRITER
PRIEST

PENCILER
GEORGES JEANTY

INKER
KARL STORY

COLORIST
MATT MILLA

LETTERER
VC'S JOE SABINO

COVER ART
MARCO CHECCHETTO

ASSISTANT EDITOR
MARTIN BIRO

ASSOCIATE EDITOR
ALANNA SMITH

EDITOR
TOM BREVOORT

SPECIAL THANKS TO **DAVE VAN DOMELEN, PHD**

COLLECTION EDITOR **DANIEL KIRCHHOFFER**
ASSISTANT MANAGING EDITOR **MAIA LOY**
ASSISTANT MANAGING EDITOR **LISA MONTALBANO**
SENIOR EDITOR, SPECIAL PROJECTS **JENNIFER GRÜNWALD**
VP, PRODUCTION & SPECIAL PROJECTS **JEFF YOUNGQUIST**
BOOK DESIGNER **STACIE ZUCKER**
SVP PRINT, SALES & MARKETING **DAVID GABRIEL**
EDITOR IN CHIEF **C.B. CEBULSKI**

U.S.AGENT: AMERICAN ZEALOT. Contains material originally published in magazine form as U.S.AGENT (2020) #1-5. First printing 2021. ISBN 978-1-302-92476-8. Published by MARVEL WORLDWIDE INC., a subsidiary of MARVEL ENTERTAINMENT, LLC. OFFICE OF PUBLICATION: 1290 Avenue of the Americas, New York, NY 10104. **Printed in Canada.** KEVIN FEIGE, Chief Creative Officer; DAN BUCKLEY, President, Marvel Entertainment; JOE QUESADA, EVP & Creative Director; DAVID BOGART, Associate Publisher & SVP of Talent Affairs; TOM BREVOORT, VP, Executive Editor; NICK LOWE, Executive Editor, VP of Content, Digital Publishing; DAVID GABRIEL, VP of Print & Digital Publishing; JEFF YOUNGQUIST, VP of Production & Special Projects; ALEX MORALES, Director of Publishing Operations; DAN EDINGTON, Managing Editor; RICKEY PURDIN, Director of Talent Relations; JENNIFER GRÜNWALD, Senior Editor, Special Projects; SUSAN CRESPI Production Manager; STAN LEE, Chairman Emeritus. For information regarding advertising in Marvel Comics or on Marvel.com, please contact Vit DeBellis, Custom Solutions & Integrated Advertising Manager, at vdebellis@marvel.com. For Marvel subscription inquiries, please call 888-511-5480. **Manufactured between 4/23/2021 and 6/1/2021 by SOLISCO PRINTERS, SCOTT, QC, CANADA.**

10 9 8 7 6 5 4 3 2 1

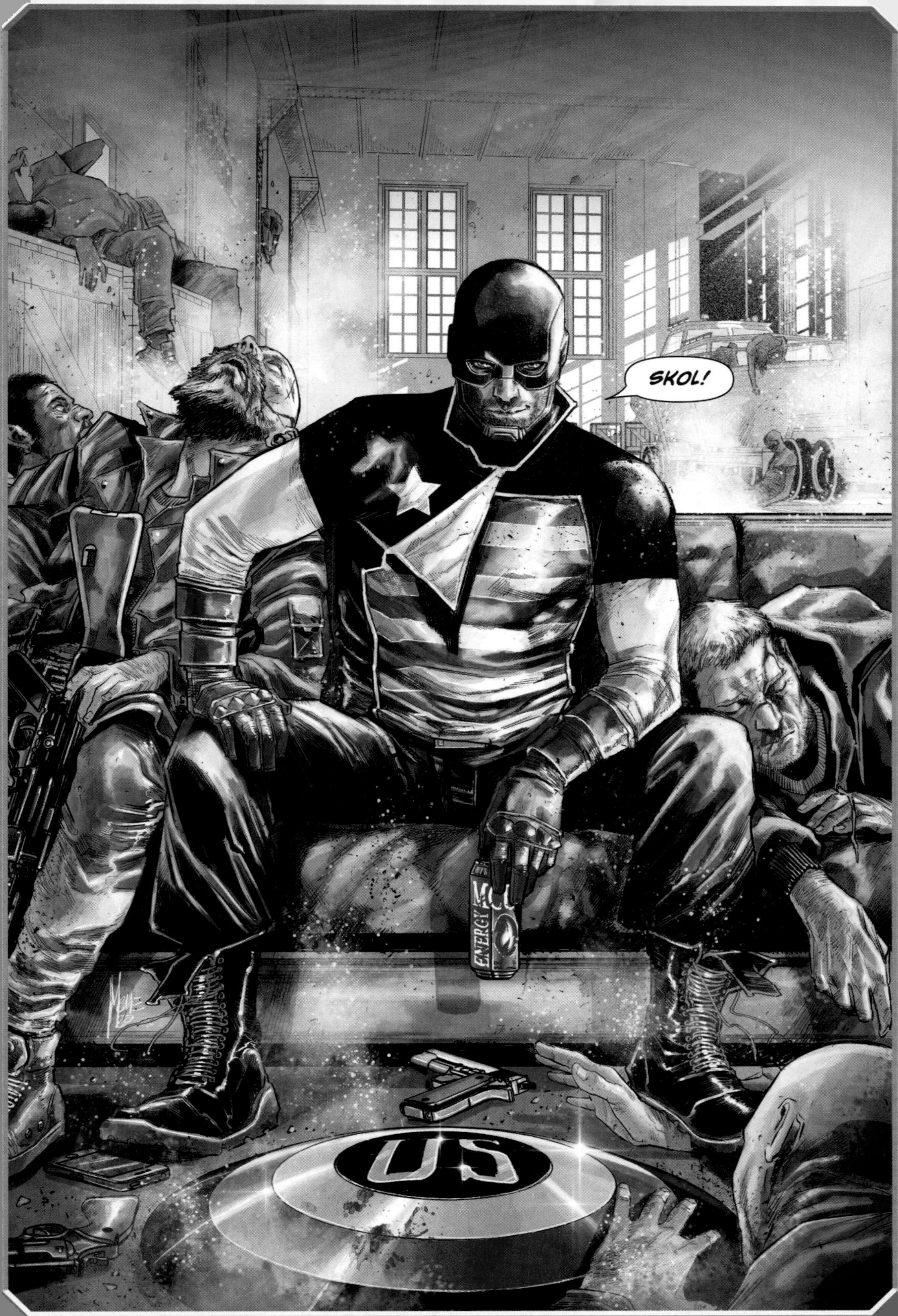
SKOL!

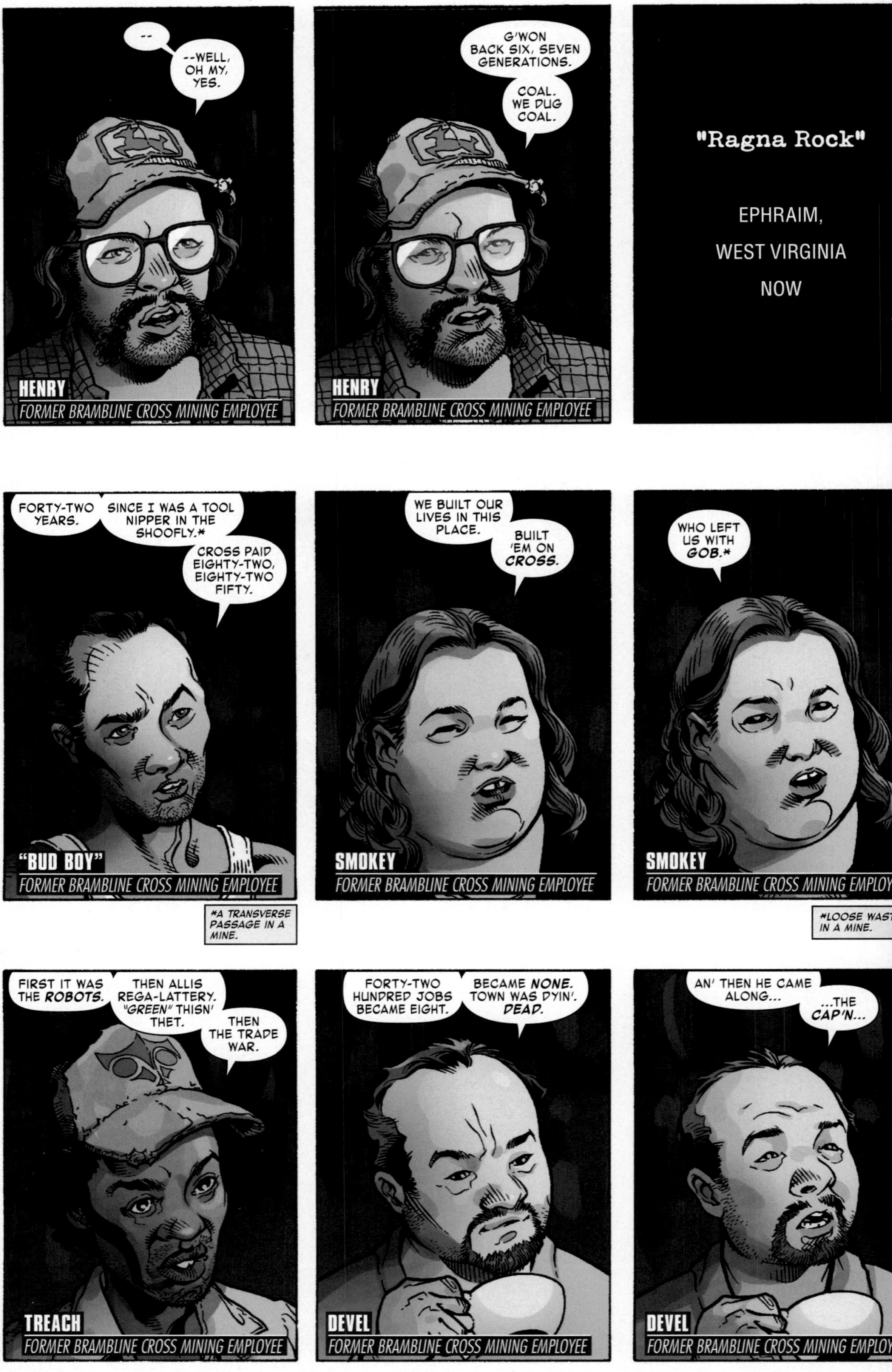
--
--WELL, OH MY, YES.
HENRY
FORMER BRAMBLINE CROSS MINING EMPLOYEE
G'WON BACK SIX, SEVEN GENERATIONS.
COAL. WE DUG COAL.
HENRY
FORMER BRAMBLINE CROSS MINING EMPLOYEE
"Ragna Rock"
EPHRAIM,
WEST VIRGINIA
NOW
FORTY-TWO YEARS.
SINCE I WAS A TOOL NIPPER IN THE SHOOFLY.*
CROSS PAID EIGHTY-TWO, EIGHTY-TWO FIFTY.
"BUD BOY"
FORMER BRAMBLINE CROSS MINING EMPLOYEE
*A TRANSVERSE PASSAGE IN A MINE.
WE BUILT OUR LIVES IN THIS PLACE.
BUILT 'EM ON CROSS.
SMOKEY
FORMER BRAMBLINE CROSS MINING EMPLOYEE
WHO LEFT US WITH GOB.*
SMOKEY
FORMER BRAMBLINE CROSS MINING EMPLOY
*LOOSE WAST IN A MINE.
FIRST IT WAS THE ROBOTS.
THEN ALLIS REGA-LATTERY. "GREEN" THISN' THET.
THEN THE TRADE WAR.
TREACH
FORMER BRAMBLINE CROSS MINING EMPLOYEE
FORTY-TWO HUNDRED JOBS BECAME EIGHT.
BECAME NONE. TOWN WAS DYIN'. DEAD.
DEVEL
FORMER BRAMBLINE CROSS MINING EMPLOYEE
AN' THEN HE CAME ALONG...
...THE CAP'N...
DEVEL
FORMER BRAMBLINE CROSS MINING EMPLOY

MARVEL COMICS PRESENTS:
JOHN WALKER
U.S.AGENT
AMERICAN ZEALOT
CHAPTER ONE: LEGEND
US

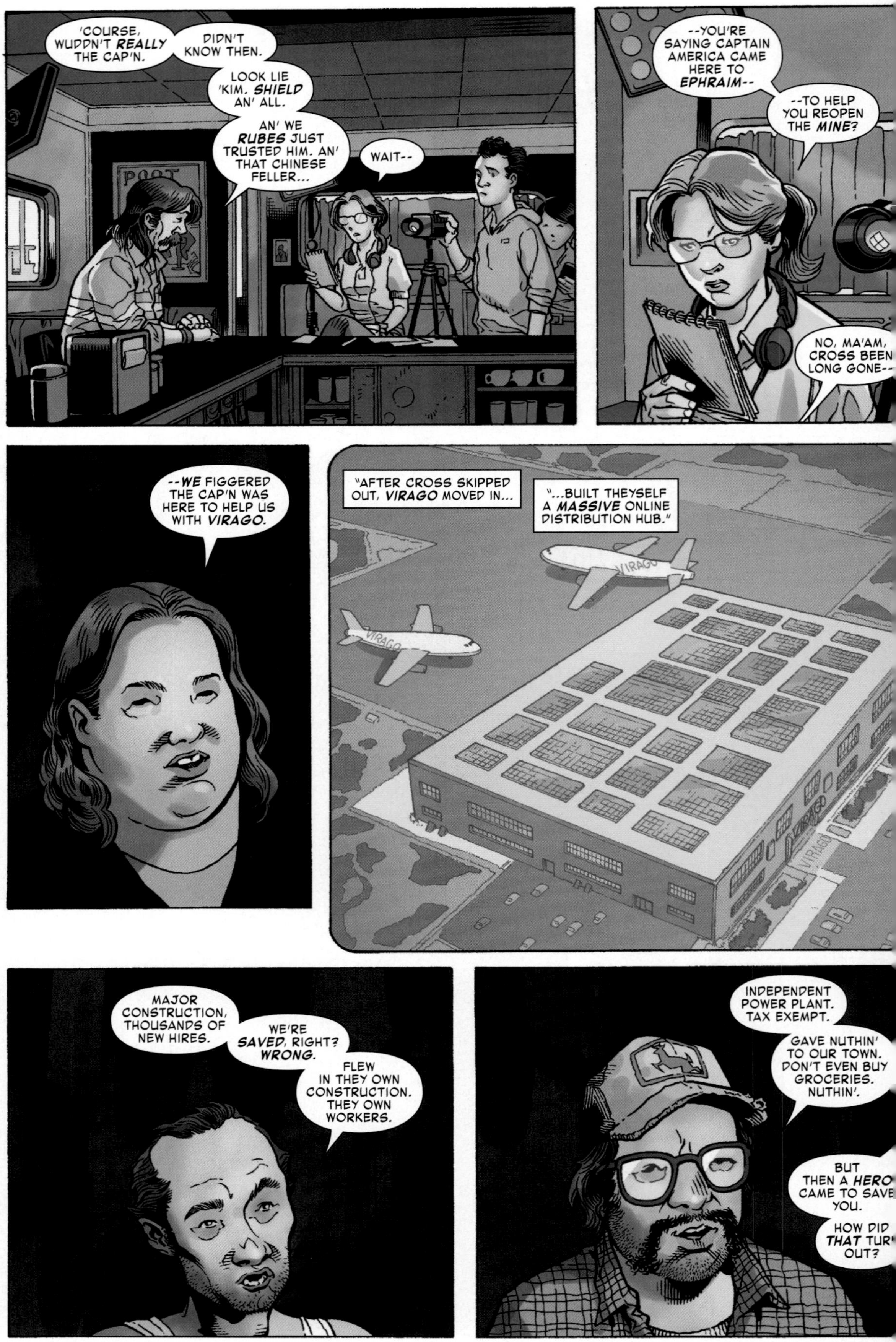

'COURSE, WUDDN'T REALLY THE CAP'N.
DIDN'T KNOW THEN.
LOOK LIE 'KIM. SHIELD AN' ALL.
AN' WE RUBES JUST TRUSTED HIM. AN' THAT CHINESE FELLER...
WAIT--
--YOU'RE SAYING CAPTAIN AMERICA CAME HERE TO EPHRAIM--
--TO HELP YOU REOPEN THE MINE?
NO, MA'AM, CROSS BEEN LONG GONE--
--WE FIGGERED THE CAP'N WAS HERE TO HELP US WITH VIRAGO.
"AFTER CROSS SKIPPED OUT, VIRAGO MOVED IN...
"...BUILT THEYSELF A MASSIVE ONLINE DISTRIBUTION HUB."
VIRAGO
VIRAGO
VIRAGO
VIRAGO
MAJOR CONSTRUCTION, THOUSANDS OF NEW HIRES.
WE'RE SAVED, RIGHT? WRONG.
FLEW IN THEY OWN CONSTRUCTION. THEY OWN WORKERS.
INDEPENDENT POWER PLANT. TAX EXEMPT.
GAVE NUTHIN' TO OUR TOWN. DON'T EVEN BUY GROCERIES. NUTHIN'.
BUT THEN A HERO CAME TO SAVE YOU.
HOW DID THAT TUR OUT?

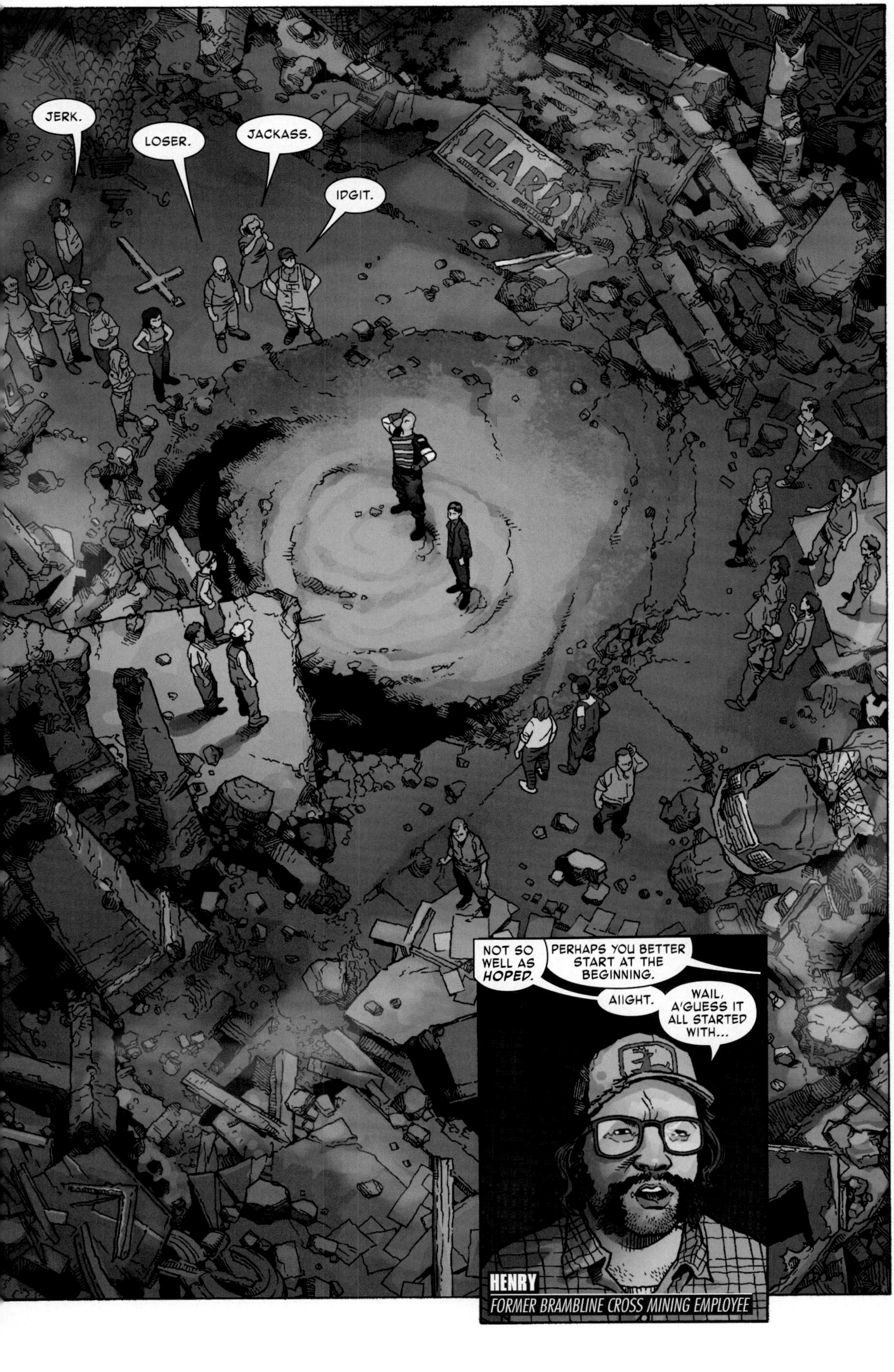
JERK.
LOSER.
JACKASS.
IDGIT.
HARD
NOT SO WELL AS *HOPED*.
PERHAPS YOU BETTER START AT THE BEGINNING.
AIIGHT.
WAIL, A'GUESS IT ALL STARTED WITH...
HENRY
FORMER BRAMBLINE CROSS MINING EMPLOYEE

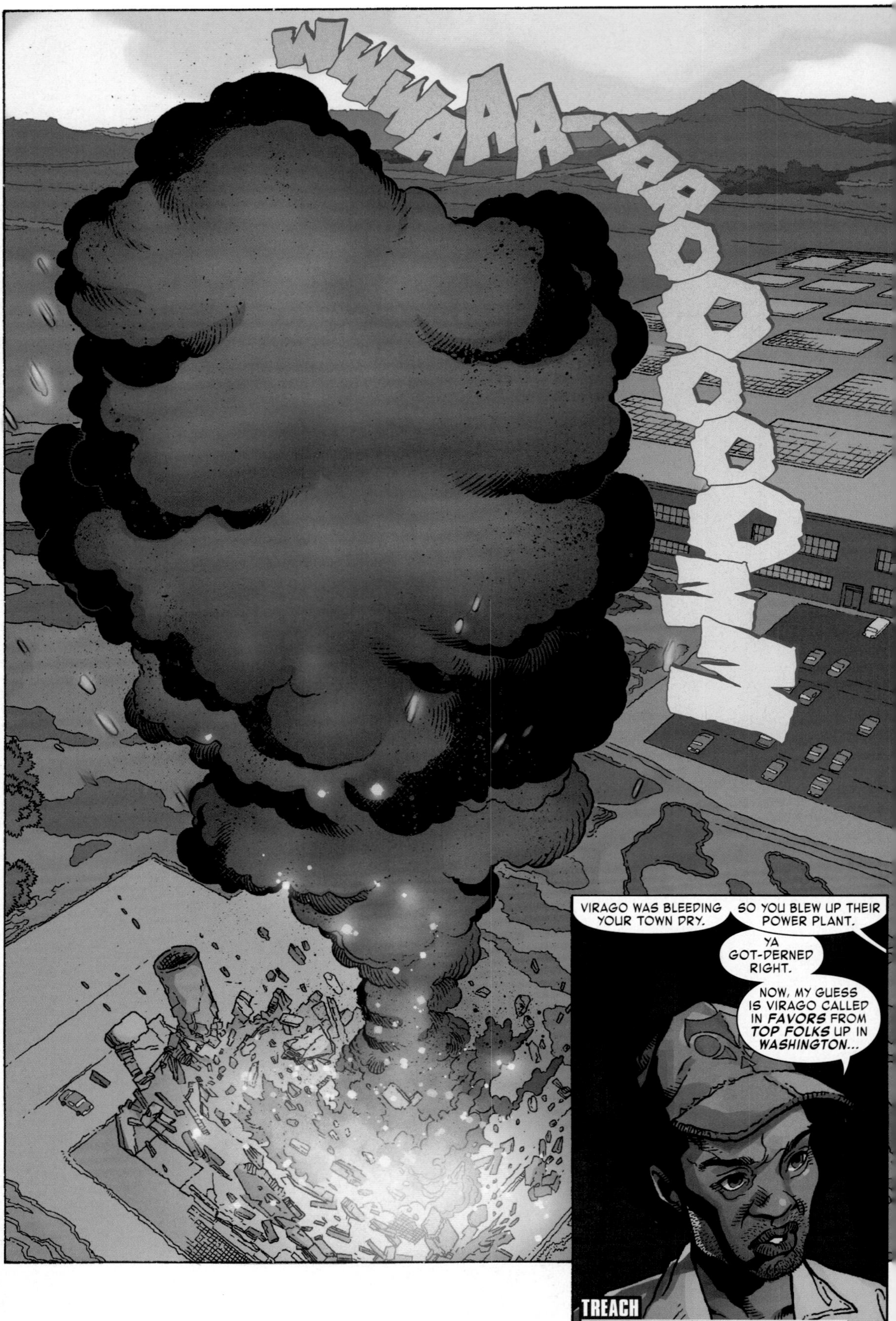
WWWAAA-'RROOOOOOOM
VIRAGO WAS BLEEDING YOUR TOWN DRY.
SO YOU BLEW UP THEIR POWER PLANT.
YA GOT-DERNED RIGHT.
NOW, MY GUESS IS VIRAGO CALLED IN *FAVORS* FROM *TOP FOLKS* UP IN *WASHINGTON*...
TREACH
FORMER BRAMBLINE CROSS MINING EMPLOYEE

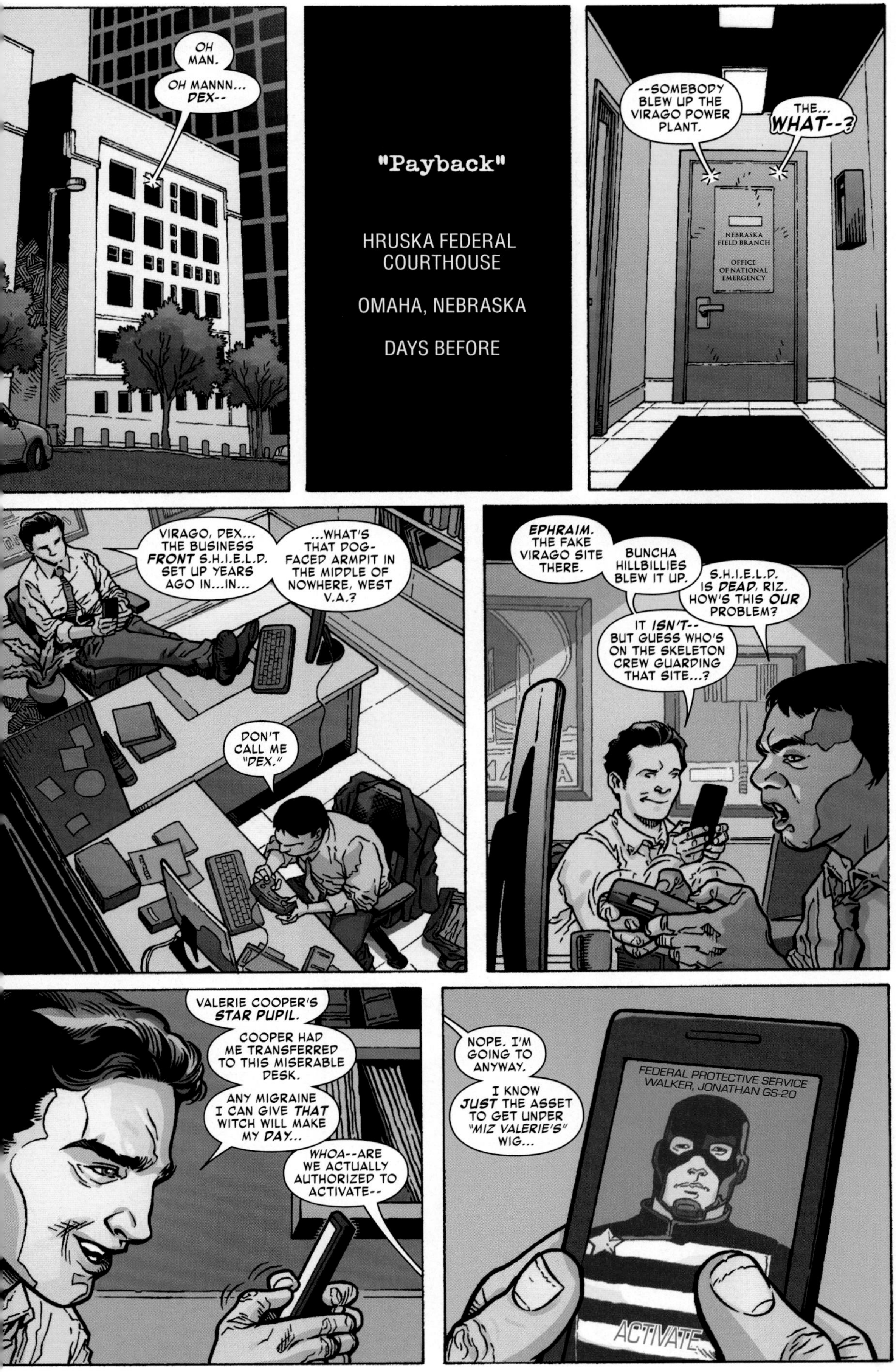
OH MAN.
OH MANNN... DEX--
"Payback"
HRUSKA FEDERAL COURTHOUSE
OMAHA, NEBRASKA
DAYS BEFORE
--SOMEBODY BLEW UP THE VIRAGO POWER PLANT.
THE... WHAT--?
NEBRASKA FIELD BRANCH
OFFICE OF NATIONAL EMERGENCY
VIRAGO, DEX... THE BUSINESS FRONT S.H.I.E.L.D. SET UP YEARS AGO IN...IN...
...WHAT'S THAT DOG-FACED ARMPIT IN THE MIDDLE OF NOWHERE, WEST V.A.?
DON'T CALL ME "DEX."
EPHRAIM. THE FAKE VIRAGO SITE THERE.
BUNCHA HILLBILLIES BLEW IT UP.
S.H.I.E.L.D. IS DEAD, RIZ. HOW'S THIS OUR PROBLEM?
IT ISN'T-- BUT GUESS WHO'S ON THE SKELETON CREW GUARDING THAT SITE...?
VALERIE COOPER'S STAR PUPIL.
COOPER HAD ME TRANSFERRED TO THIS MISERABLE DESK.
ANY MIGRAINE I CAN GIVE THAT WITCH WILL MAKE MY DAY...
WHOA--ARE WE ACTUALLY AUTHORIZED TO ACTIVATE--
NOPE. I'M GOING TO ANYWAY.
I KNOW JUST THE ASSET TO GET UNDER "MIZ VALERIE'S" WIG...
FEDERAL PROTECTIVE SERVICE
WALKER, JONATHAN GS-20
ACTIVATE

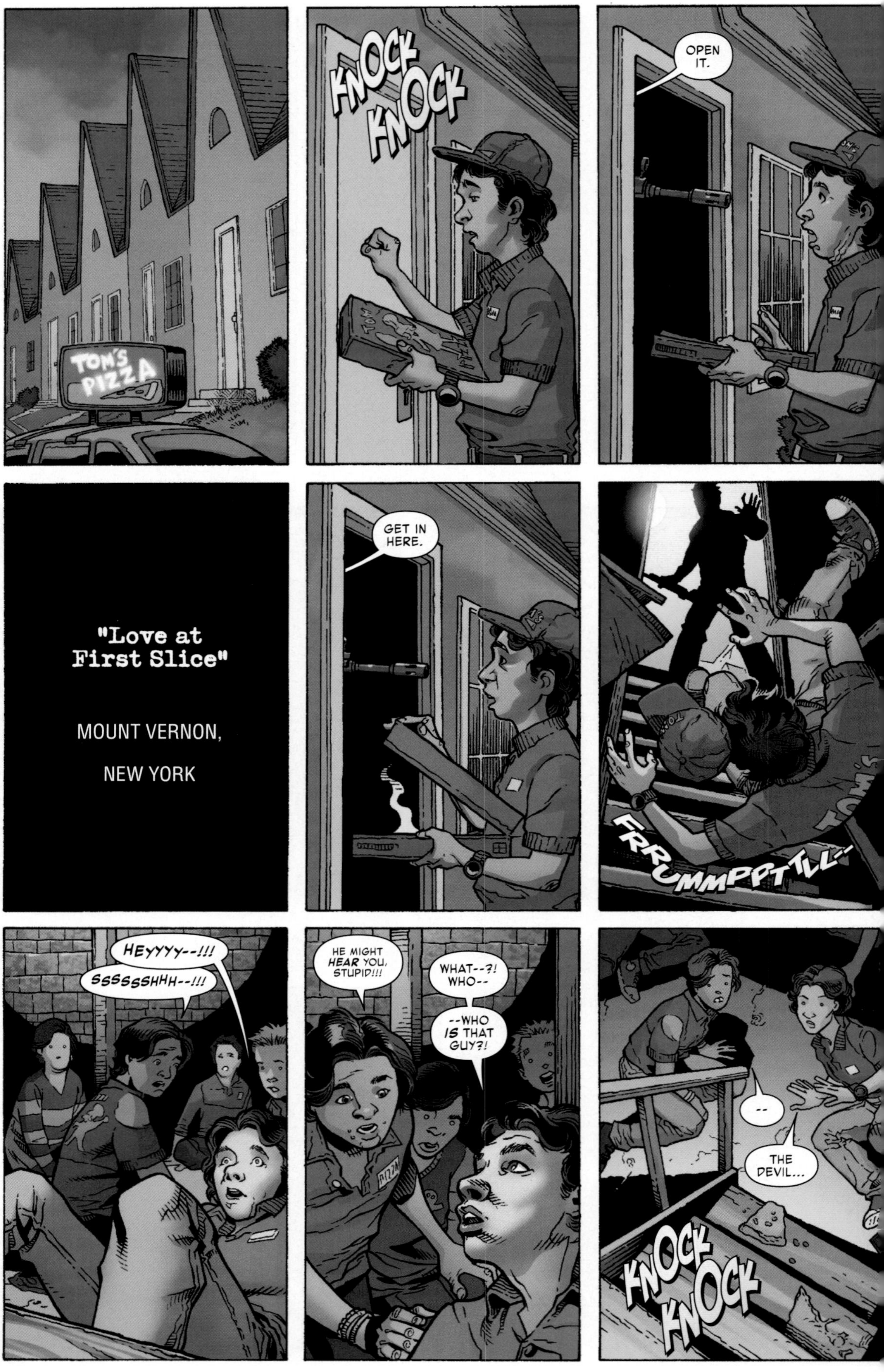
TOM'S PIZZA
KNOCK KNOCK
OPEN IT.
"Love at First Slice"
MOUNT VERNON,
NEW YORK
GET IN HERE.
FRRUMMPPTTLL--
HEYYYY--!!!
SSSSSSHHH--!!!
HE MIGHT HEAR YOU, STUPID!!!
WHAT--?! WHO--
--WHO IS THAT GUY?!
--
THE DEVIL...
KNOCK KNOCK

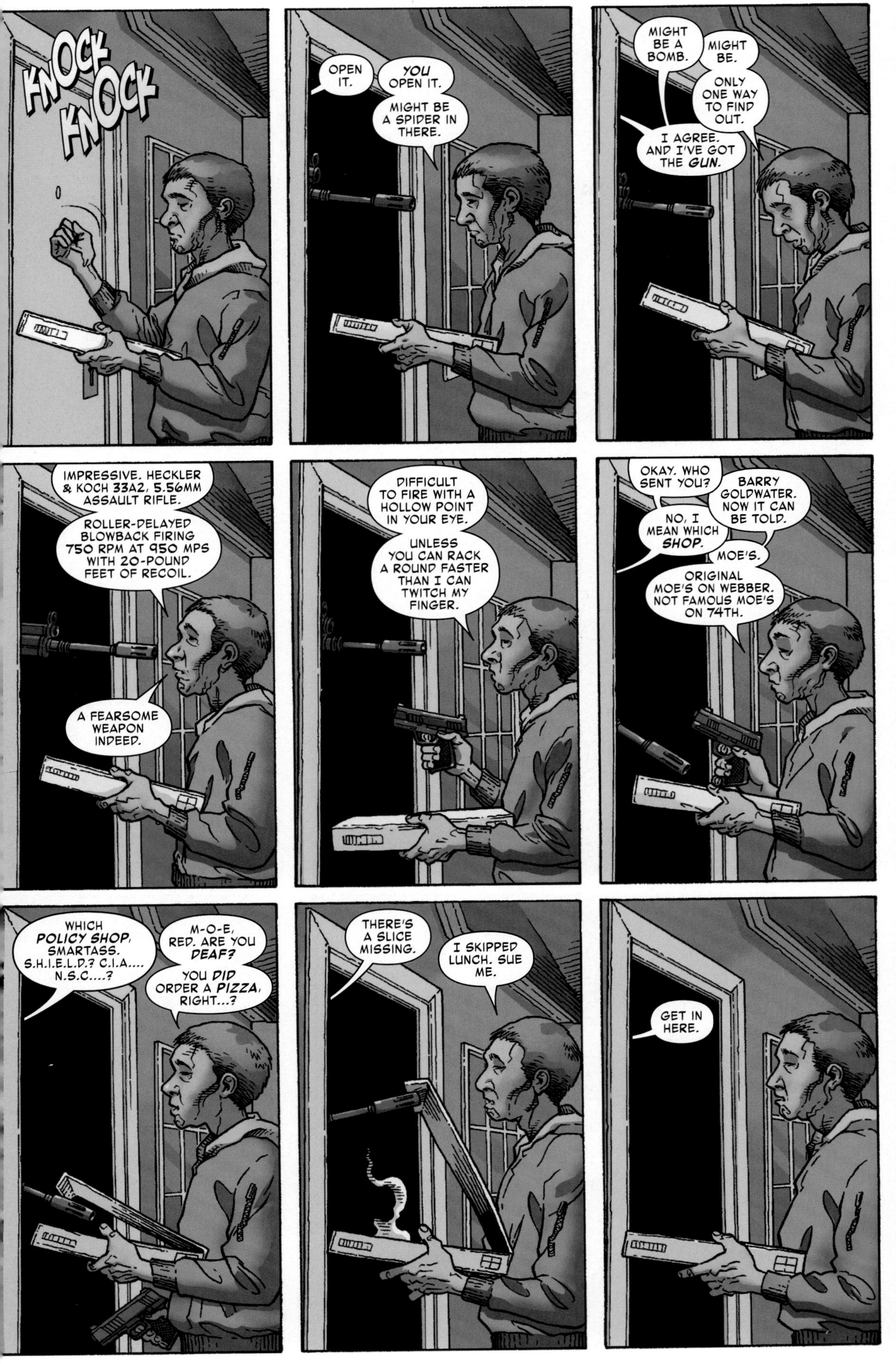
KNOCK KNOCK
OPEN IT.
YOU OPEN IT.
MIGHT BE A SPIDER IN THERE.
MIGHT BE A BOMB.
MIGHT BE.
ONLY ONE WAY TO FIND OUT.
I AGREE. AND I'VE GOT THE GUN.
IMPRESSIVE. HECKLER & KOCH 33A2, 5.56MM ASSAULT RIFLE.
ROLLER-DELAYED BLOWBACK FIRING 750 RPM AT 950 MPS WITH 20-POUND FEET OF RECOIL.
A FEARSOME WEAPON INDEED.
DIFFICULT TO FIRE WITH A HOLLOW POINT IN YOUR EYE.
UNLESS YOU CAN RACK A ROUND FASTER THAN I CAN TWITCH MY FINGER.
OKAY. WHO SENT YOU?
BARRY GOLDWATER. NOW IT CAN BE TOLD.
NO, I MEAN WHICH SHOP.
MOE'S.
ORIGINAL MOE'S ON WEBBER. NOT FAMOUS MOE'S ON 74TH.
WHICH POLICY SHOP, SMARTASS. S.H.I.E.L.D.? C.I.A.... N.S.C....?
M-O-E, RED. ARE YOU DEAF?
YOU DID ORDER A PIZZA, RIGHT...?
THERE'S A SLICE MISSING.
I SKIPPED LUNCH. SUE ME.
GET IN HERE.

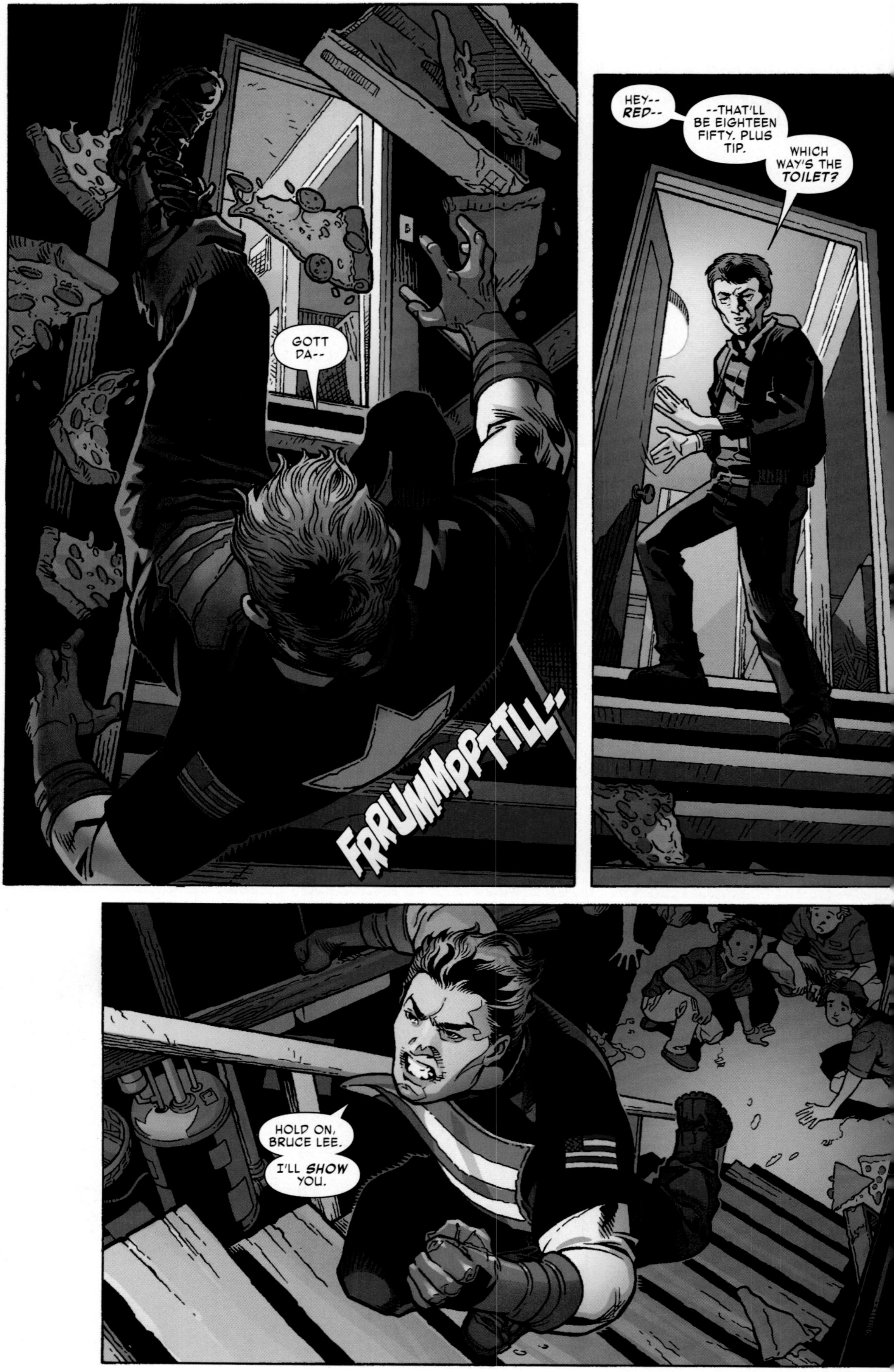
GOTT DA--
FRRUMMPPTTLL--
HEY-- RED--
--THAT'LL BE EIGHTEEN FIFTY. PLUS TIP.
WHICH WAY'S THE TOILET?
HOLD ON, BRUCE LEE.
I'LL SHOW YOU.

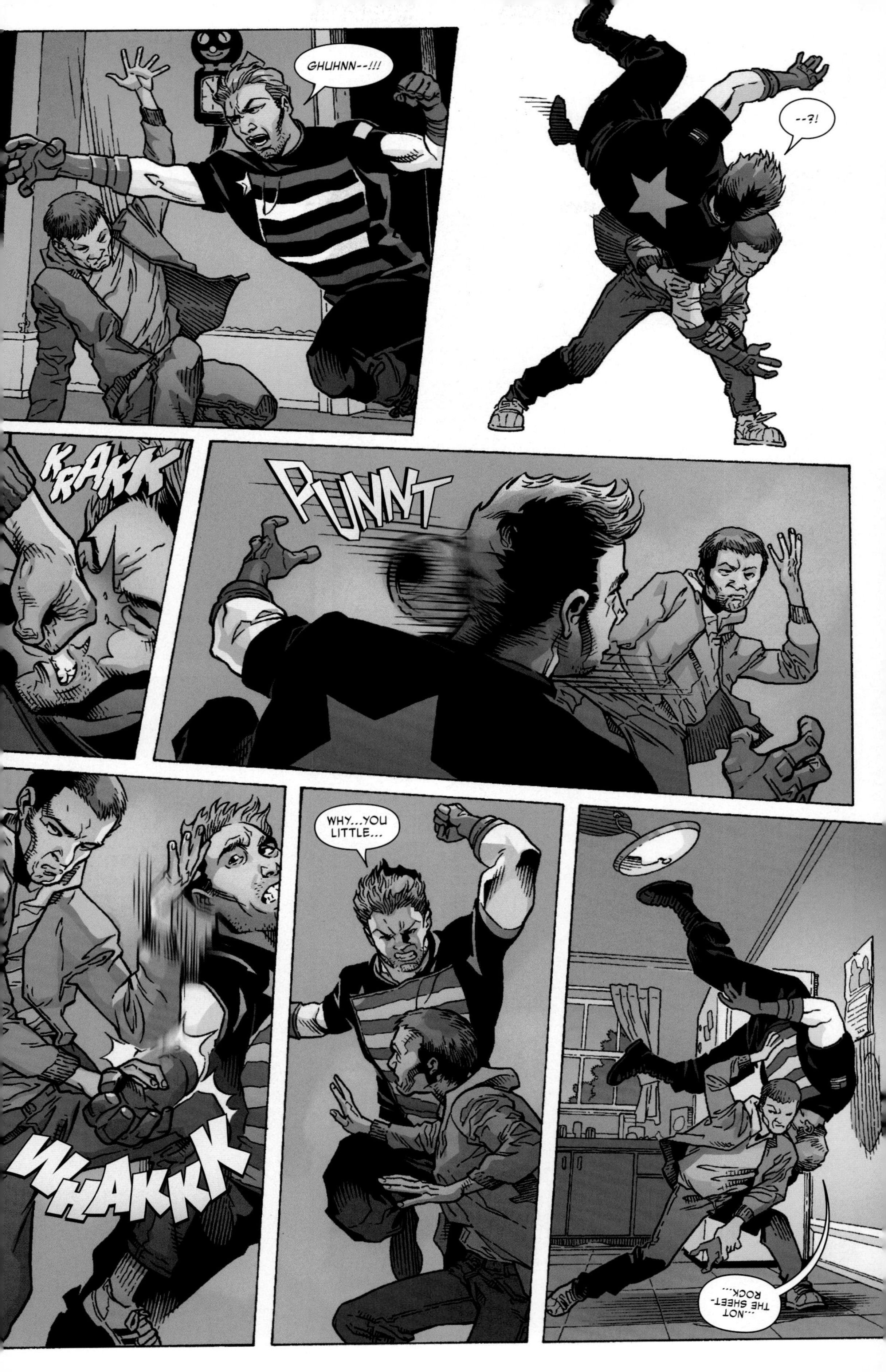
GHUHNN--!!!
--?!
KRAKK
PUNNT
WHAKKK
WHY...YOU LITTLE...
...NOT THE SHEET-ROCK...

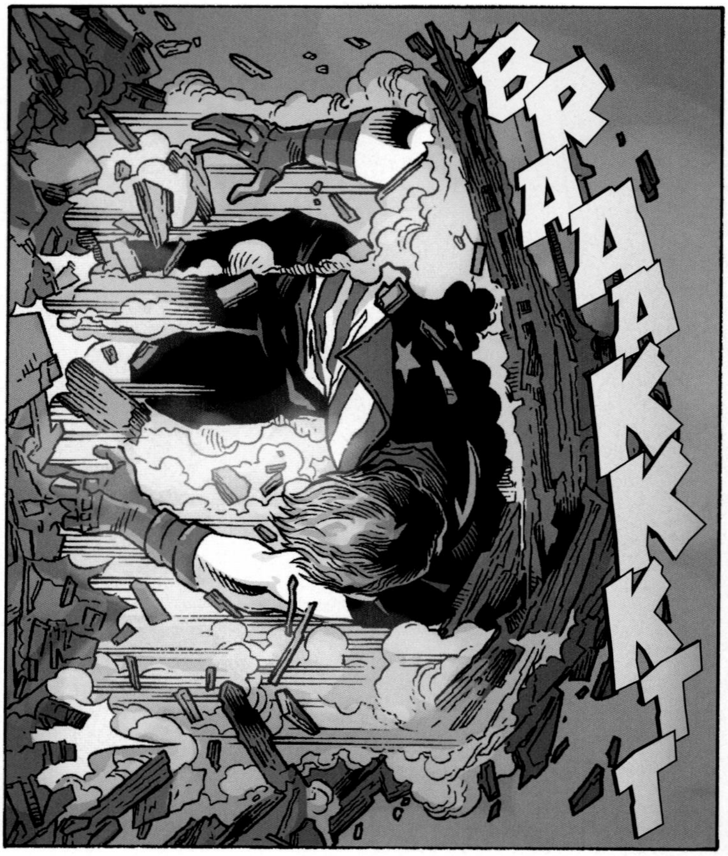
BRAAAKKTTT

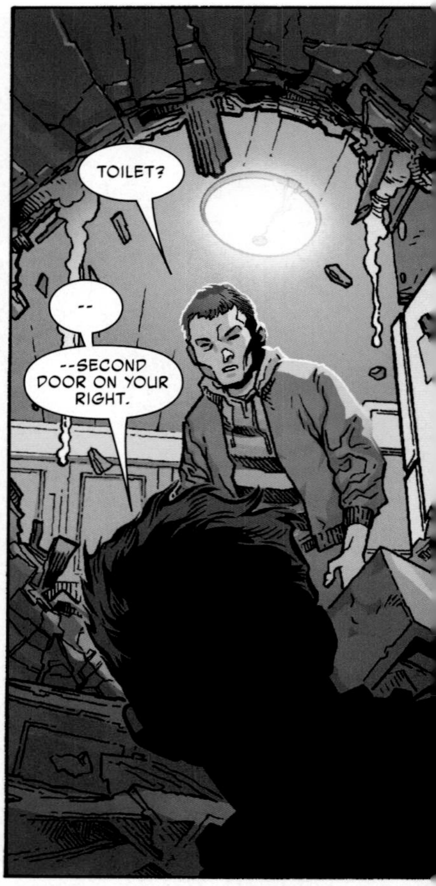
TOILET?
--
--SECOND DOOR ON YOUR RIGHT.

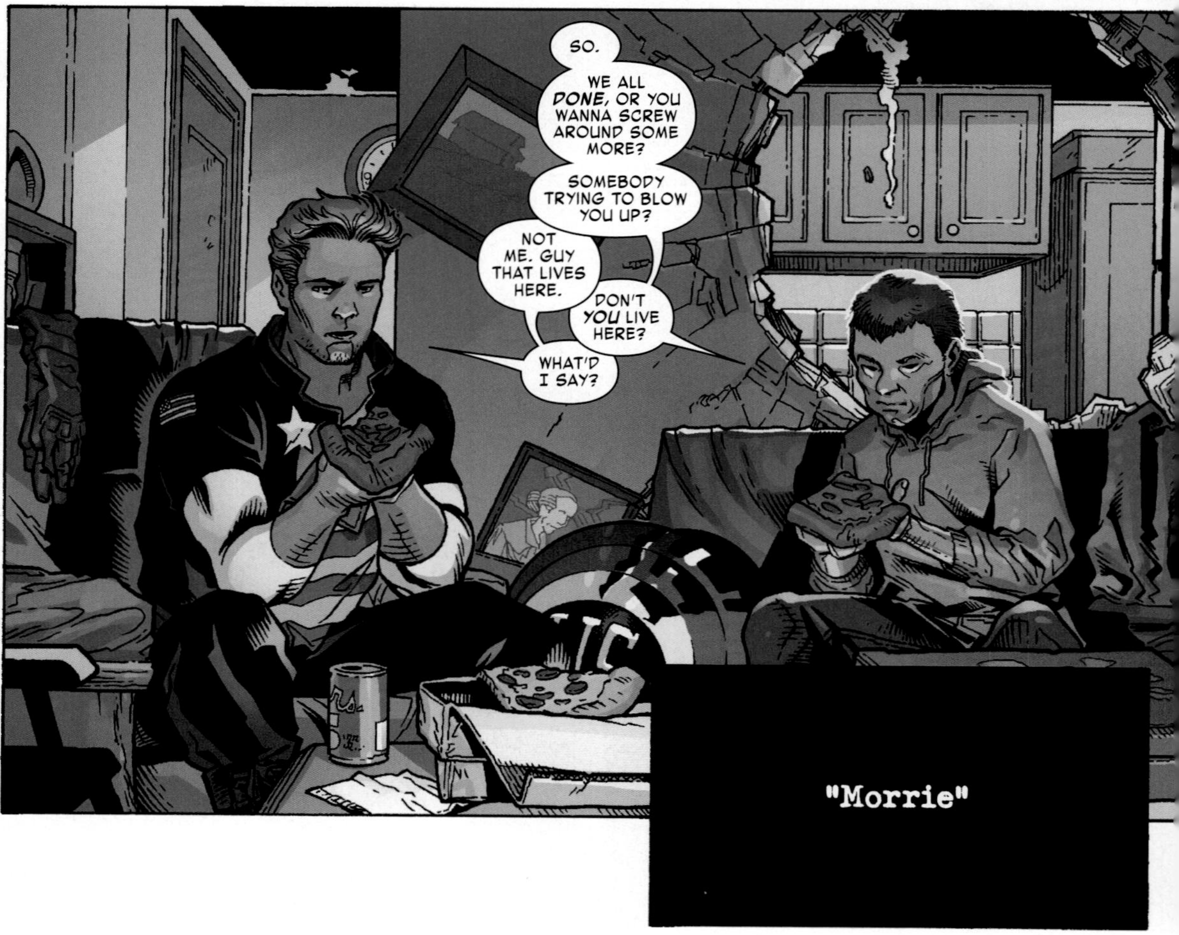
SO.
WE ALL *DONE,* OR YOU WANNA SCREW AROUND SOME MORE?
SOMEBODY TRYING TO BLOW YOU UP?
NOT ME. GUY THAT LIVES HERE.
DON'T *YOU* LIVE HERE?
WHAT'D I SAY?

"Morrie"

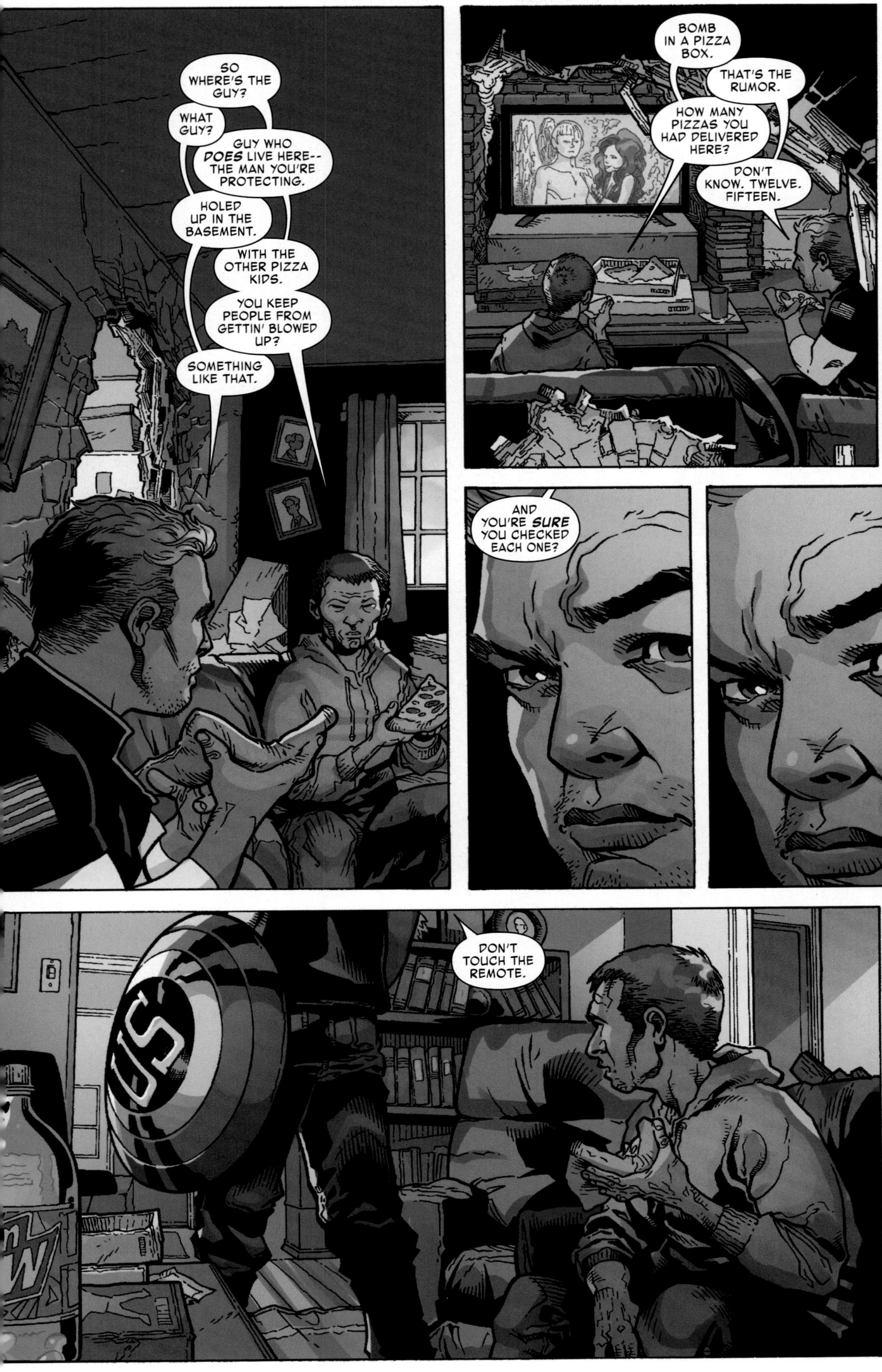
SO WHERE'S THE GUY?
WHAT GUY?
GUY WHO DOES LIVE HERE-- THE MAN YOU'RE PROTECTING.
HOLED UP IN THE BASEMENT.
WITH THE OTHER PIZZA KIDS.
YOU KEEP PEOPLE FROM GETTIN' BLOWED UP?
SOMETHING LIKE THAT.
BOMB IN A PIZZA BOX.
THAT'S THE RUMOR.
HOW MANY PIZZAS YOU HAD DELIVERED HERE?
DON'T KNOW. TWELVE. FIFTEEN.
AND YOU'RE SURE YOU CHECKED EACH ONE?
DON'T TOUCH THE REMOTE.
US

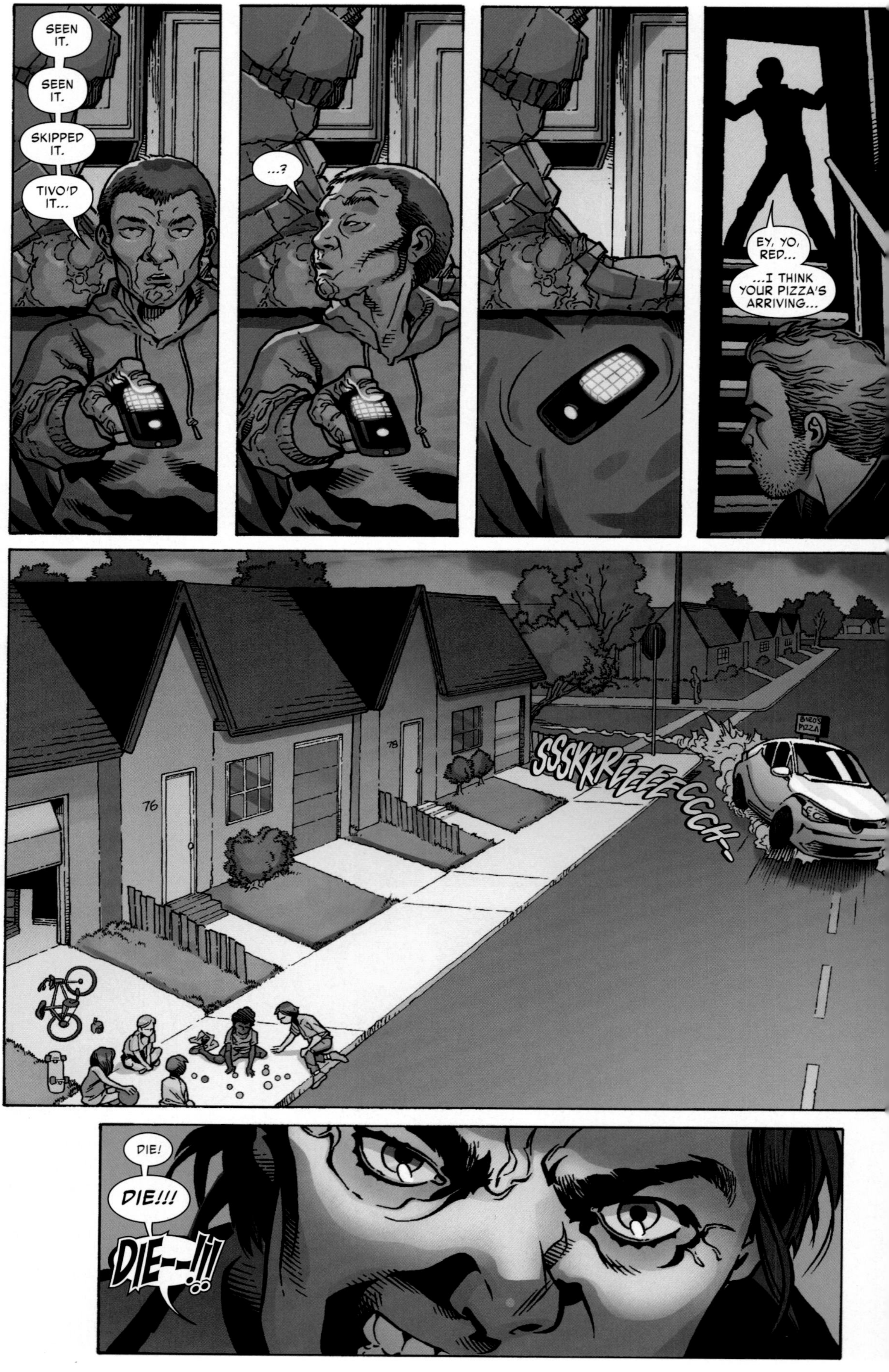
SEEN IT.
SEEN IT.
SKIPPED IT.
TIVO'D IT...
...?
EY, YO, RED...
...I THINK YOUR PIZZA'S ARRIVING...
SSSKKREEEEECCCH-
DIE!
DIE!!!
DIE--!!!

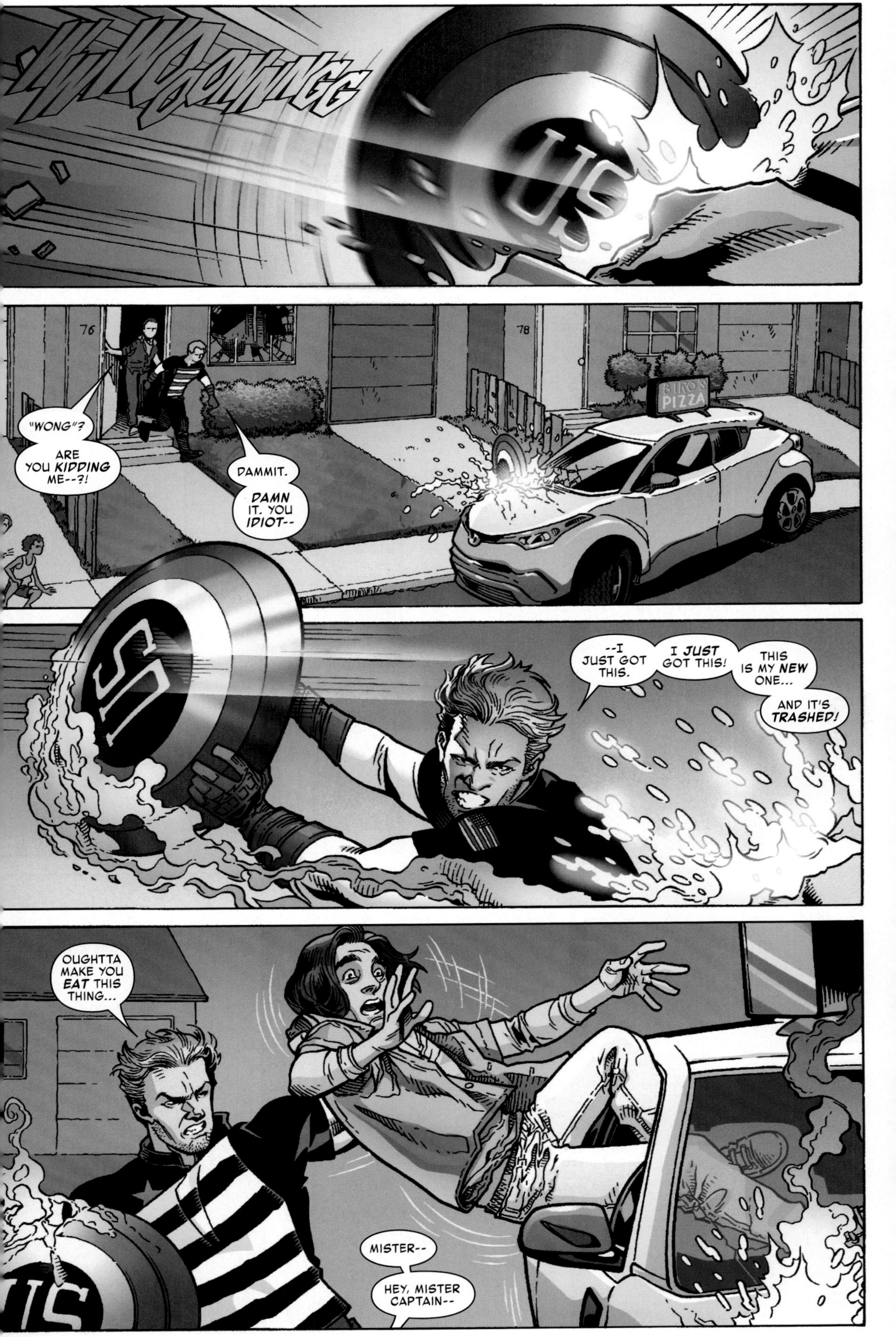
76
78
BIRO'S PIZZA
"WONG"? ARE YOU KIDDING ME--?!
DAMMIT. DAMN IT. YOU IDIOT--
--I JUST GOT THIS.
I JUST GOT THIS!
THIS IS MY NEW ONE...
AND IT'S TRASHED!
OUGHTTA MAKE YOU EAT THIS THING...
MISTER--
HEY, MISTER CAPTAIN--

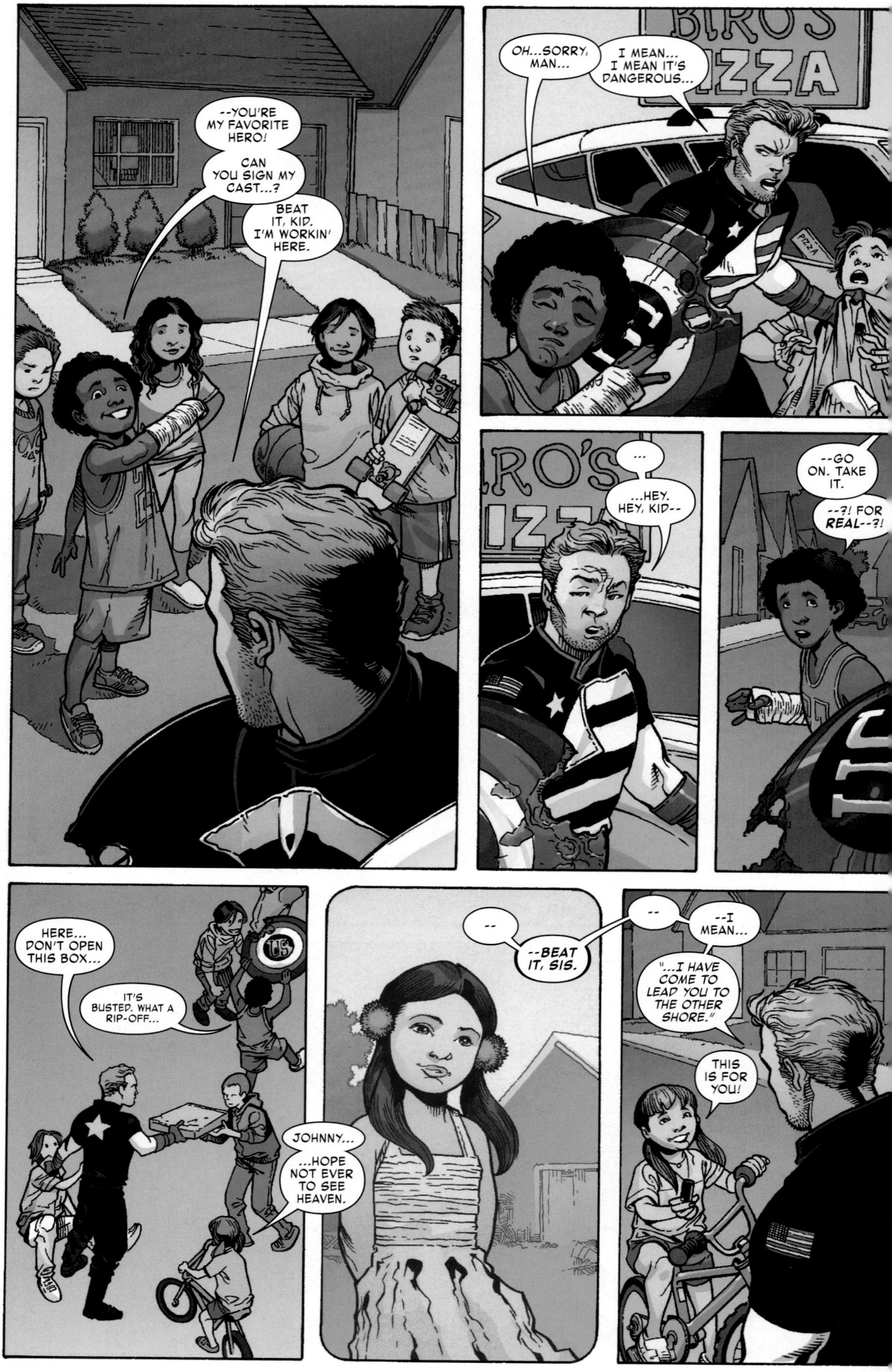
--YOU'RE MY FAVORITE HERO!
CAN YOU SIGN MY CAST...?
BEAT IT, KID. I'M WORKIN' HERE.
BIRO'S PIZZA
OH...SORRY, MAN...
I MEAN... I MEAN IT'S DANGEROUS...
...
...HEY. HEY, KID--
--GO ON. TAKE IT.
--?! FOR REAL--?!
HERE... DON'T OPEN THIS BOX...
IT'S BUSTED. WHAT A RIP-OFF...
JOHNNY...
...HOPE NOT EVER TO SEE HEAVEN.
--
--BEAT IT, SIS.
--
--I MEAN...
"...I HAVE COME TO LEAD YOU TO THE OTHER SHORE."
THIS IS FOR YOU!

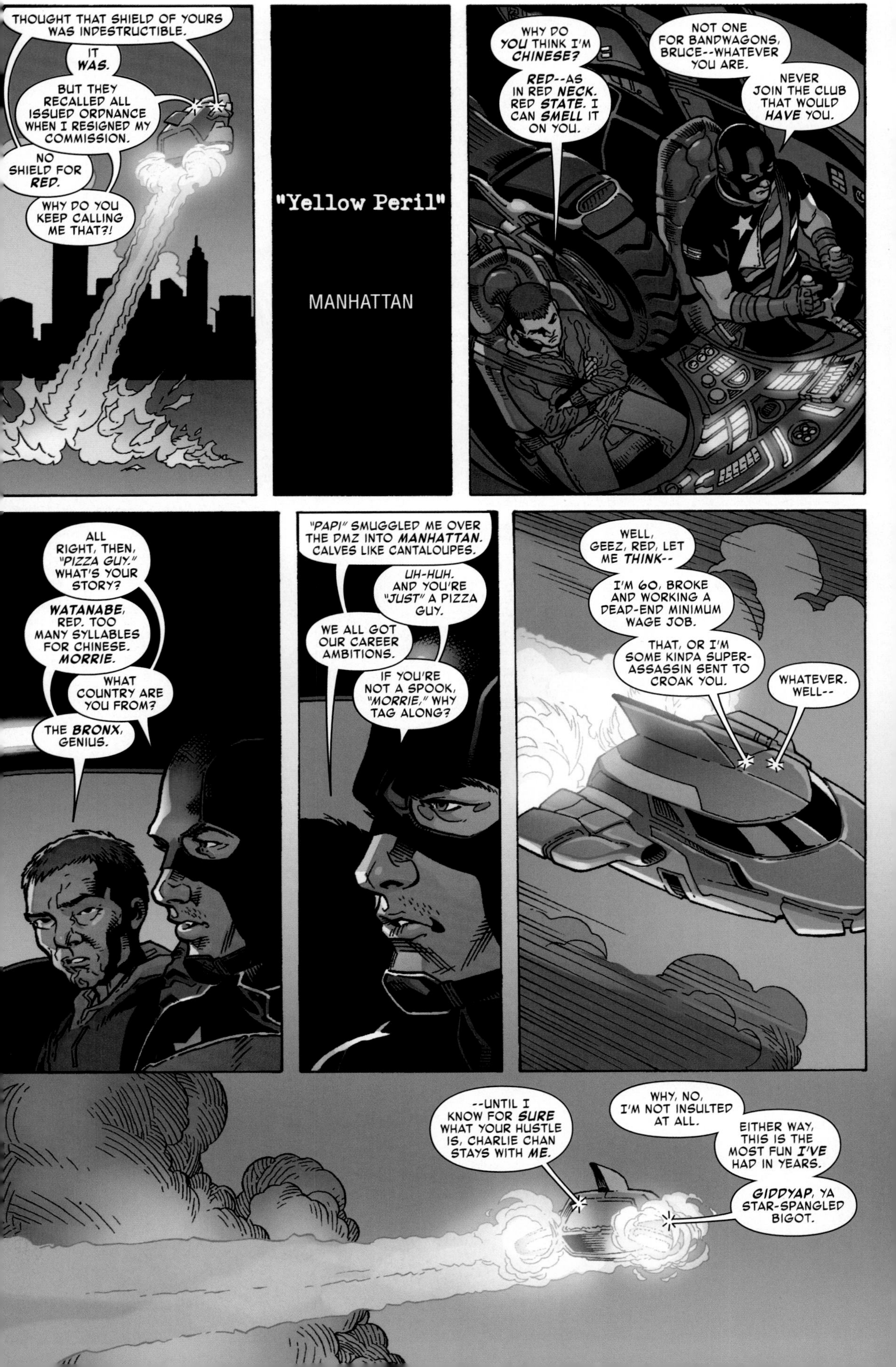
THOUGHT THAT SHIELD OF YOURS WAS INDESTRUCTIBLE.
IT WAS.
BUT THEY RECALLED ALL ISSUED ORDNANCE WHEN I RESIGNED MY COMMISSION.
NO SHIELD FOR RED.
WHY DO YOU KEEP CALLING ME THAT?!
"Yellow Peril"
MANHATTAN
WHY DO YOU THINK I'M CHINESE?
RED--AS IN RED NECK. RED STATE. I CAN SMELL IT ON YOU.
NOT ONE FOR BANDWAGONS, BRUCE--WHATEVER YOU ARE.
NEVER JOIN THE CLUB THAT WOULD HAVE YOU.
ALL RIGHT, THEN, "PIZZA GUY." WHAT'S YOUR STORY?
WATANABE, RED. TOO MANY SYLLABLES FOR CHINESE. MORRIE.
WHAT COUNTRY ARE YOU FROM?
THE BRONX, GENIUS.
"PAPI" SMUGGLED ME OVER THE DMZ INTO MANHATTAN. CALVES LIKE CANTALOUPES.
UH-HUH. AND YOU'RE "JUST" A PIZZA GUY.
WE ALL GOT OUR CAREER AMBITIONS.
IF YOU'RE NOT A SPOOK, "MORRIE," WHY TAG ALONG?
WELL, GEEZ, RED, LET ME THINK--
I'M 60, BROKE AND WORKING A DEAD-END MINIMUM WAGE JOB.
THAT, OR I'M SOME KINDA SUPER-ASSASSIN SENT TO CROAK YOU.
WHATEVER. WELL--
--UNTIL I KNOW FOR SURE WHAT YOUR HUSTLE IS, CHARLIE CHAN STAYS WITH ME.
WHY, NO, I'M NOT INSULTED AT ALL.
EITHER WAY, THIS IS THE MOST FUN I'VE HAD IN YEARS.
GIDDYAP, YA STAR-SPANGLED BIGOT.

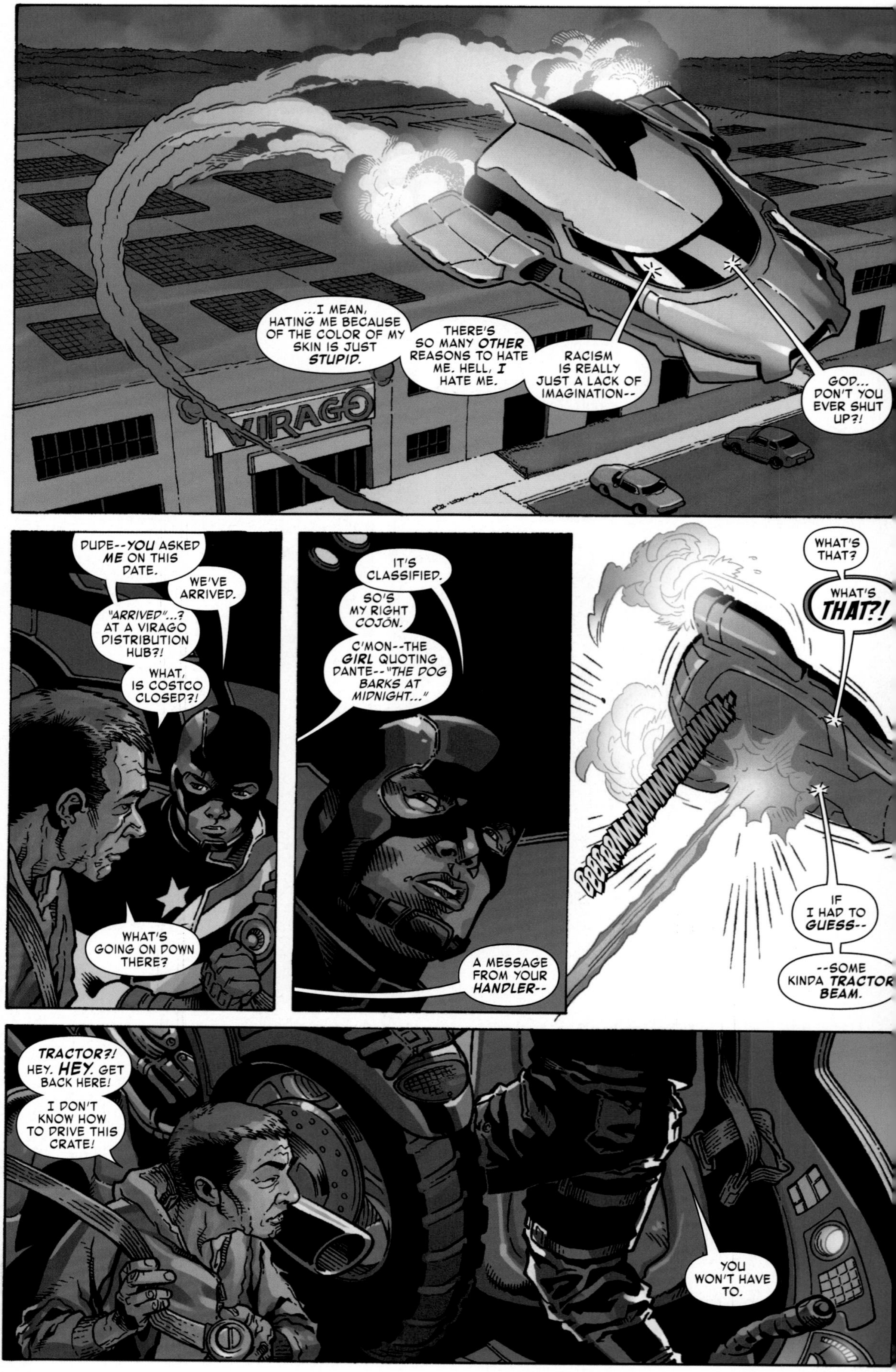
...I MEAN, HATING ME BECAUSE OF THE COLOR OF MY SKIN IS JUST STUPID.
THERE'S SO MANY OTHER REASONS TO HATE ME. HELL, I HATE ME.
RACISM IS REALLY JUST A LACK OF IMAGINATION--
GOD... DON'T YOU EVER SHUT UP?!
VIRAGO
DUDE--YOU ASKED ME ON THIS DATE.
WE'VE ARRIVED.
"ARRIVED"...? AT A VIRAGO DISTRIBUTION HUB?!
WHAT, IS COSTCO CLOSED?!
WHAT'S GOING ON DOWN THERE?
IT'S CLASSIFIED.
SO'S MY RIGHT COJÓN.
C'MON--THE GIRL QUOTING DANTE--"THE DOG BARKS AT MIDNIGHT..."
A MESSAGE FROM YOUR HANDLER--
WHAT'S THAT?
WHAT'S THAT?!
IF I HAD TO GUESS--
--SOME KINDA TRACTOR BEAM.
TRACTOR?! HEY. HEY. GET BACK HERE!
I DON'T KNOW HOW TO DRIVE THIS CRATE!
YOU WON'T HAVE TO.

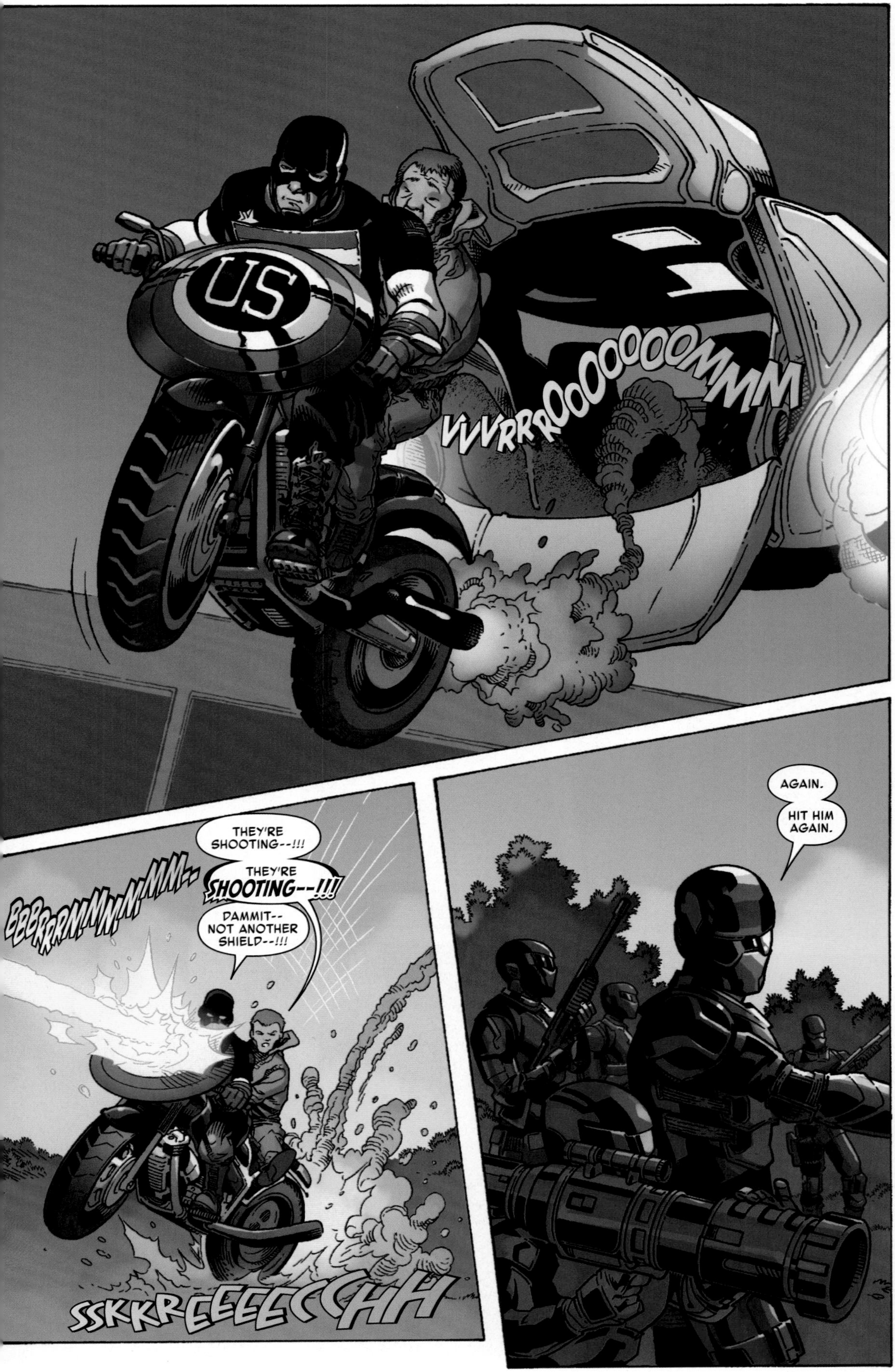
VVVRRROOOOOOOMMM
AGAIN.
HIT HIM AGAIN.
BBBRRRMMMMMM--
THEY'RE SHOOTING--!!!
THEY'RE SHOOTING--!!!
DAMMIT-- NOT ANOTHER SHIELD--!!!
SSKKREEEEECCHH

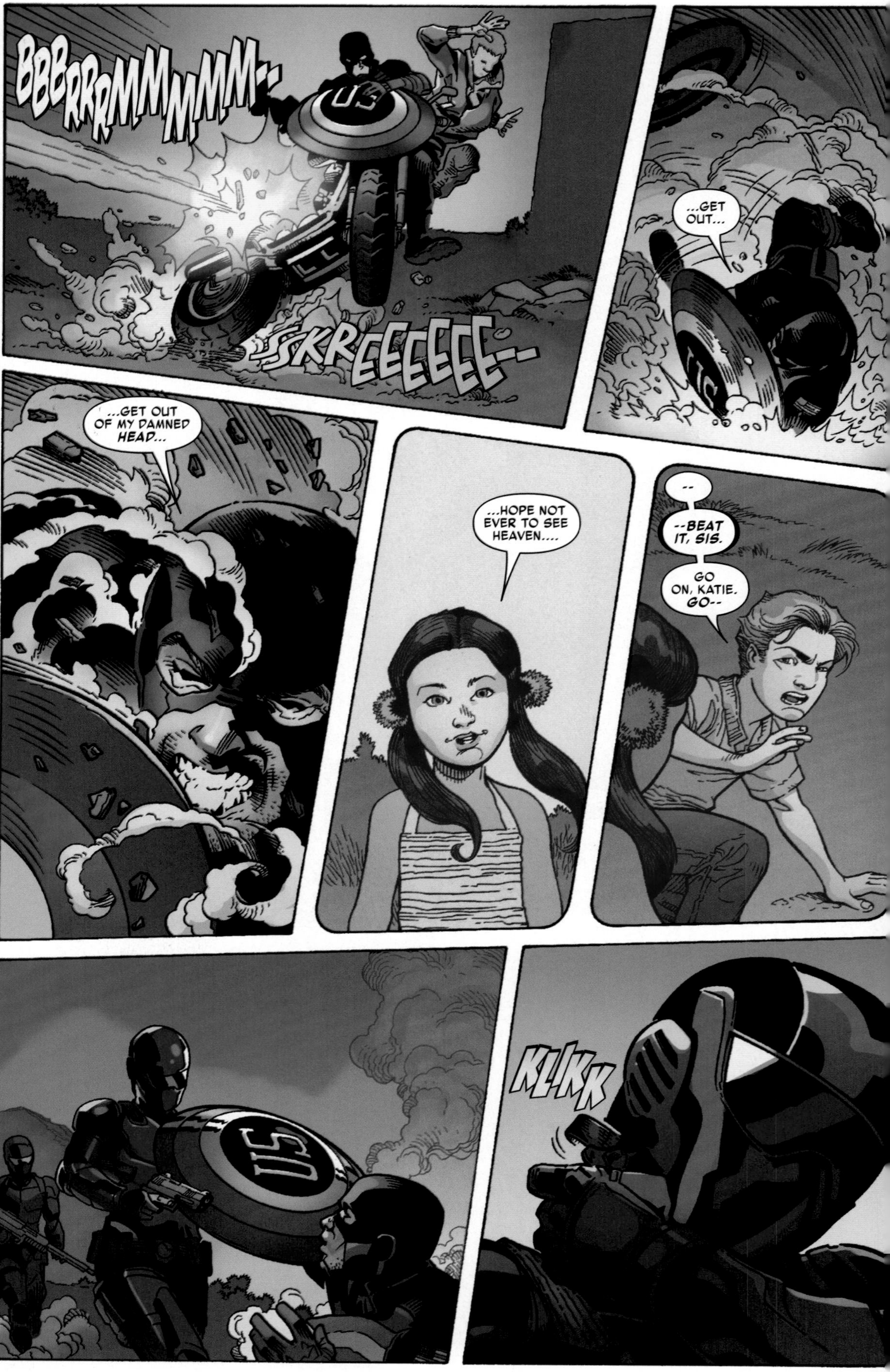
BBBRRRMMMMMM--
SSKREEEEEEE--
...GET OUT...
...GET OUT OF MY DAMNED HEAD...
...HOPE NOT EVER TO SEE HEAVEN....
--
--BEAT IT, SIS.
GO ON, KATIE. GO--
KLIKK

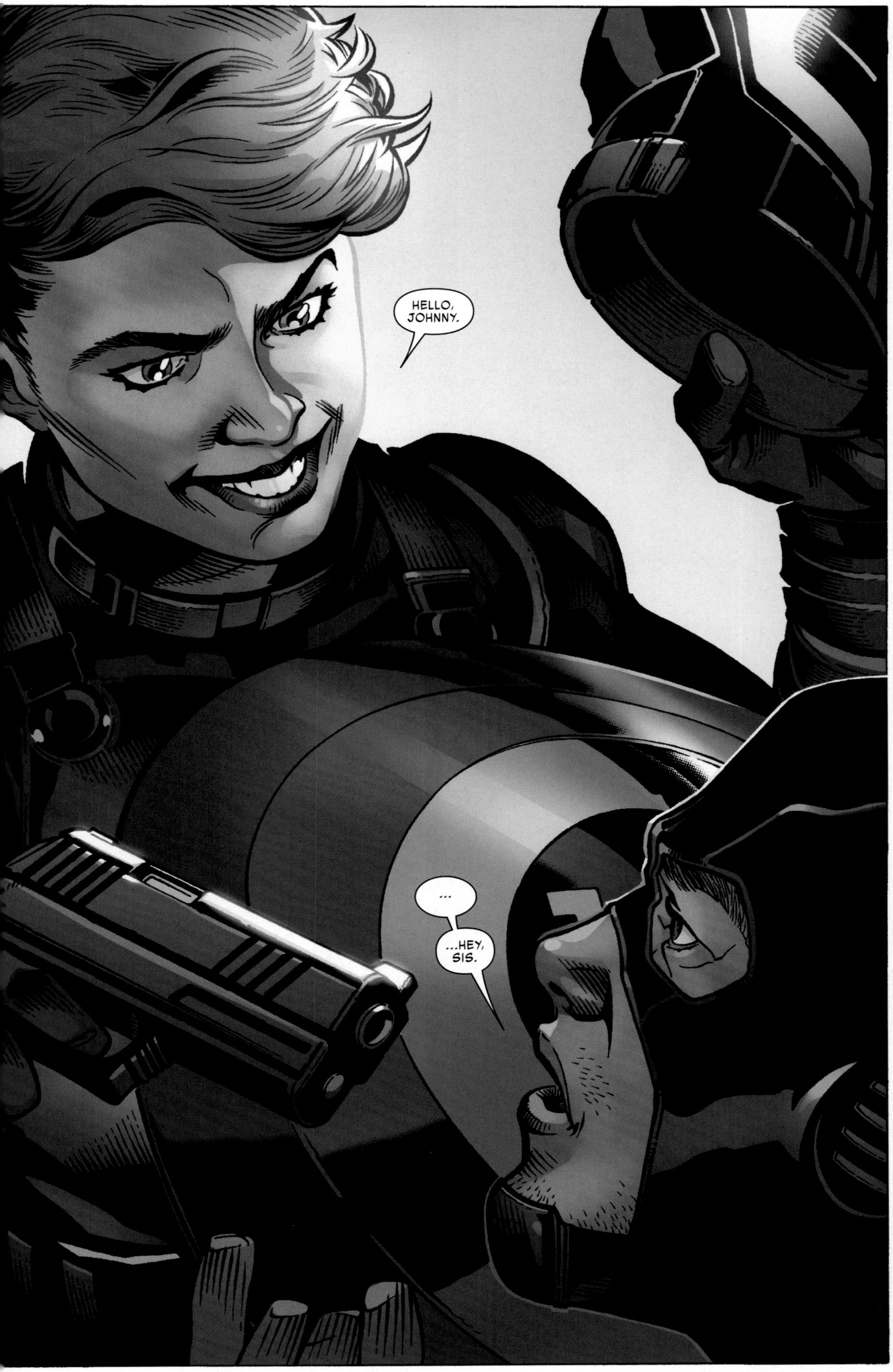
HELLO, JOHNNY.
...
...HEY, SIS.

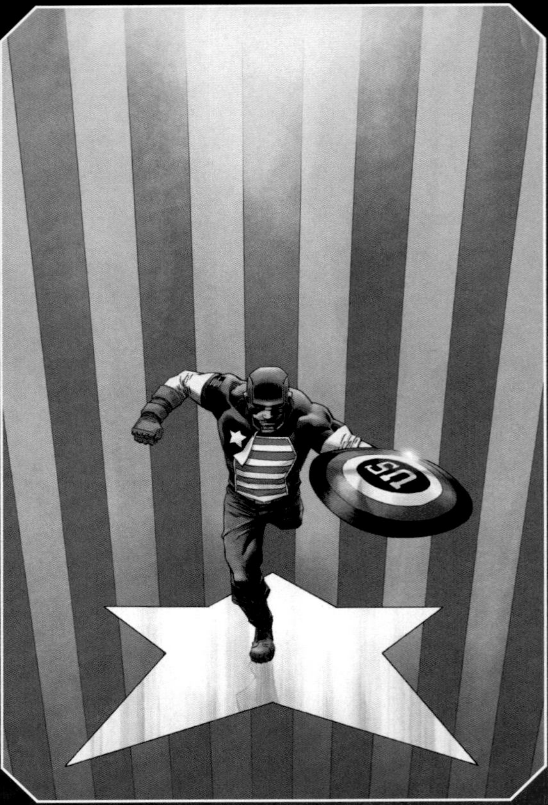
US

#1 VARIANT BY
DECLAN SHALVEY

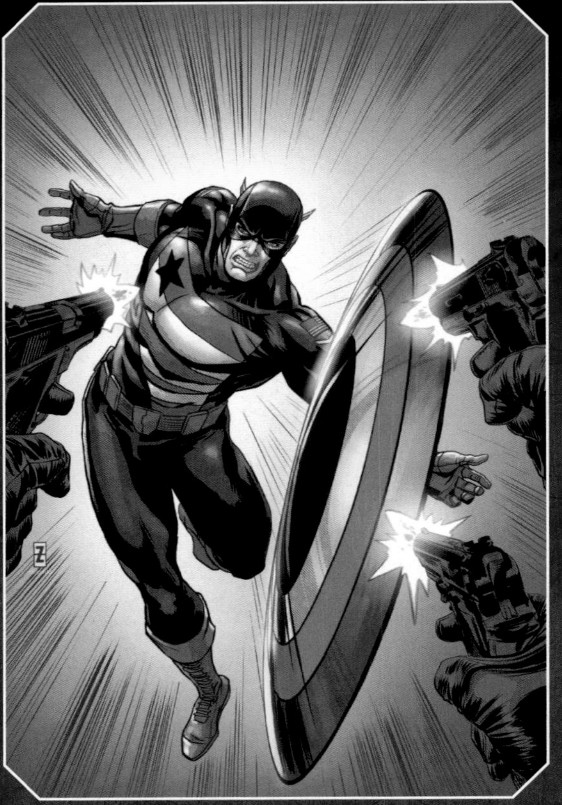

#1 VARIANT BY
PATCH ZIRCHER & EDGAR DELGADO

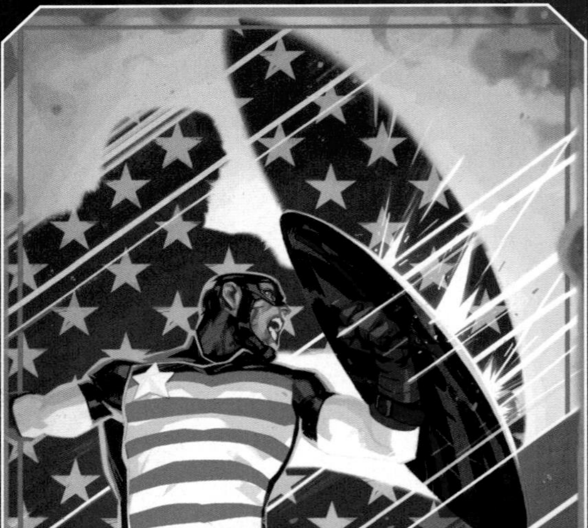

#1 VARIANT BY
TONI INFANTE

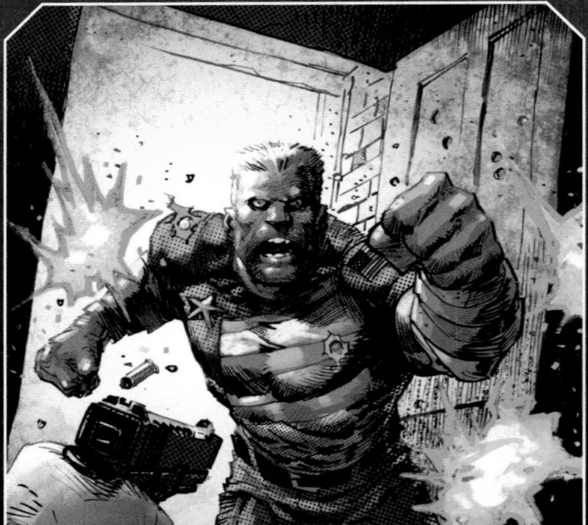
PANOSIAN

#2 VARIANT BY
DAN PANOSIAN

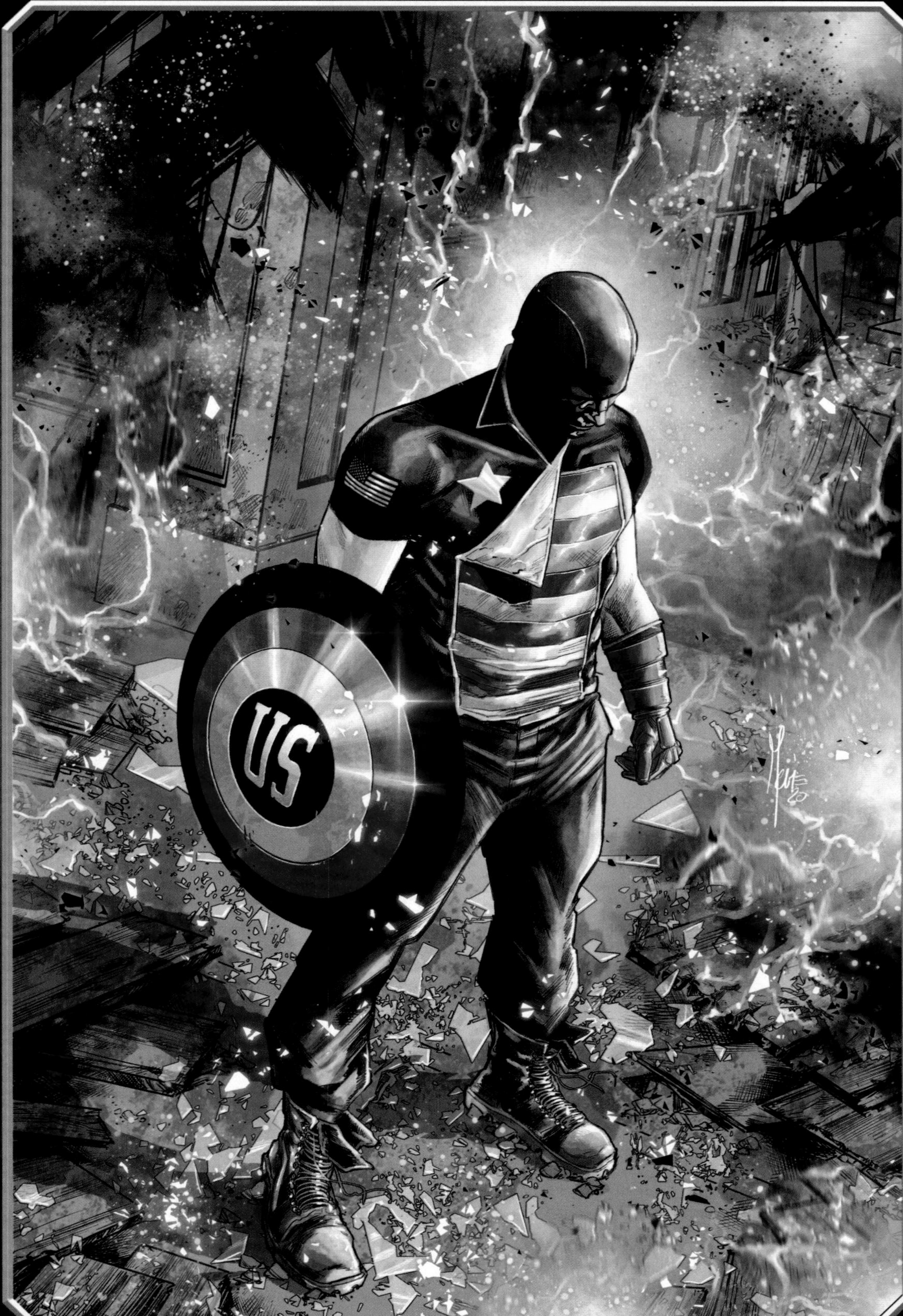
US

2

SO, THE COAL MINE CLOSED. *VIRAGO* MOVED IN BUT DIDN'T HELP THE TOWN.

SO YOU BLEW UP VIRAGO'S POWER PLANT.

SHUT 'EM RIGHT DOWN.

FIGGERED THAT'D GIT THEY 'TENTION.

SMOKEY
FORMER BRAMBLINE CROSS MINING EMPLOYEE

DID IT?

RECKON.

I MEAN, THE CAP'N SHOWIN' UP AN' ALL.

DEVEL
FORMER BRAMBLINE CROSS MINING EMPLOYEE

AND THEN THAT *OTHER* FELLER.

DEVEL
FORMER BRAMBLINE CROSS MINING EMPLOYEE

...WHICH IN TURN CREATED SECURITIZATION VEHICLES FOR NOTES SPUN OFF FROM THE SHADOW BANKING MARKET.

MANY INVESTORS SAW THOSE INSTRUMENTS AS TOXIC WASTE.

WHICH WAS WHERE TALF* CAME IN.

*TERM ASSET-BACKED SECURITIES LOAN FACILITY. --T.O.M.

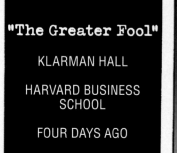

"The Greater Fool"

KLARMAN HALL

HARVARD BUSINESS SCHOOL

FOUR DAYS AGO

THE GOAL WAS HIGH EMBEDDED GROWTH FOR THE MAJORITY UNITY HOLDER--

--JUST REMEMBER TO READ YIELDS LOW SO YOU GET THAT GROWTH.

AND LEVERAGE THE GREATER FOOL THEORY.

THANKS FOR HAVING ME.

MY GOSH, MR. MANNING-- WE'RE SO HONORED...

APRIL MANNING

BAINBRIDGE OPPORTUNITY FUND

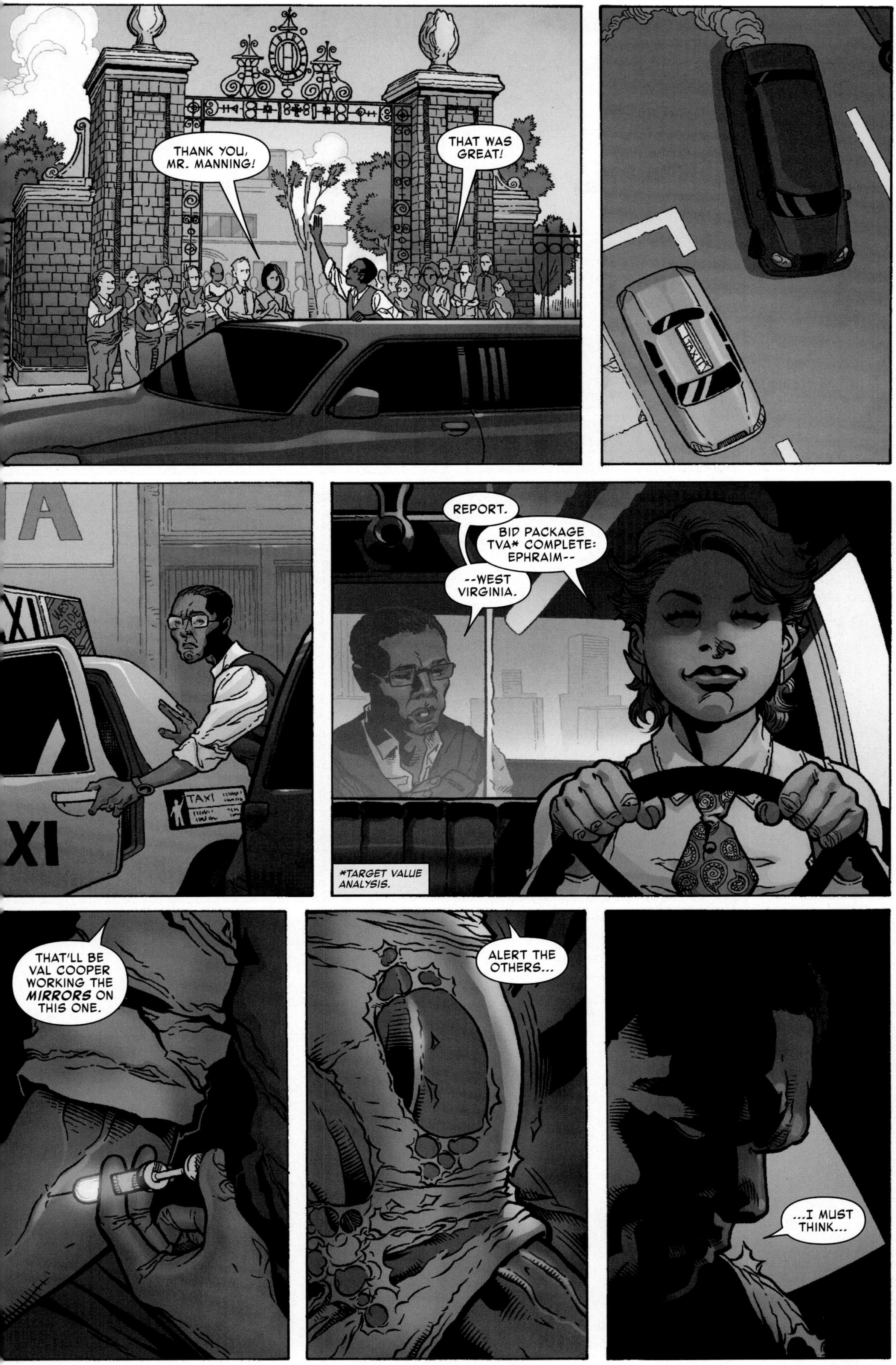
THANK YOU, MR. MANNING!
THAT WAS GREAT!
TAXI
TAXI
WEST SIDE
XI
REPORT.
BID PACKAGE TVA* COMPLETE: EPHRAIM--
--WEST VIRGINIA.
*TARGET VALUE ANALYSIS.
THAT'LL BE VAL COOPER WORKING THE MIRRORS ON THIS ONE.
ALERT THE OTHERS...
...I MUST THINK...

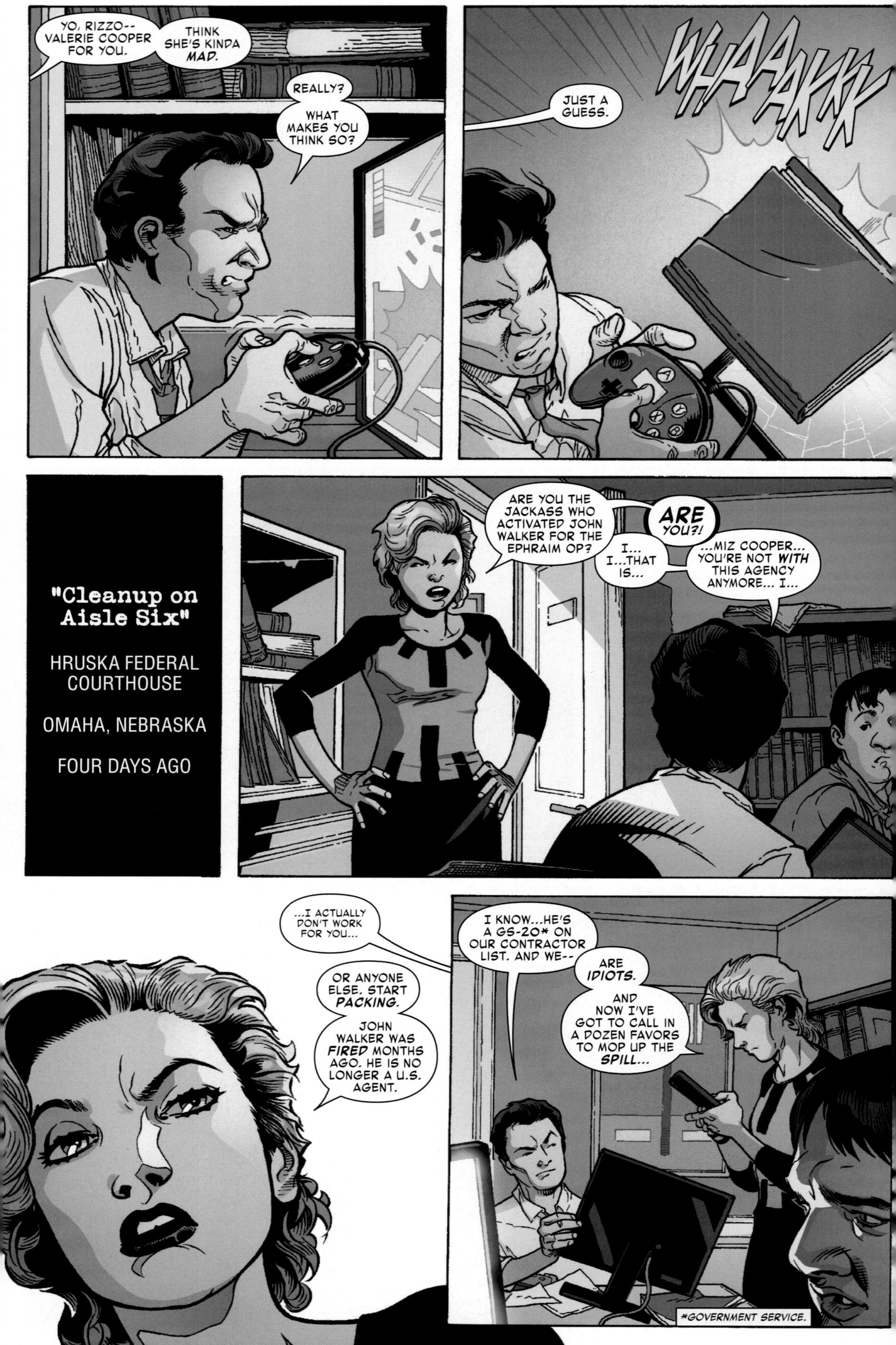
YO, RIZZO-- VALERIE COOPER FOR YOU.
THINK SHE'S KINDA *MAD.*
REALLY?
WHAT MAKES YOU THINK SO?
JUST A GUESS.
WHAAAKKK
"Cleanup on Aisle Six"
HRUSKA FEDERAL COURTHOUSE
OMAHA, NEBRASKA
FOUR DAYS AGO
ARE YOU THE JACKASS WHO ACTIVATED JOHN WALKER FOR THE EPHRAIM OP?
ARE YOU?!
I... I...THAT IS...
...MIZ COOPER... YOU'RE NOT *WITH* THIS AGENCY ANYMORE... I...
...I ACTUALLY DON'T WORK FOR YOU...
OR ANYONE ELSE. START *PACKING.*
JOHN WALKER WAS *FIRED* MONTHS AGO. HE IS NO LONGER A U.S. AGENT.
I KNOW...HE'S A GS-20* ON OUR CONTRACTOR LIST. AND WE--
ARE *IDIOTS.*
AND NOW I'VE GOT TO CALL IN A DOZEN FAVORS TO MOP UP THE *SPILL...*
*GOVERNMENT SERVICE.

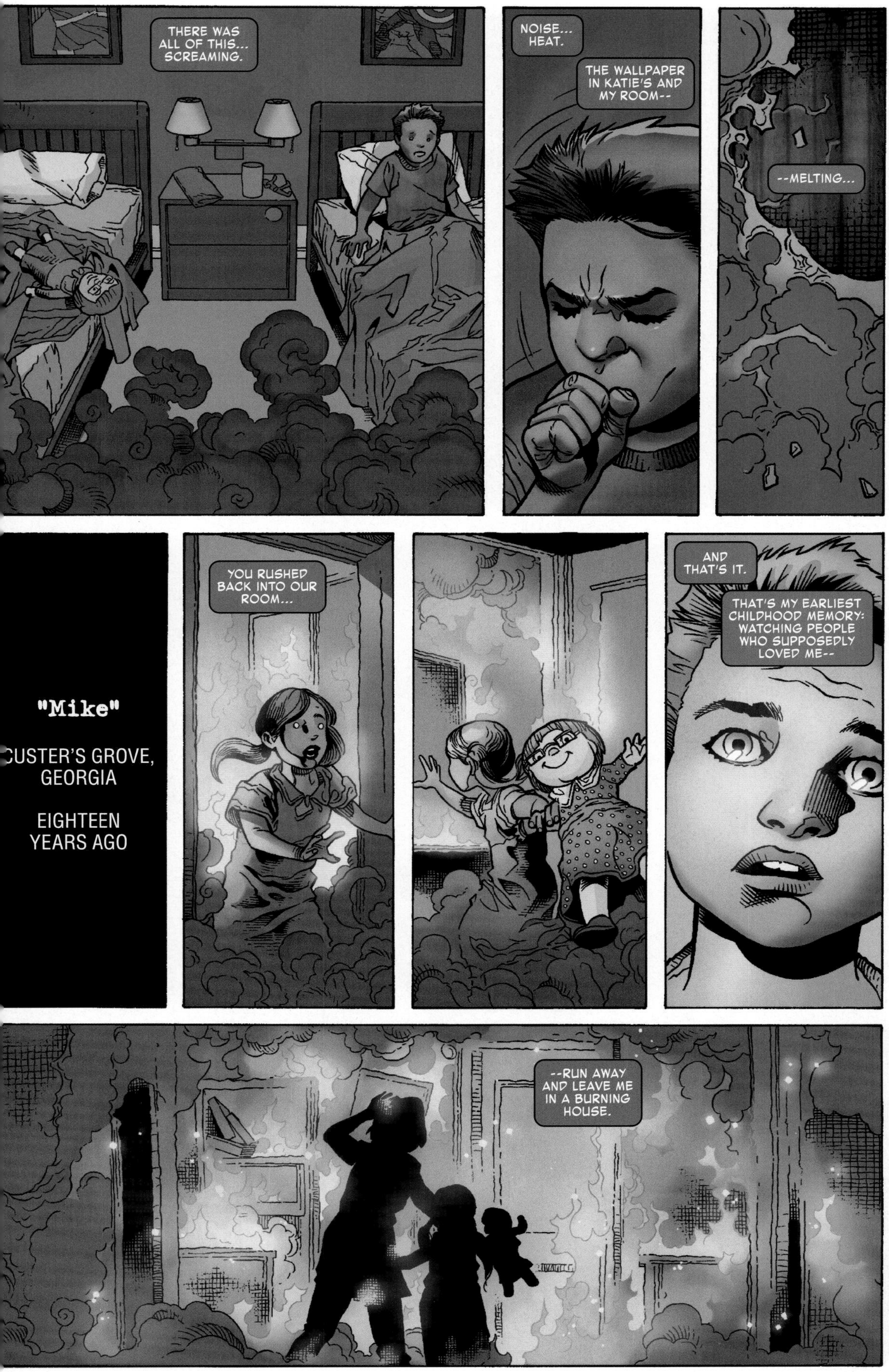
THERE WAS ALL OF THIS... SCREAMING.
NOISE... HEAT.
THE WALLPAPER IN KATIE'S AND MY ROOM--
--MELTING...
"Mike"
CUSTER'S GROVE, GEORGIA
EIGHTEEN YEARS AGO
YOU RUSHED BACK INTO OUR ROOM...
AND THAT'S IT.
THAT'S MY EARLIEST CHILDHOOD MEMORY: WATCHING PEOPLE WHO SUPPOSEDLY LOVED ME--
--RUN AWAY AND LEAVE ME IN A BURNING HOUSE.

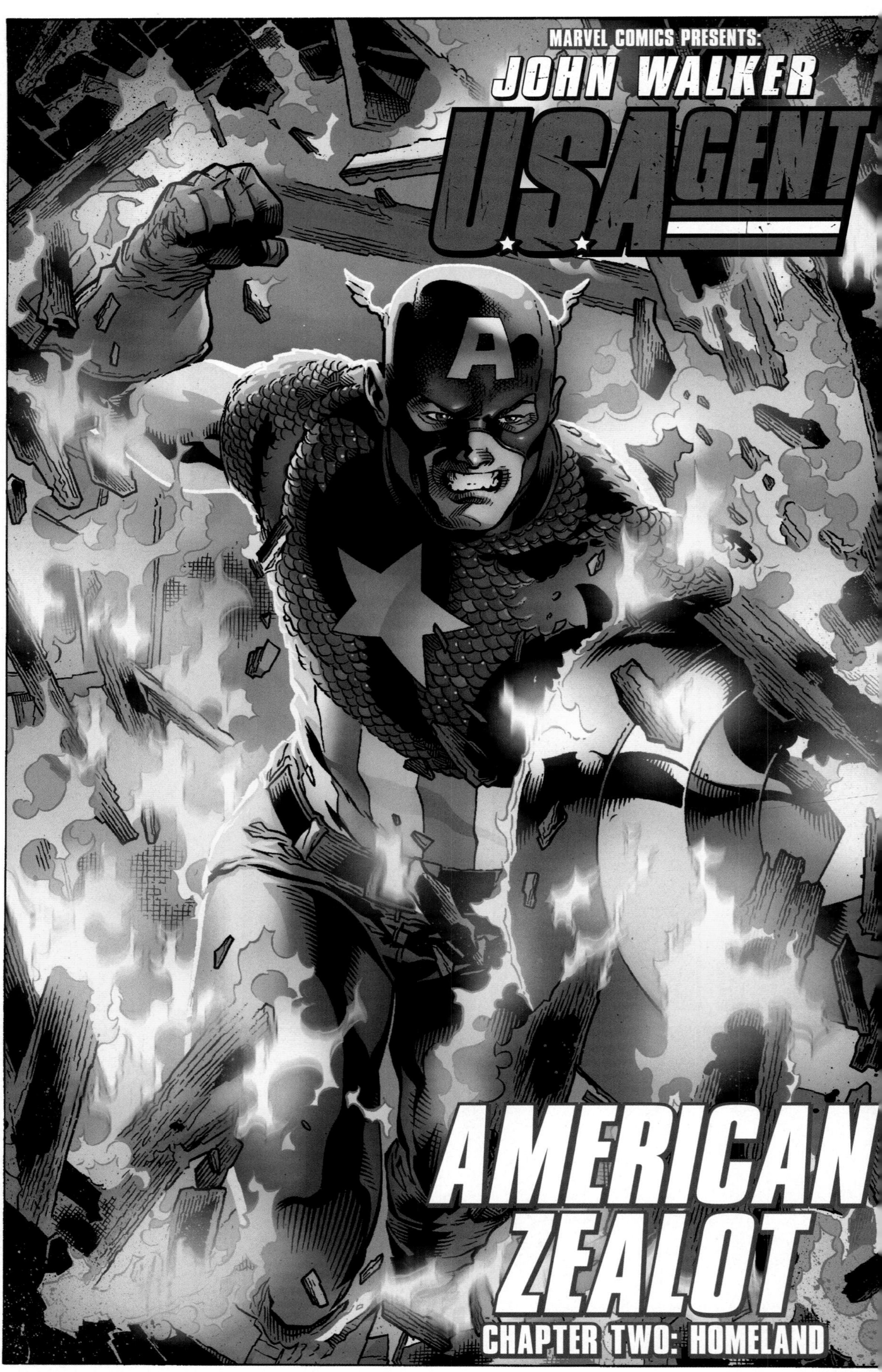
MARVEL COMICS PRESENTS:
JOHN WALKER
U.S.AGENT
AMERICAN ZEALOT
CHAPTER TWO: HOMELAND

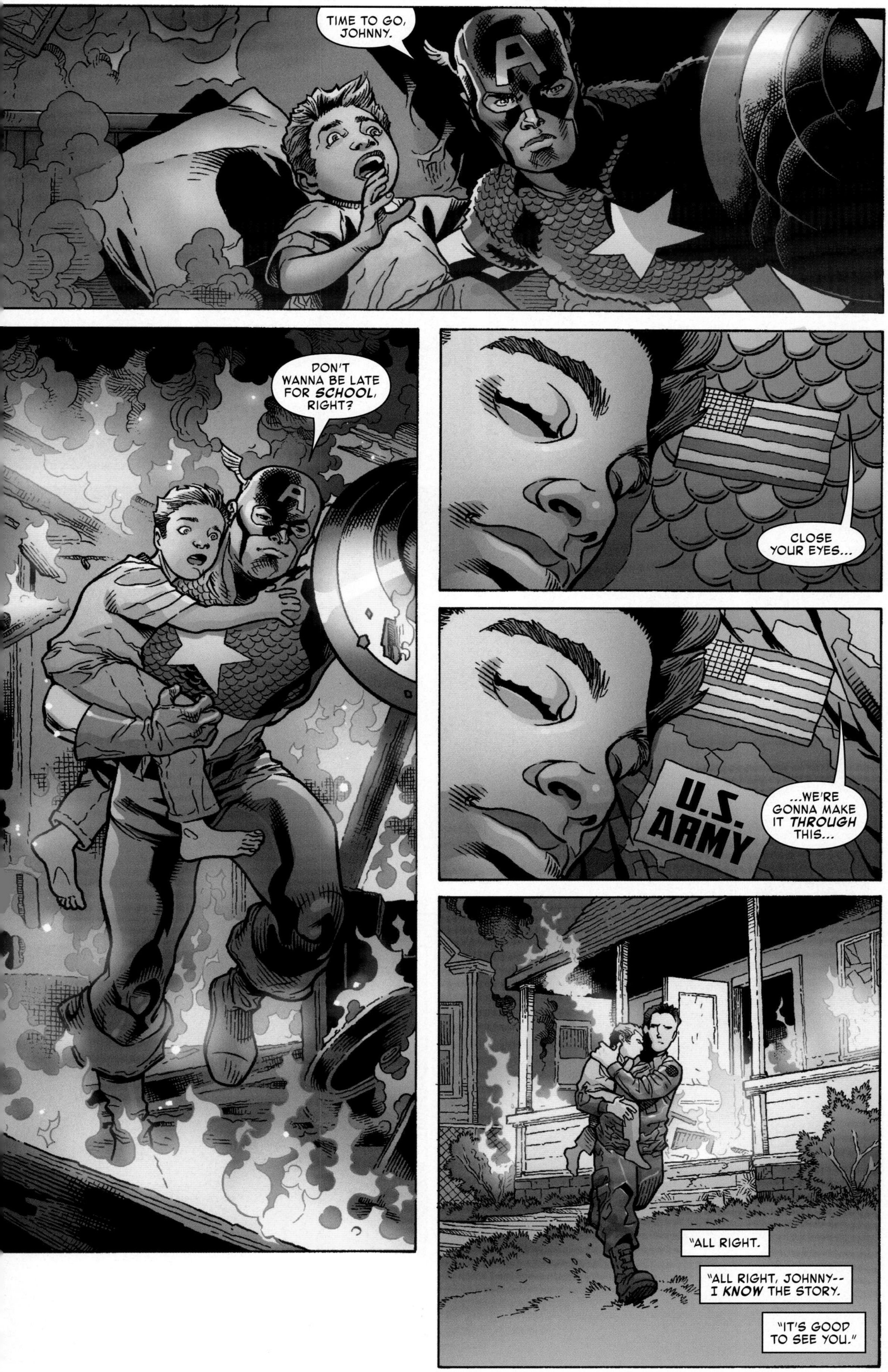

TIME TO GO, JOHNNY.
DON'T WANNA BE LATE FOR SCHOOL, RIGHT?
CLOSE YOUR EYES...
U.S. ARMY
...WE'RE GONNA MAKE IT THROUGH THIS...
"ALL RIGHT.
"ALL RIGHT, JOHNNY-- I KNOW THE STORY.
"IT'S GOOD TO SEE YOU."

-- --GOOD TO SEE YOU TOO, HBO.

"HBO." HUH. HONEY BATCHES OF OATS--OUR FAVORITE BREAKFAST CEREAL.

BEEN A MINUTE SINCE ANYONE'S CALLED ME THAT.

SO-- S.H.I.E.L.D. IS HIRING 14-YEAR-OLDS NOW? "JUNIOR SPOOK ROTC."

23, JOHNNY. AND THERE IS NO S.H.I.E.L.D. JUST DECOMMISSIONED WRECKS--

--LIKE YOU.

WHICH MAKES YOU WHAT, KATIE--

--HIGH SCHOOL INTERN FOR THOSE GRUNTS?

A SAFE POSTING OUT OF HARM'S WAY. VAL COOPER IS YOUR RABBI.

VALERIE COOPER CREATED YOU, JOHNNY--

"--RECRUITED THE 'SUPER-PATRIOT' TO REPLACE THE REAL CAPTAIN AMERICA.*

"AFTER YOU GOT YOURSELF AMPED UP BY A GUY CALLED THE POWER BROKER."

*CAPTAIN AMERICA #333. --TOM

GIVE ME THAT.

DON'T PUT MUSTARD IN THE EGGS.

NICE HAIR. W HAPPENED

LO B

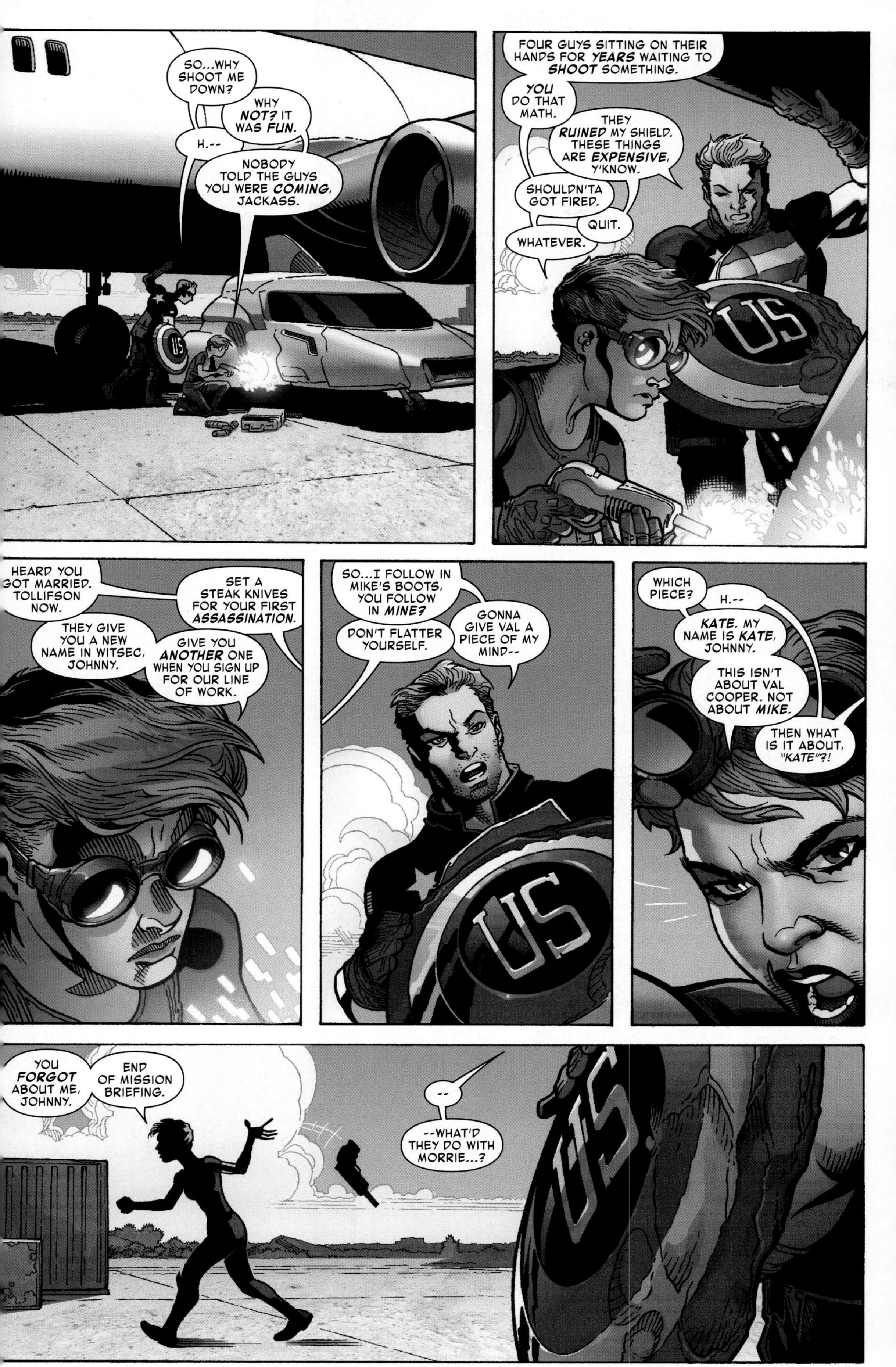
SO...WHY SHOOT ME DOWN?
WHY NOT? IT WAS FUN.
H.--
NOBODY TOLD THE GUYS YOU WERE COMING, JACKASS.
FOUR GUYS SITTING ON THEIR HANDS FOR YEARS WAITING TO SHOOT SOMETHING.
YOU DO THAT MATH.
THEY RUINED MY SHIELD. THESE THINGS ARE EXPENSIVE, Y'KNOW.
SHOULDN'TA GOT FIRED.
QUIT.
WHATEVER.
HEARD YOU GOT MARRIED. TOLLIFSON NOW.
SET A STEAK KNIVES FOR YOUR FIRST ASSASSINATION.
THEY GIVE YOU A NEW NAME IN WITSEC, JOHNNY.
GIVE YOU ANOTHER ONE WHEN YOU SIGN UP FOR OUR LINE OF WORK.
SO...I FOLLOW IN MIKE'S BOOTS, YOU FOLLOW IN MINE?
DON'T FLATTER YOURSELF.
GONNA GIVE VAL A PIECE OF MY MIND--
WHICH PIECE?
H.--
KATE. MY NAME IS KATE, JOHNNY.
THIS ISN'T ABOUT VAL COOPER. NOT ABOUT MIKE.
THEN WHAT IS IT ABOUT, "KATE"?!
YOU FORGOT ABOUT ME, JOHNNY.
END OF MISSION BRIEFING.
--
--WHAT'D THEY DO WITH MORRIE...?

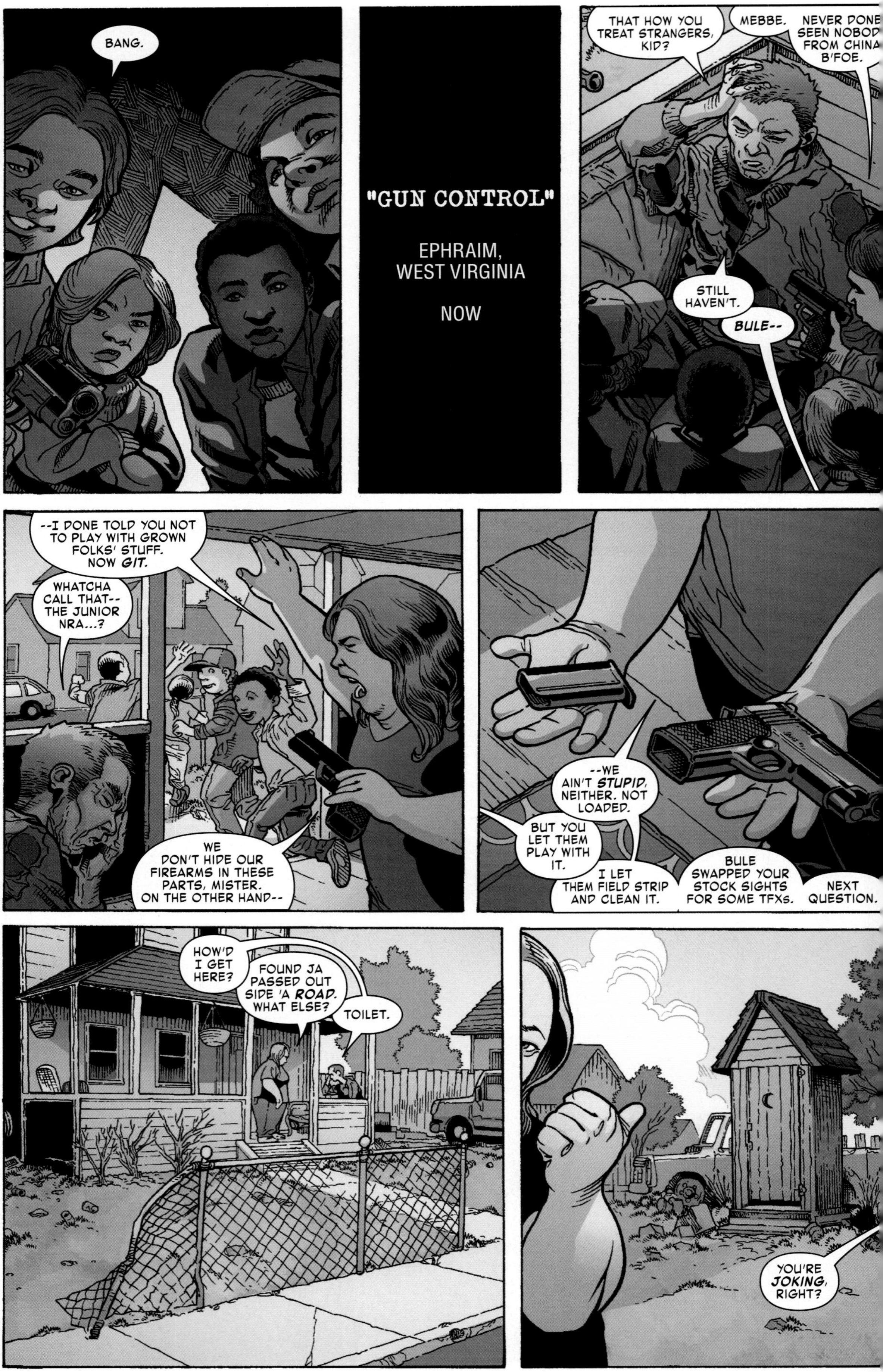
BANG.
"GUN CONTROL"
EPHRAIM, WEST VIRGINIA
NOW
THAT HOW YOU TREAT STRANGERS, KID?
MEBBE.
NEVER DONE SEEN NOBOD FROM CHINA B'FOE.
STILL HAVEN'T.
BULE--
--I DONE TOLD YOU NOT TO PLAY WITH GROWN FOLKS' STUFF. NOW GIT.
WHATCHA CALL THAT-- THE JUNIOR NRA...?
WE DON'T HIDE OUR FIREARMS IN THESE PARTS, MISTER. ON THE OTHER HAND--
--WE AIN'T STUPID, NEITHER. NOT LOADED.
BUT YOU LET THEM PLAY WITH IT.
I LET THEM FIELD STRIP AND CLEAN IT.
BULE SWAPPED YOUR STOCK SIGHTS FOR SOME TFXs.
NEXT QUESTION.
HOW'D I GET HERE?
FOUND JA PASSED OUT SIDE 'A ROAD. WHAT ELSE?
TOILET.
YOU'RE JOKING, RIGHT?

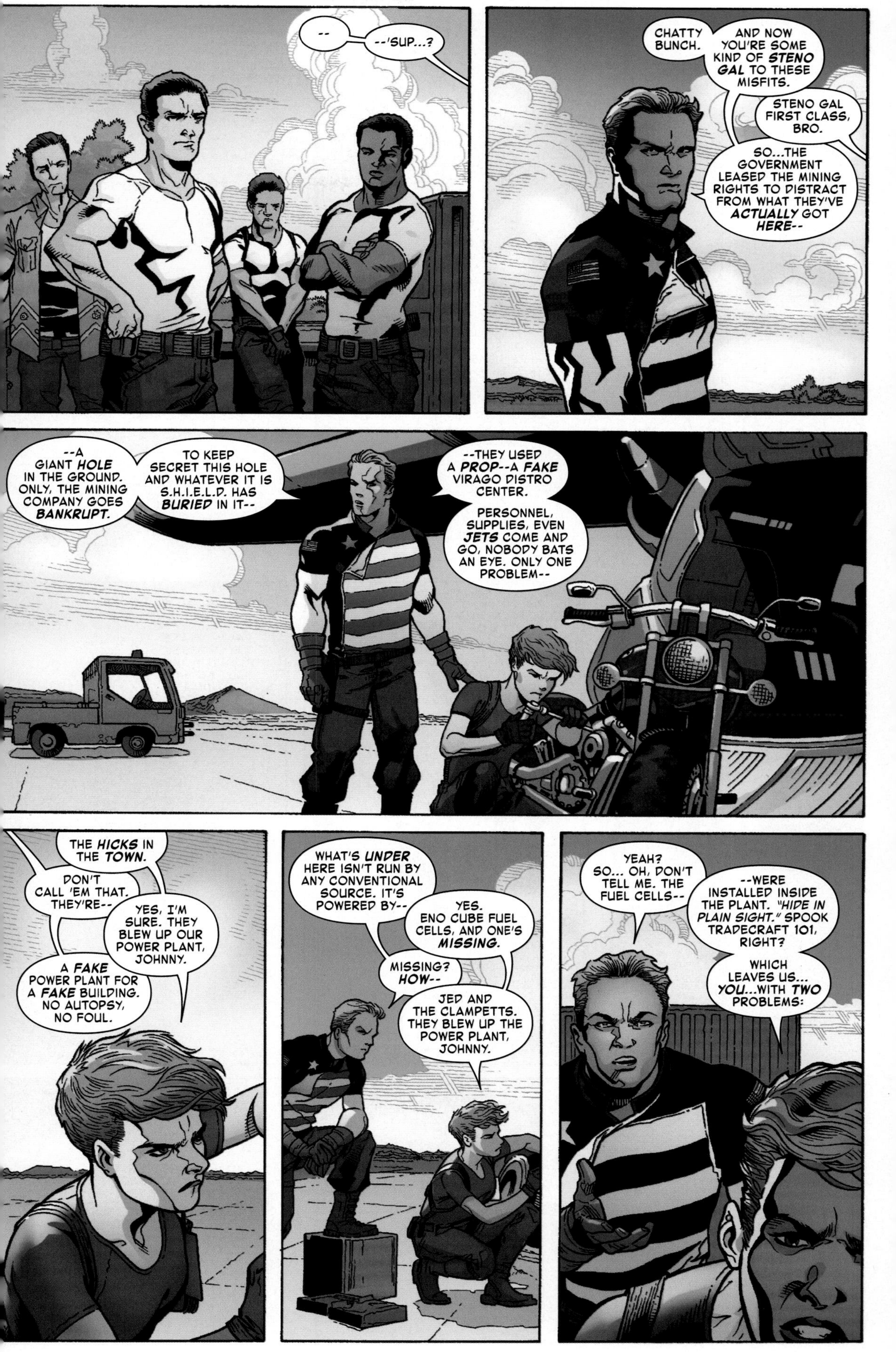
--
--'SUP...?
CHATTY BUNCH.
AND NOW YOU'RE SOME KIND OF STENO GAL TO THESE MISFITS.
STENO GAL FIRST CLASS, BRO.
SO...THE GOVERNMENT LEASED THE MINING RIGHTS TO DISTRACT FROM WHAT THEY'VE ACTUALLY GOT HERE--
--A GIANT HOLE IN THE GROUND. ONLY, THE MINING COMPANY GOES BANKRUPT.
TO KEEP SECRET THIS HOLE AND WHATEVER IT IS S.H.I.E.L.D. HAS BURIED IN IT--
--THEY USED A PROP--A FAKE VIRAGO DISTRO CENTER.
PERSONNEL, SUPPLIES, EVEN JETS COME AND GO, NOBODY BATS AN EYE. ONLY ONE PROBLEM--
THE HICKS IN THE TOWN.
DON'T CALL 'EM THAT. THEY'RE--
YES, I'M SURE. THEY BLEW UP OUR POWER PLANT, JOHNNY.
A FAKE POWER PLANT FOR A FAKE BUILDING. NO AUTOPSY, NO FOUL.
WHAT'S UNDER HERE ISN'T RUN BY ANY CONVENTIONAL SOURCE. IT'S POWERED BY--
YES. ENO CUBE FUEL CELLS, AND ONE'S MISSING.
MISSING? HOW--
JED AND THE CLAMPETTS. THEY BLEW UP THE POWER PLANT, JOHNNY.
YEAH? SO... OH, DON'T TELL ME. THE FUEL CELLS--
--WERE INSTALLED INSIDE THE PLANT. "HIDE IN PLAIN SIGHT." SPOOK TRADECRAFT 101, RIGHT?
WHICH LEAVES US... YOU...WITH TWO PROBLEMS:

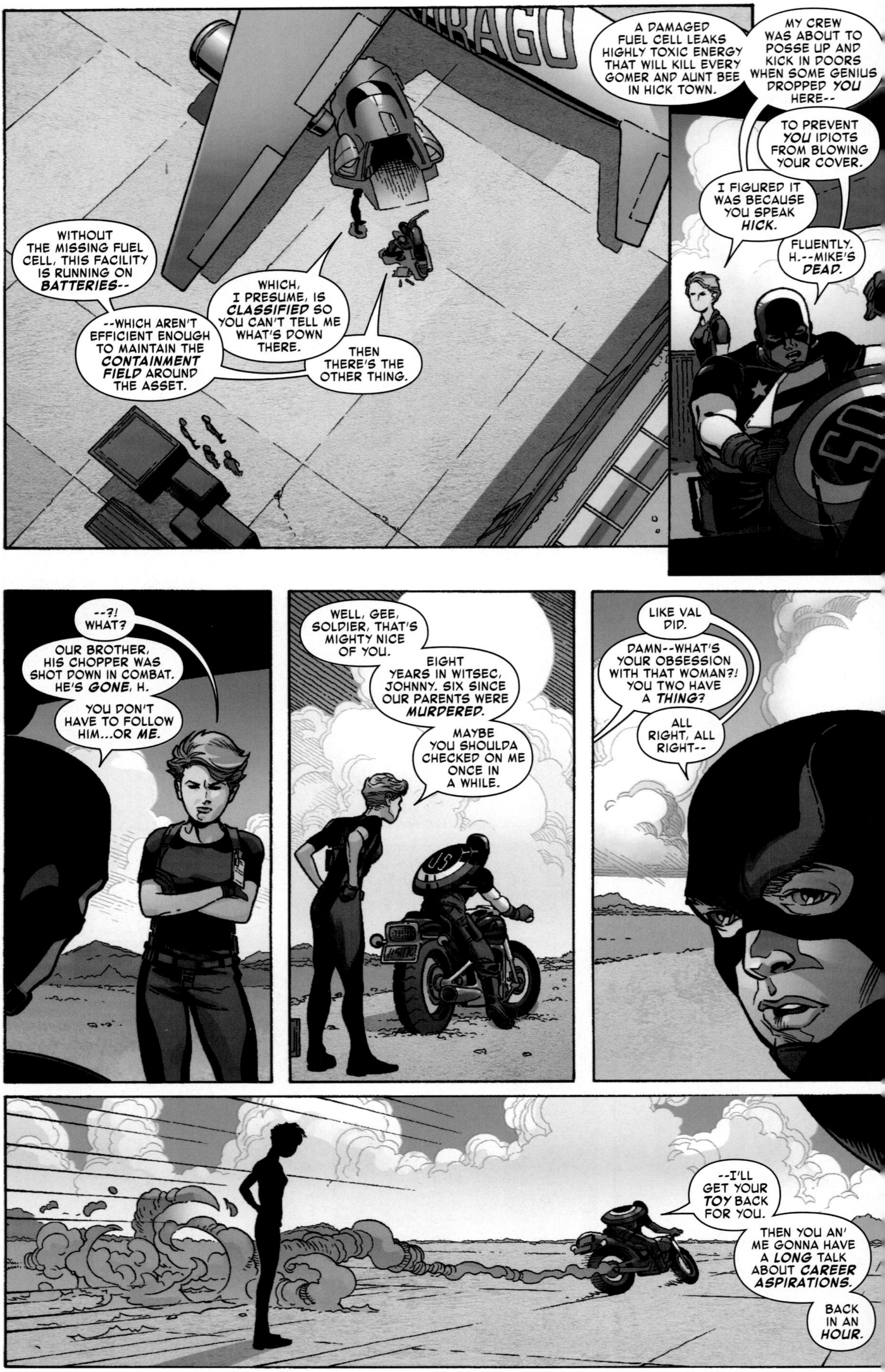
MIRAGO
A DAMAGED FUEL CELL LEAKS HIGHLY TOXIC ENERGY THAT WILL KILL EVERY GOMER AND AUNT BEE IN HICK TOWN.
MY CREW WAS ABOUT TO POSSE UP AND KICK IN DOORS WHEN SOME GENIUS DROPPED YOU HERE--
TO PREVENT YOU IDIOTS FROM BLOWING YOUR COVER.
I FIGURED IT WAS BECAUSE YOU SPEAK HICK.
FLUENTLY. H.--MIKE'S DEAD.
WITHOUT THE MISSING FUEL CELL, THIS FACILITY IS RUNNING ON BATTERIES--
--WHICH AREN'T EFFICIENT ENOUGH TO MAINTAIN THE CONTAINMENT FIELD AROUND THE ASSET.
WHICH, I PRESUME, IS CLASSIFIED SO YOU CAN'T TELL ME WHAT'S DOWN THERE.
THEN THERE'S THE OTHER THING.
--?! WHAT?
OUR BROTHER, HIS CHOPPER WAS SHOT DOWN IN COMBAT. HE'S GONE, H.
YOU DON'T HAVE TO FOLLOW HIM...OR ME.
WELL, GEE, SOLDIER, THAT'S MIGHTY NICE OF YOU.
EIGHT YEARS IN WITSEC, JOHNNY. SIX SINCE OUR PARENTS WERE MURDERED.
MAYBE YOU SHOULDA CHECKED ON ME ONCE IN A WHILE.
LIKE VAL DID.
DAMN--WHAT'S YOUR OBSESSION WITH THAT WOMAN?! YOU TWO HAVE A THING?
ALL RIGHT, ALL RIGHT--
--I'LL GET YOUR TOY BACK FOR YOU.
THEN YOU AN' ME GONNA HAVE A LONG TALK ABOUT CAREER ASPIRATIONS.
BACK IN AN HOUR.

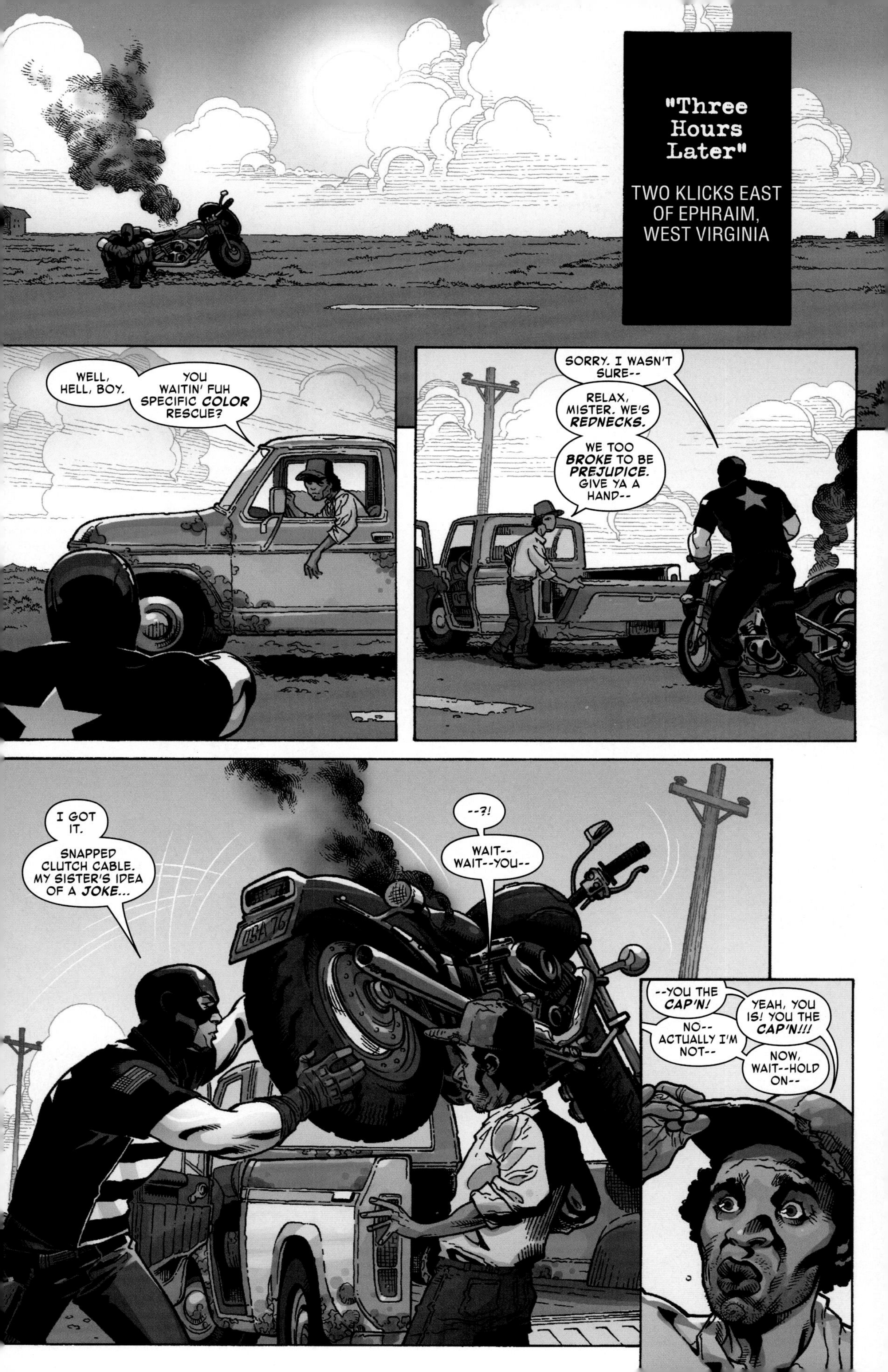

"Three Hours Later"
TWO KLICKS EAST OF EPHRAIM, WEST VIRGINIA
WELL, HELL, BOY.
YOU WAITIN' FUH SPECIFIC COLOR RESCUE?
SORRY. I WASN'T SURE--
RELAX, MISTER. WE'S REDNECKS.
WE TOO BROKE TO BE PREJUDICE. GIVE YA A HAND--
I GOT IT.
SNAPPED CLUTCH CABLE. MY SISTER'S IDEA OF A JOKE...
--?!
WAIT-- WAIT--YOU--
--YOU THE CAP'N!
NO-- ACTUALLY I'M NOT--
YEAH, YOU IS! YOU THE CAP'N!!!
NOW, WAIT--HOLD ON--

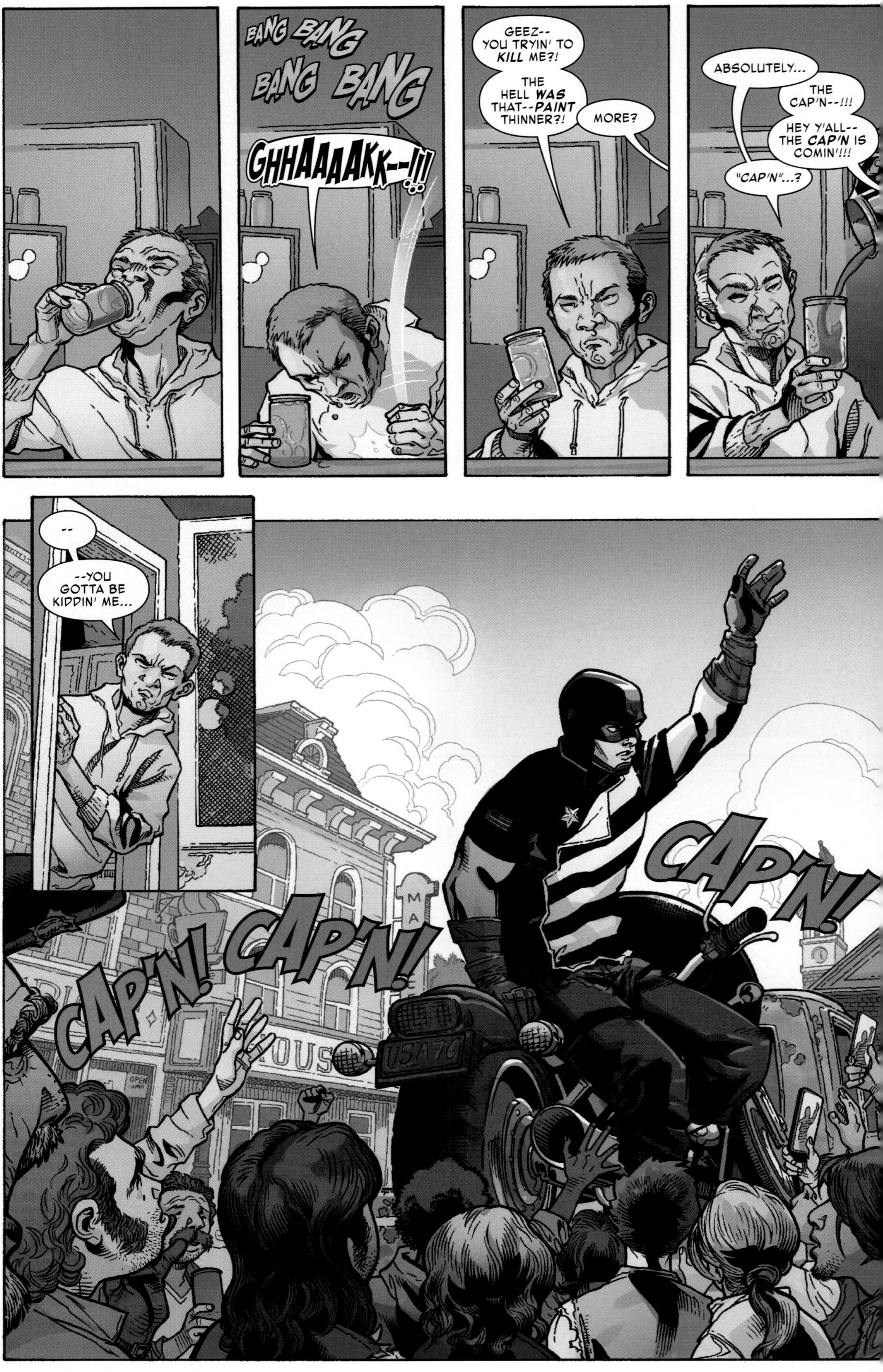

BANG BANG
BANG BANG
GHHAAAAKK--!!!
GEEZ-- YOU TRYIN' TO KILL ME?!
THE HELL WAS THAT--PAINT THINNER?!
MORE?
ABSOLUTELY...
"CAP'N"...?
THE CAP'N--!!!
HEY Y'ALL-- THE CAP'N IS COMIN'!!!
--
--YOU GOTTA BE KIDDIN' ME...
CAP'N!
CAP'N!
CAP'N!
OPEN
USA 76

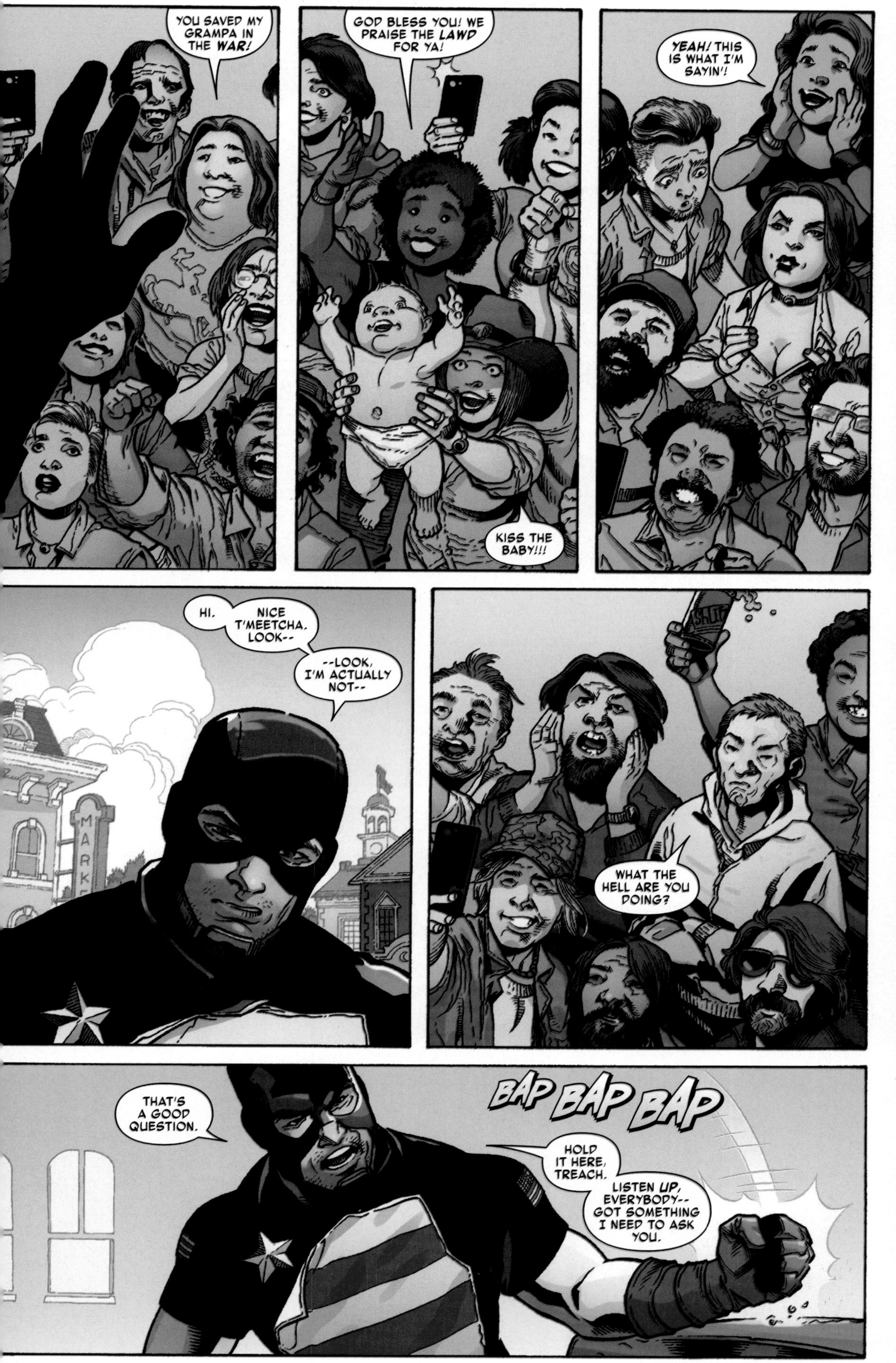
YOU SAVED MY GRAMPA IN THE WAR!
GOD BLESS YOU! WE PRAISE THE LAWD FOR YA!
KISS THE BABY!!!
YEAH! THIS IS WHAT I'M SAYIN'!
HI.
NICE T'MEETCHA. LOOK--
--LOOK, I'M ACTUALLY NOT--
WHAT THE HELL ARE YOU DOING?
THAT'S A GOOD QUESTION.
BAP BAP BAP
HOLD IT HERE, TREACH.
LISTEN UP, EVERYBODY-- GOT SOMETHING I NEED TO ASK YOU.

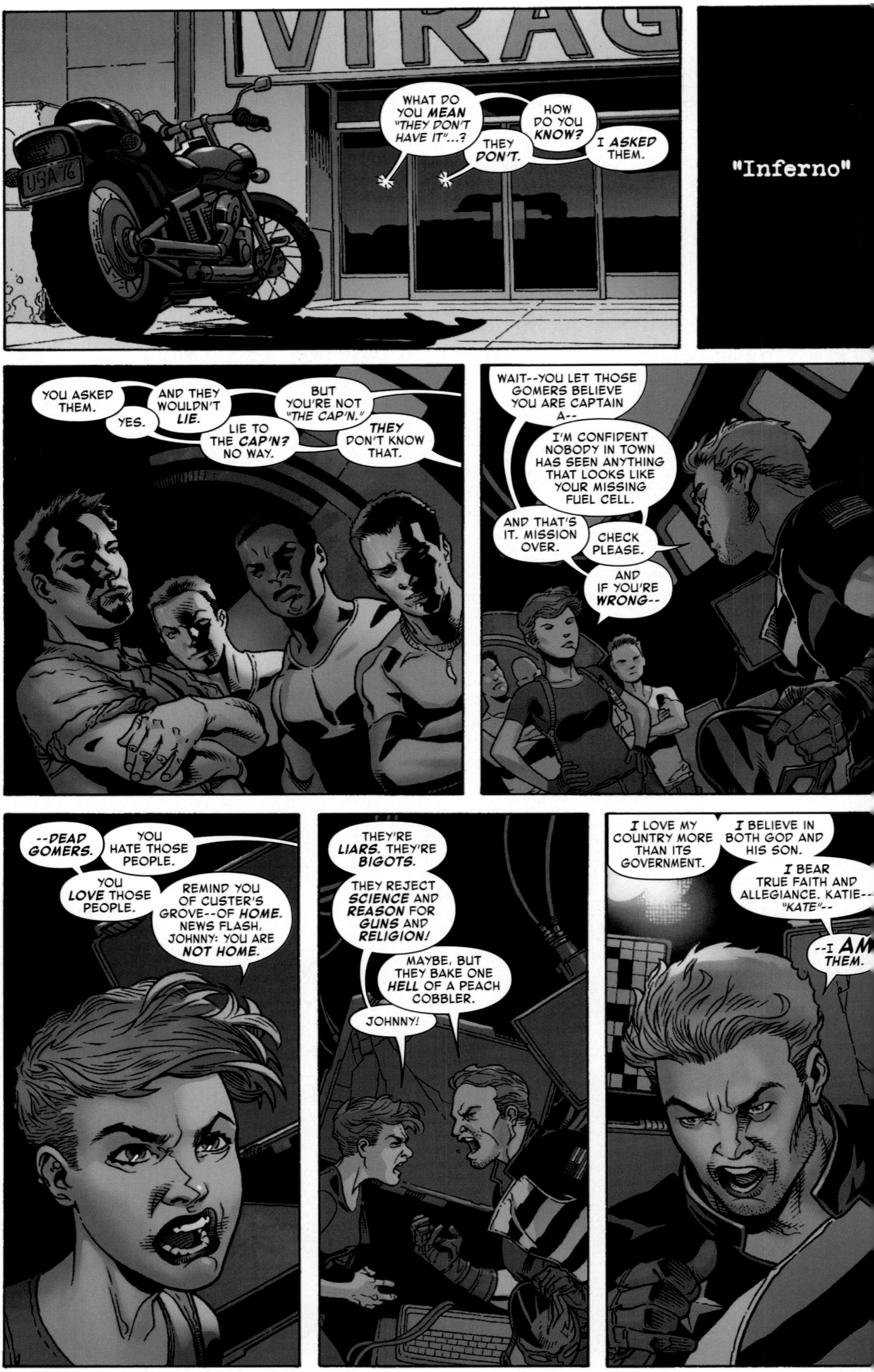
WHAT DO YOU MEAN "THEY DON'T HAVE IT"...?
THEY DON'T.
HOW DO YOU KNOW?
I ASKED THEM.
"Inferno"
YOU ASKED THEM.
YES.
AND THEY WOULDN'T LIE.
LIE TO THE CAP'N? NO WAY.
BUT YOU'RE NOT "THE CAP'N."
THEY DON'T KNOW THAT.
WAIT--YOU LET THOSE GOMERS BELIEVE YOU ARE CAPTAIN A--
I'M CONFIDENT NOBODY IN TOWN HAS SEEN ANYTHING THAT LOOKS LIKE YOUR MISSING FUEL CELL.
AND THAT'S IT. MISSION OVER.
CHECK PLEASE.
AND IF YOU'RE WRONG--
--DEAD GOMERS.
YOU HATE THOSE PEOPLE.
YOU LOVE THOSE PEOPLE.
REMIND YOU OF CUSTER'S GROVE--OF HOME. NEWS FLASH, JOHNNY: YOU ARE NOT HOME.
THEY'RE LIARS. THEY'RE BIGOTS.
THEY REJECT SCIENCE AND REASON FOR GUNS AND RELIGION!
MAYBE, BUT THEY BAKE ONE HELL OF A PEACH COBBLER.
JOHNNY!
I LOVE MY COUNTRY MORE THAN ITS GOVERNMENT.
I BELIEVE IN BOTH GOD AND HIS SON.
I BEAR TRUE FAITH AND ALLEGIANCE. KATIE-- "KATE"--
--I AM THEM.

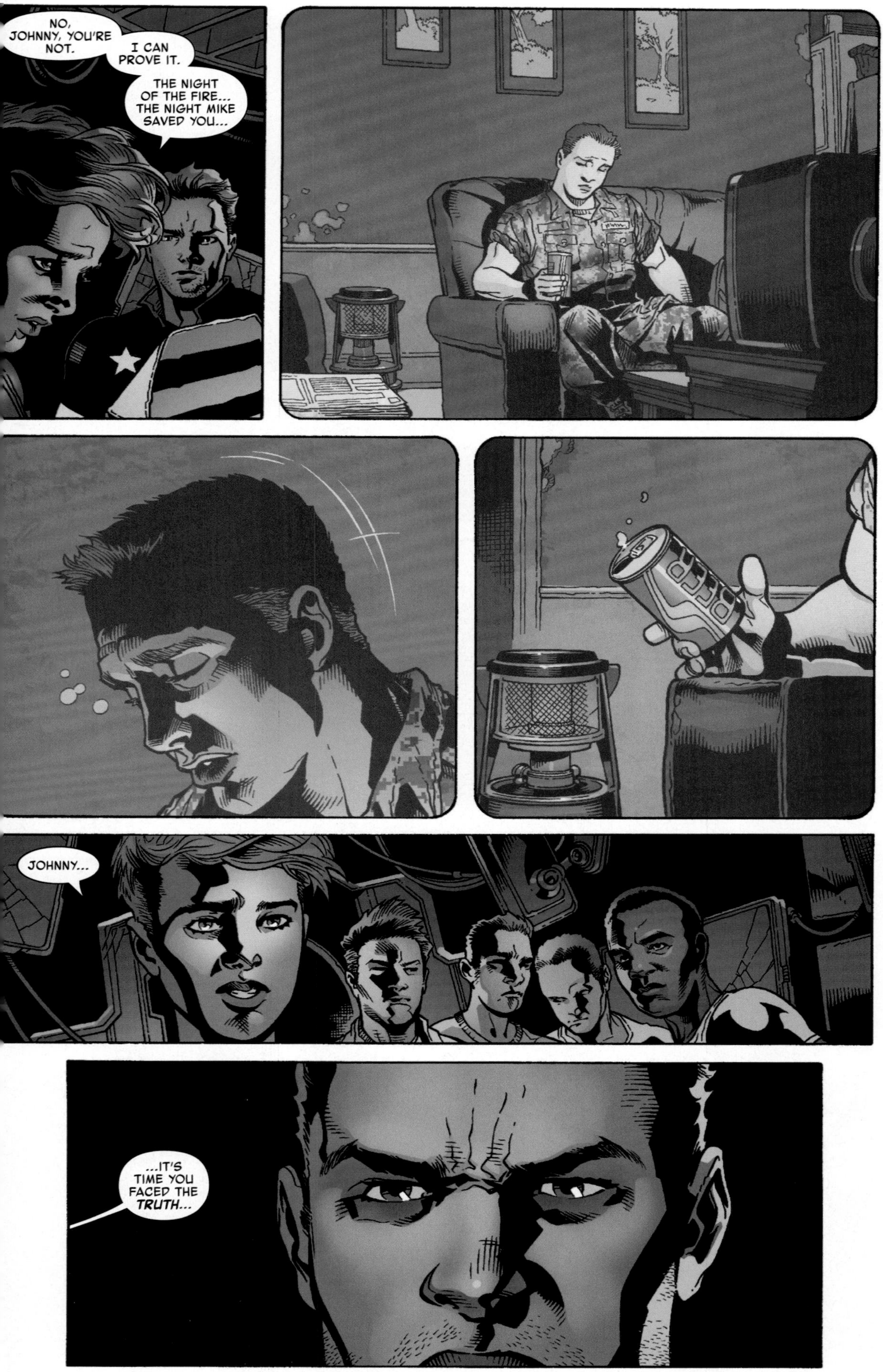
NO, JOHNNY, YOU'RE NOT.
I CAN PROVE IT.
THE NIGHT OF THE FIRE... THE NIGHT MIKE SAVED YOU...
JOHNNY...
...IT'S TIME YOU FACED THE *TRUTH*...

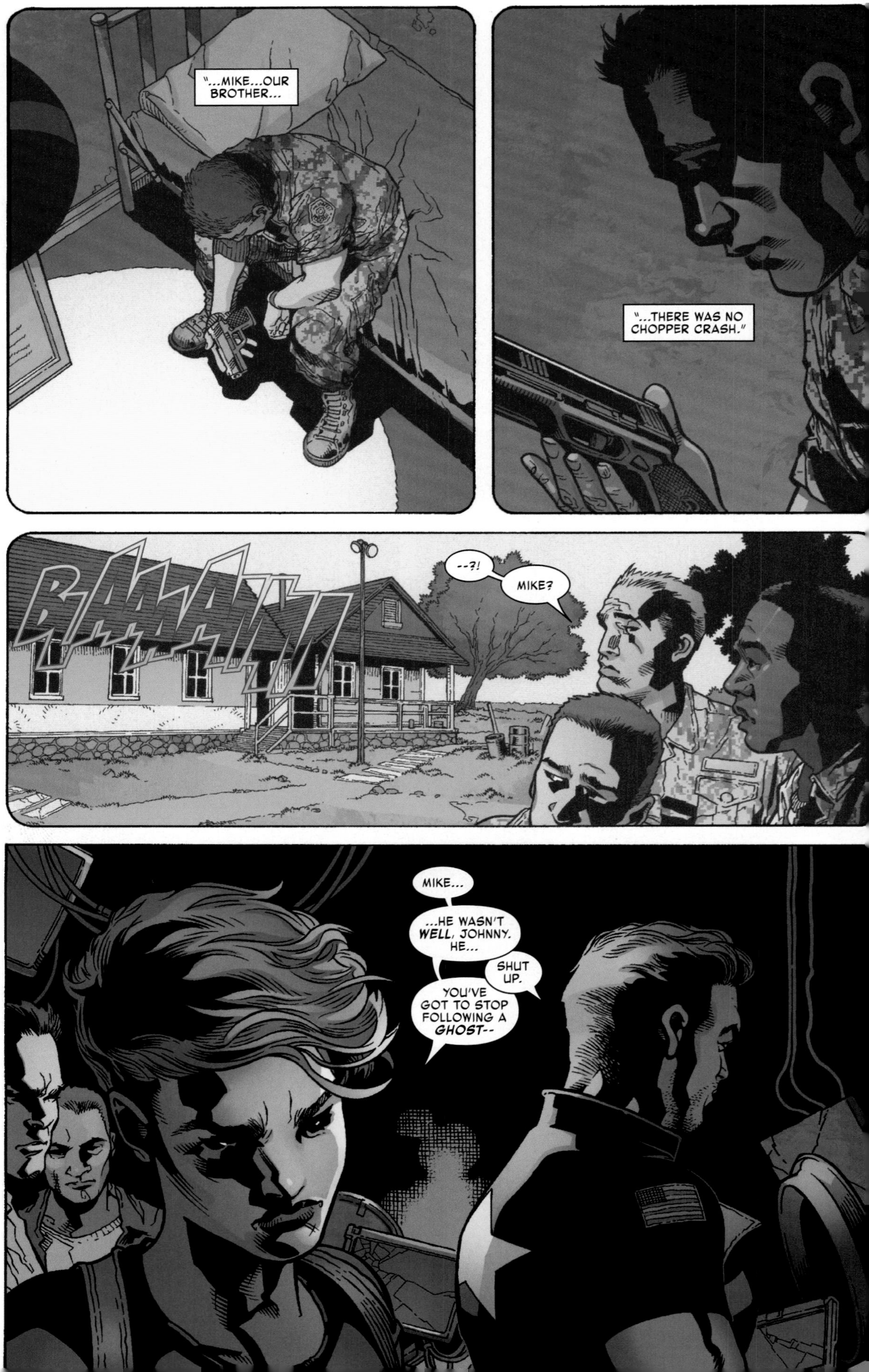
"...MIKE...OUR BROTHER...
"...THERE WAS NO CHOPPER CRASH."
BLAAAM!!
--?!
MIKE?
MIKE...
...HE WASN'T WELL, JOHNNY. HE...
SHUT UP.
YOU'VE GOT TO STOP FOLLOWING A GHOST--

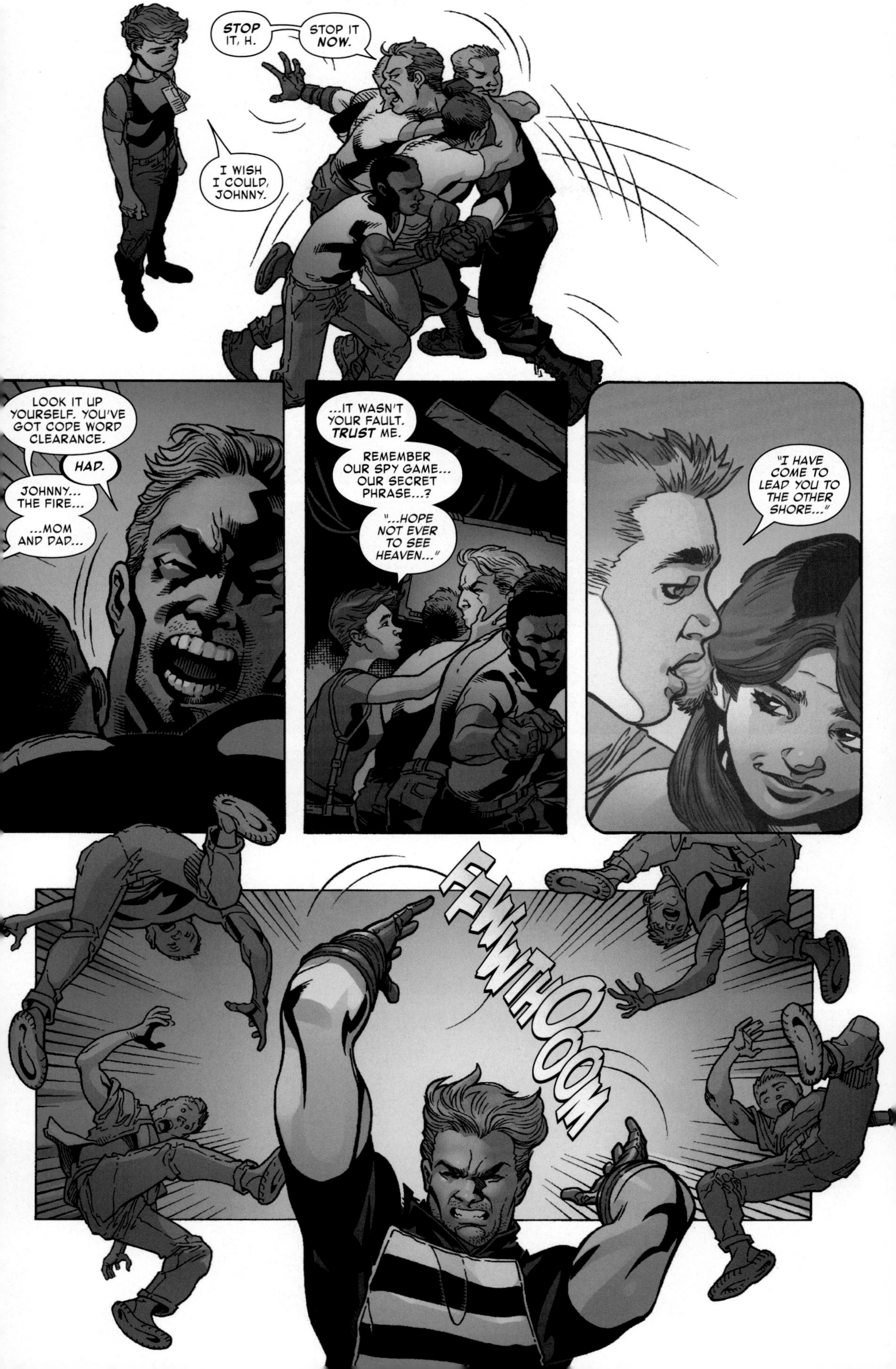
STOP IT, H.
STOP IT NOW.
I WISH I COULD, JOHNNY.
LOOK IT UP YOURSELF. YOU'VE GOT CODE WORD CLEARANCE.
HAD.
JOHNNY... THE FIRE...
...MOM AND DAD...
...IT WASN'T YOUR FAULT. TRUST ME.
REMEMBER OUR SPY GAME... OUR SECRET PHRASE...?
"...HOPE NOT EVER TO SEE HEAVEN..."
"I HAVE COME TO LEAD YOU TO THE OTHER SHORE..."
FFWHTHOOOM

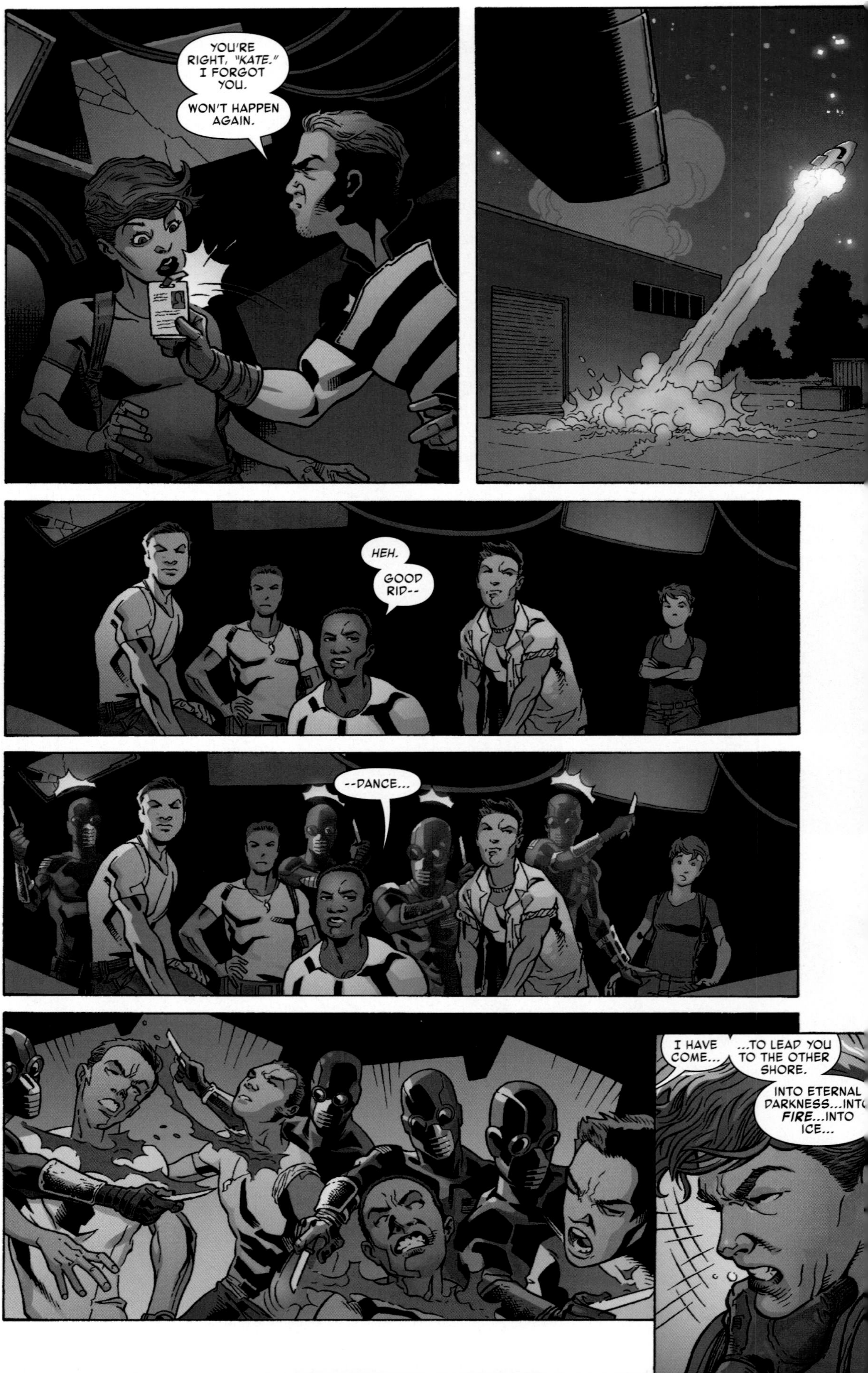
YOU'RE RIGHT, "KATE." I FORGOT YOU.
WON'T HAPPEN AGAIN.
HEH.
GOOD RID--
--DANCE...
I HAVE COME...
...TO LEAD YOU TO THE OTHER SHORE.
INTO ETERNAL DARKNESS...INTO FIRE...INTO ICE...

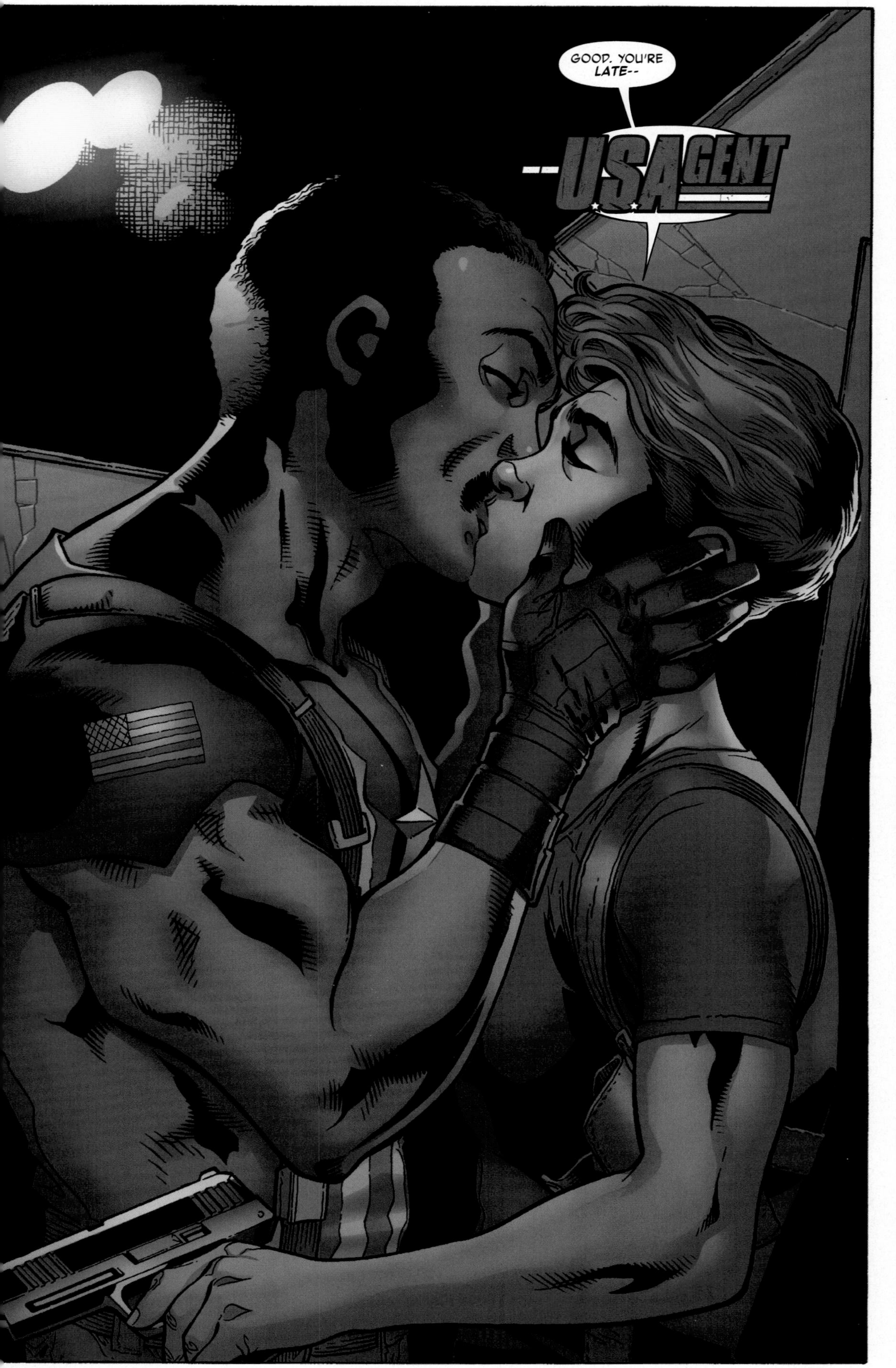
GOOD. YOU'RE LATE--
--USAGENT

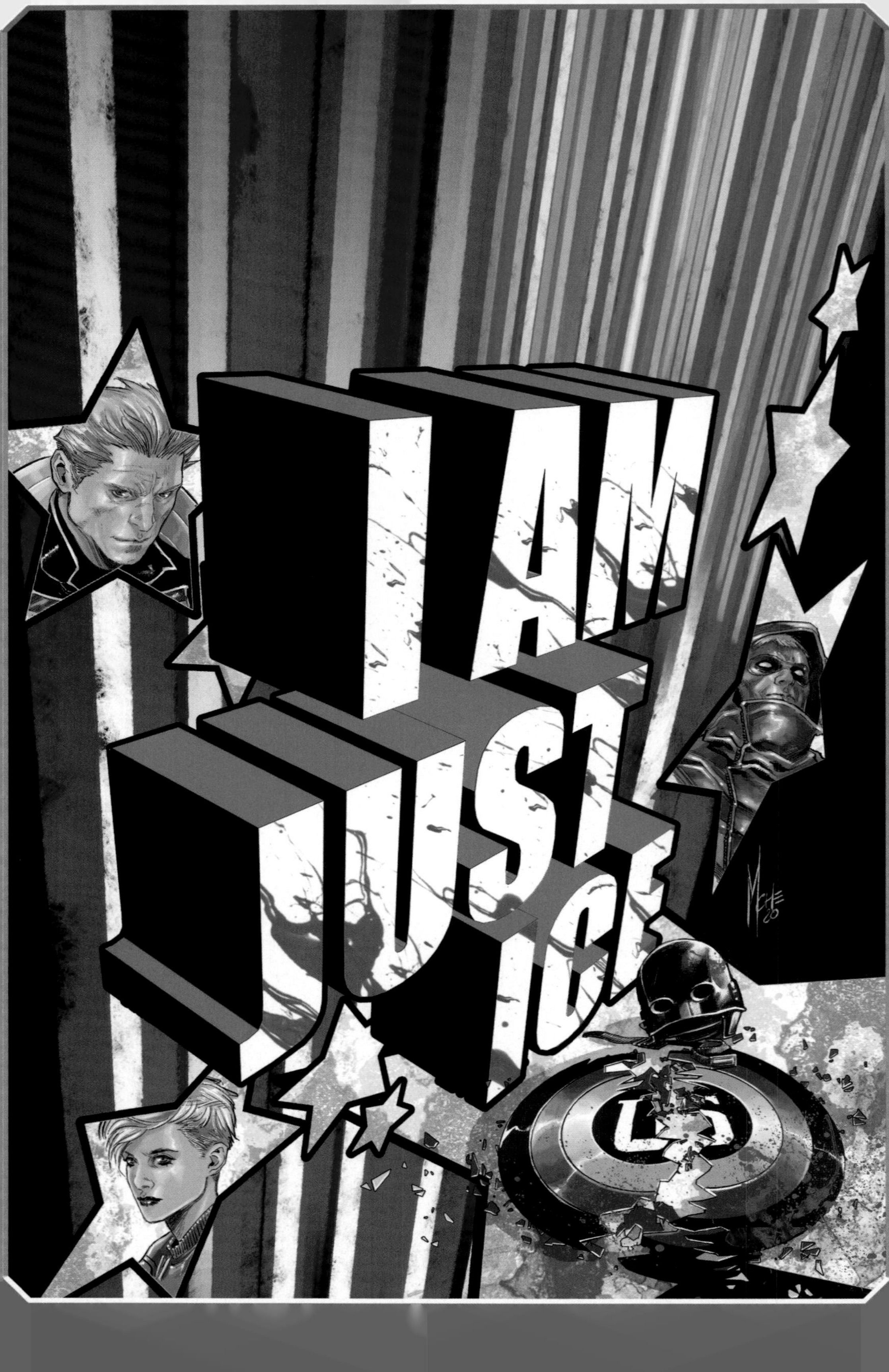
I AM
JUST
ICE

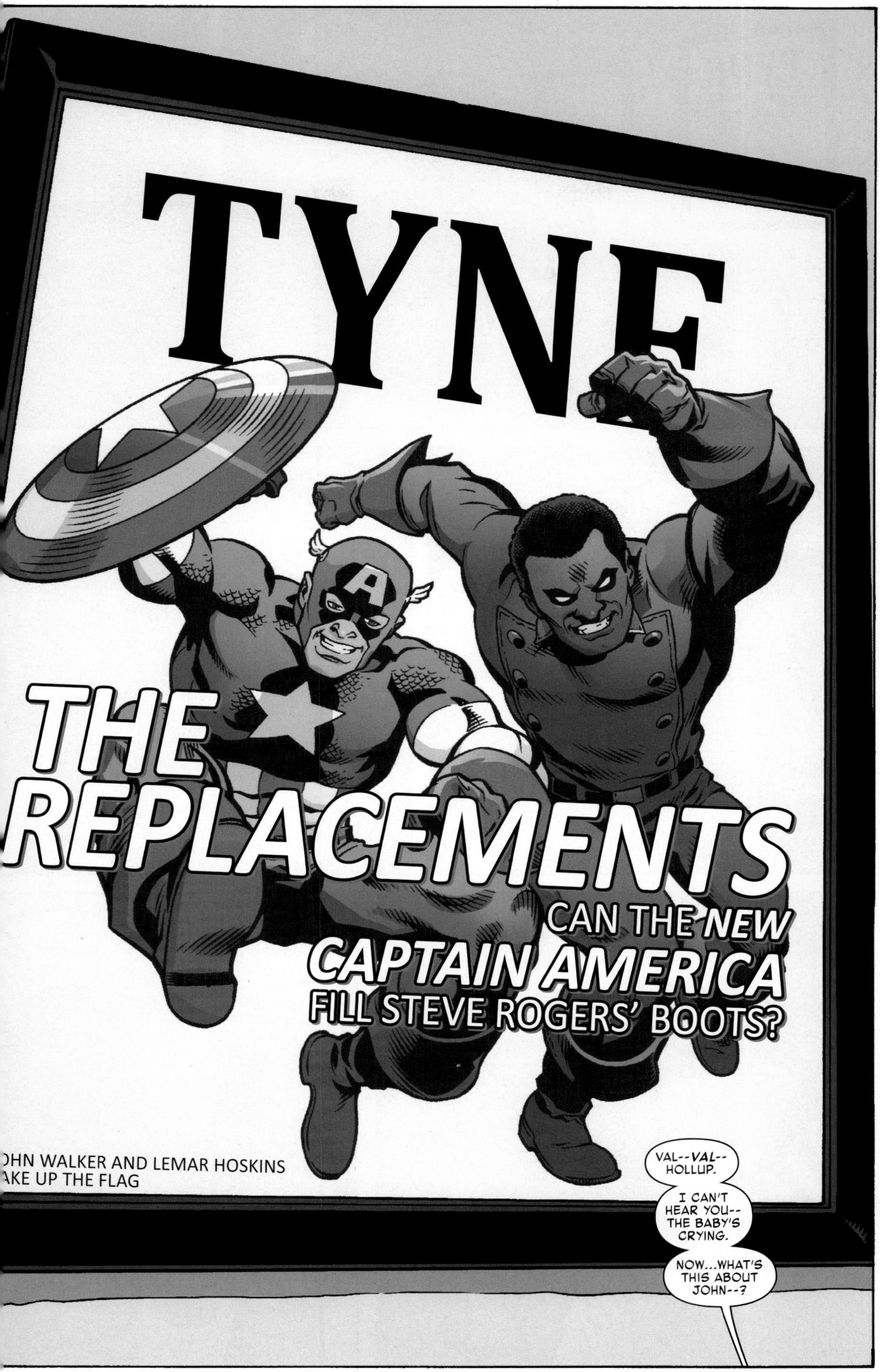
TYNE
THE REPLACEMENTS
CAN THE NEW CAPTAIN AMERICA FILL STEVE ROGERS' BOOTS?
OHN WALKER AND LEMAR HOSKINS
AKE UP THE FLAG
VAL--VAL--HOLLUP.
I CAN'T HEAR YOU--THE BABY'S CRYING.
NOW...WHAT'S THIS ABOUT JOHN--?

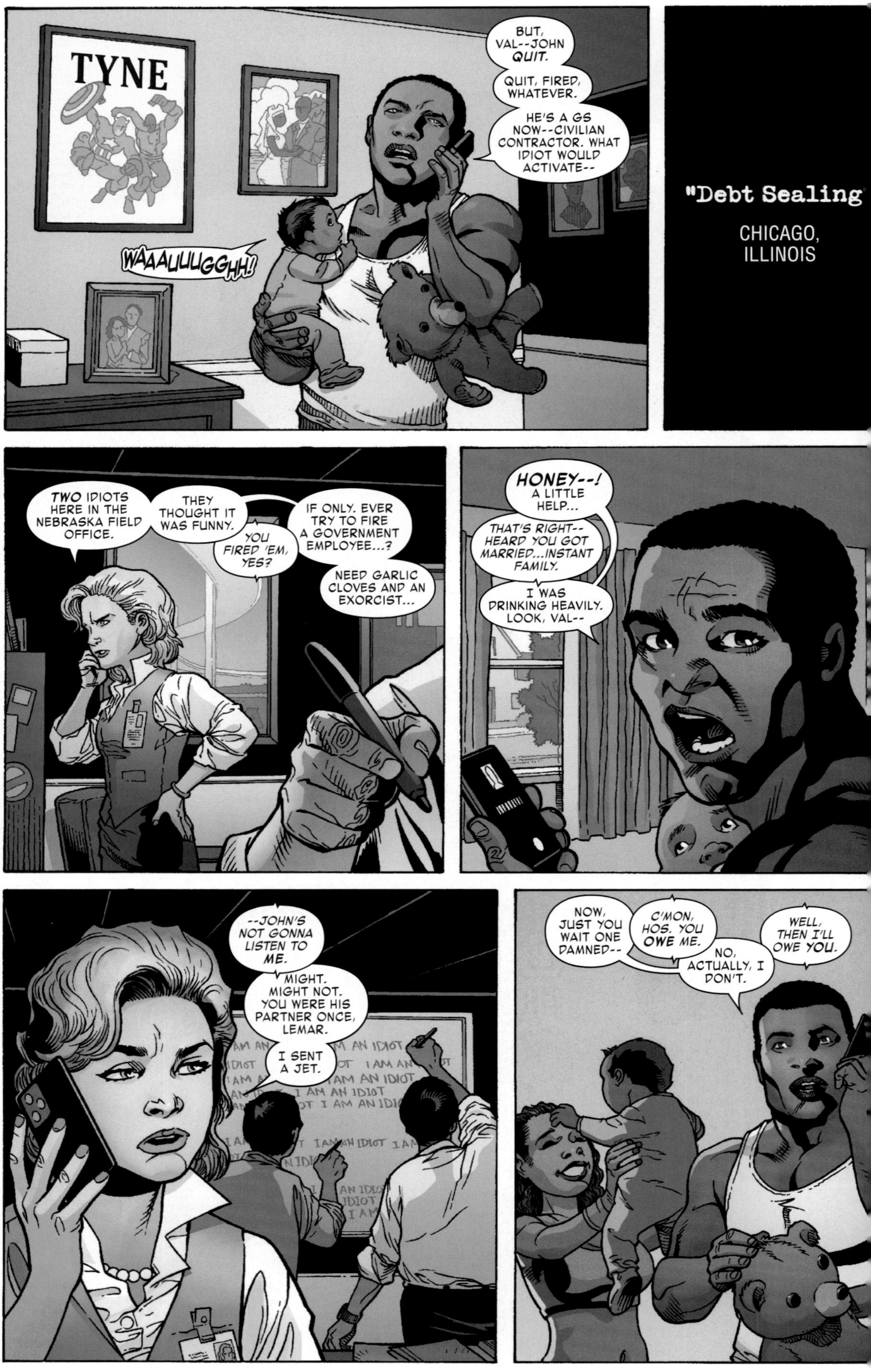

"Debt Sealing"
CHICAGO, ILLINOIS
TYNE
BUT, VAL--JOHN QUIT.
QUIT, FIRED, WHATEVER.
HE'S A GS NOW--CIVILIAN CONTRACTOR. WHAT IDIOT WOULD ACTIVATE--
WAAAUUUGGHH!
TWO IDIOTS HERE IN THE NEBRASKA FIELD OFFICE.
THEY THOUGHT IT WAS FUNNY.
YOU FIRED 'EM, YES?
IF ONLY. EVER TRY TO FIRE A GOVERNMENT EMPLOYEE...?
NEED GARLIC CLOVES AND AN EXORCIST...
HONEY--! A LITTLE HELP...
THAT'S RIGHT--HEARD YOU GOT MARRIED...INSTANT FAMILY.
I WAS DRINKING HEAVILY. LOOK, VAL--
--JOHN'S NOT GONNA LISTEN TO ME.
MIGHT. MIGHT NOT. YOU WERE HIS PARTNER ONCE, LEMAR.
I SENT A JET.
I AM AN IDIOT
NOW, JUST YOU WAIT ONE DAMNED--
C'MON, HOS. YOU OWE ME.
NO, ACTUALLY, I DON'T.
WELL, THEN I'LL OWE YOU.

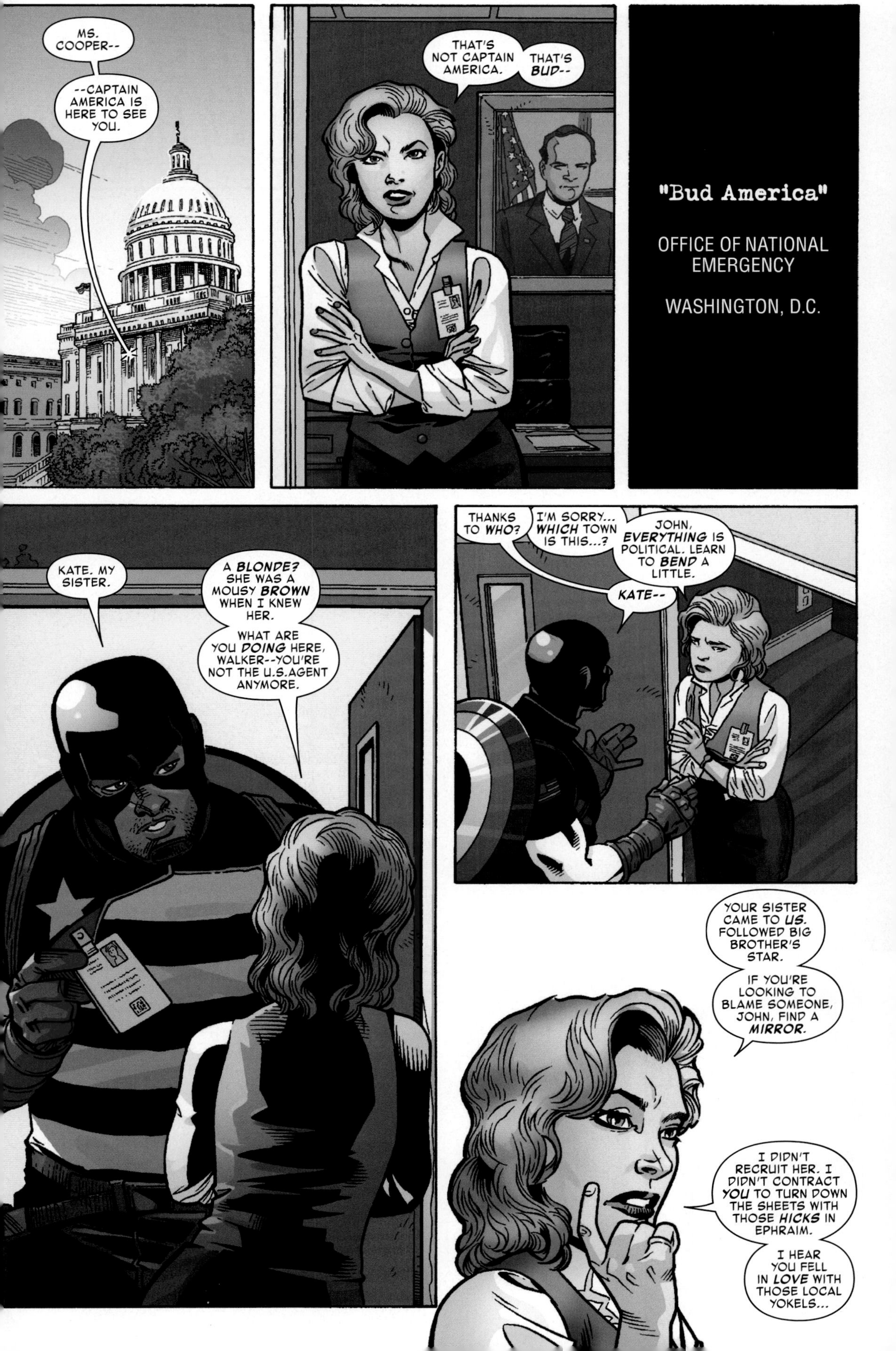
MS. COOPER--
--CAPTAIN AMERICA IS HERE TO SEE YOU.
THAT'S NOT CAPTAIN AMERICA.
THAT'S *BUD*--
"Bud America"
OFFICE OF NATIONAL EMERGENCY
WASHINGTON, D.C.
KATE. MY SISTER.
A *BLONDE?* SHE WAS A MOUSY *BROWN* WHEN I KNEW HER.
WHAT ARE YOU *DOING* HERE, WALKER--YOU'RE NOT THE U.S.AGENT ANYMORE.
THANKS TO *WHO?*
I'M SORRY... *WHICH* TOWN IS THIS...?
JOHN, *EVERYTHING* IS POLITICAL. LEARN TO *BEND* A LITTLE.
KATE--
YOUR SISTER CAME TO *US*. FOLLOWED BIG BROTHER'S STAR.
IF YOU'RE LOOKING TO BLAME SOMEONE, JOHN, FIND A *MIRROR*.
I DIDN'T RECRUIT HER. I DIDN'T CONTRACT *YOU* TO TURN DOWN THE SHEETS WITH THOSE *HICKS* IN EPHRAIM.
I HEAR YOU FELL IN *LOVE* WITH THOSE LOCAL YOKELS...

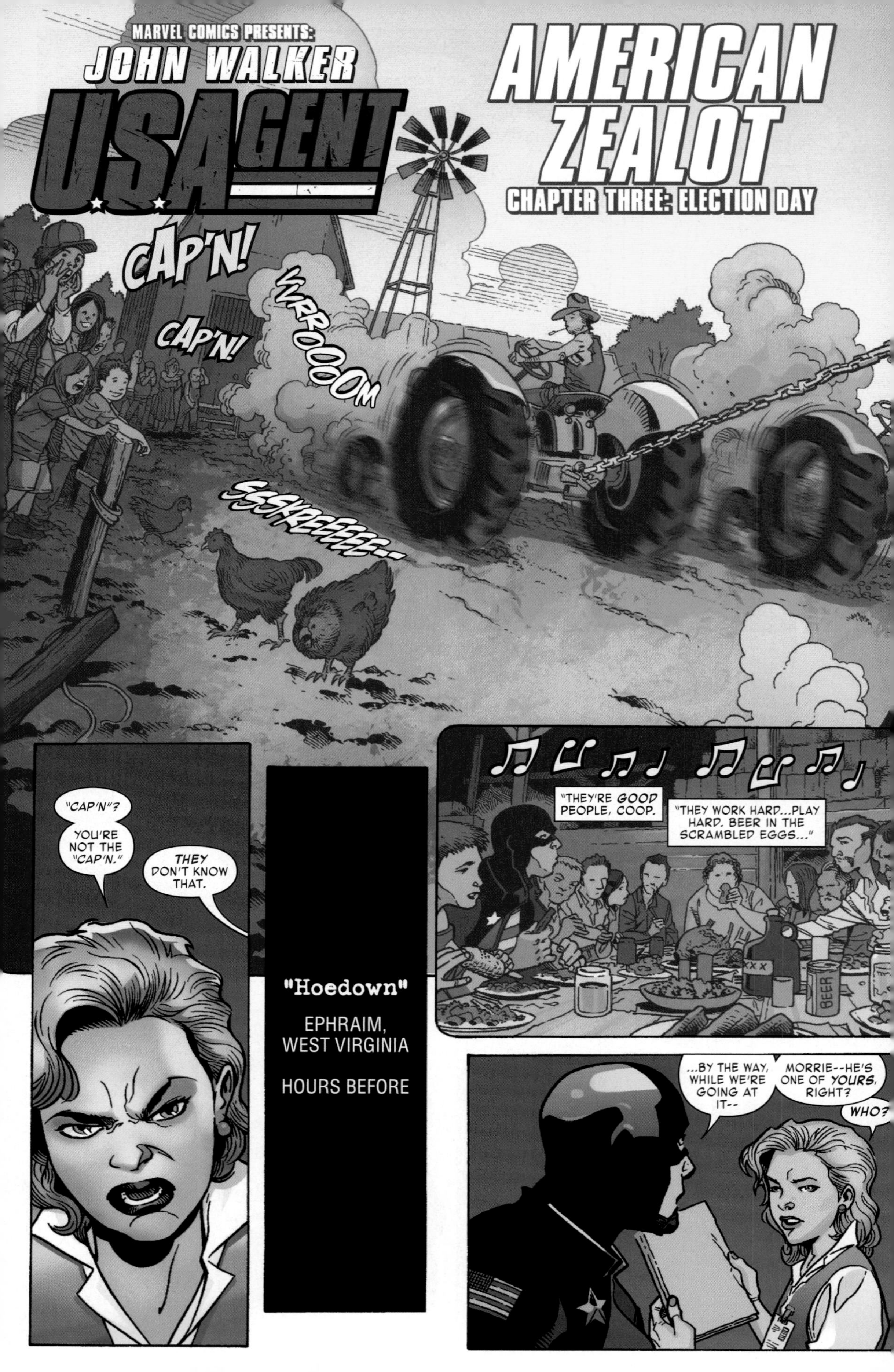
MARVEL COMICS PRESENTS:
JOHN WALKER
U.S.AGENT
AMERICAN ZEALOT
CHAPTER THREE: ELECTION DAY
CAP'N!
CAP'N!
VVRROOOOOM
SSSKREEEEEE--
"CAP'N"? YOU'RE NOT THE "CAP'N."
THEY DON'T KNOW THAT.
"Hoedown"
EPHRAIM, WEST VIRGINIA
HOURS BEFORE
"THEY'RE GOOD PEOPLE, COOP.
"THEY WORK HARD...PLAY HARD. BEER IN THE SCRAMBLED EGGS..."
XXX
BEER
...BY THE WAY, WHILE WE'RE GOING AT IT--
MORRIE--HE'S ONE OF YOURS, RIGHT?
WHO?

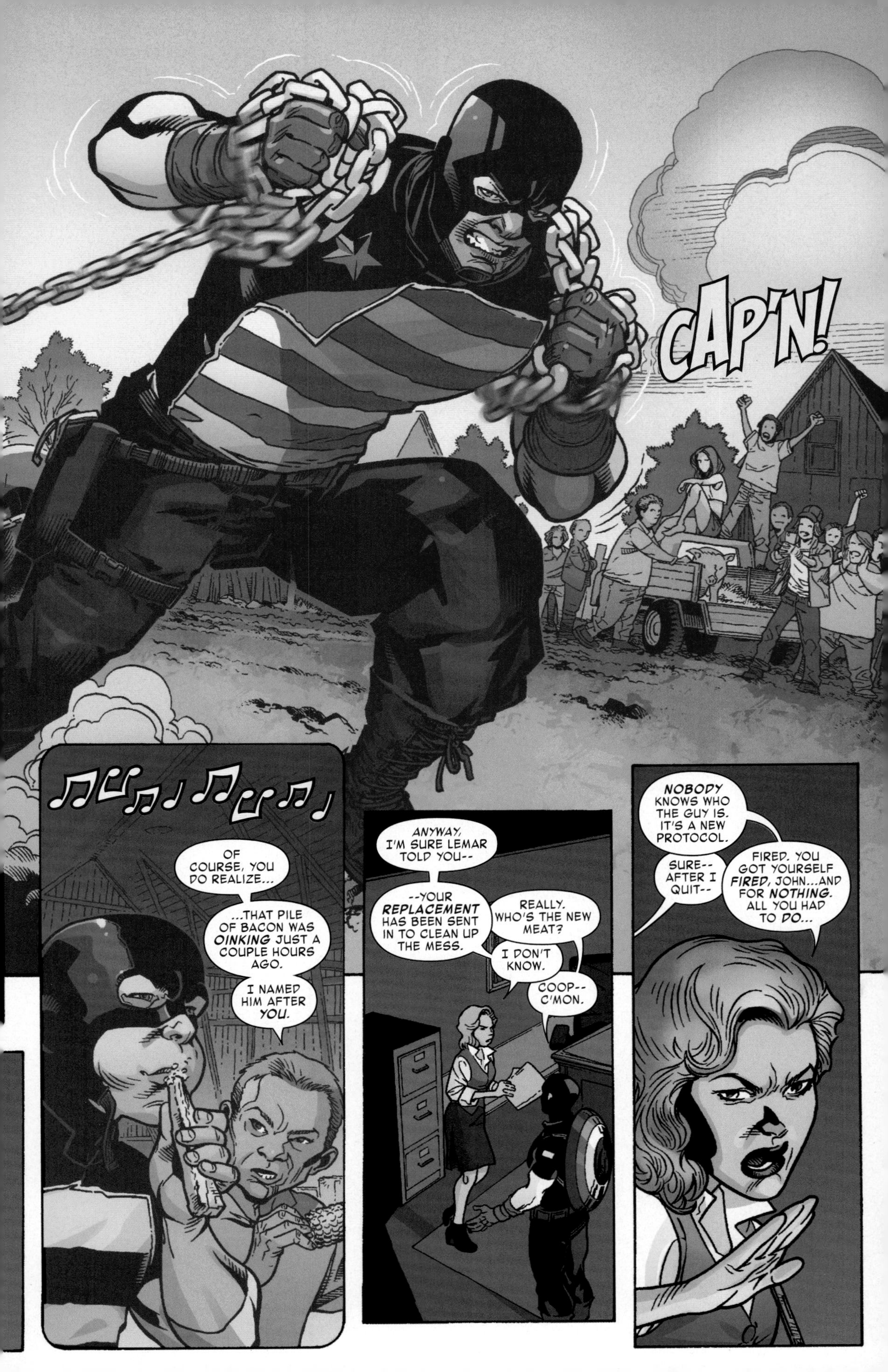
CAP'N!
OF COURSE, YOU DO REALIZE...
...THAT PILE OF BACON WAS OINKING JUST A COUPLE HOURS AGO.
I NAMED HIM AFTER YOU.
ANYWAY, I'M SURE LEMAR TOLD YOU--
--YOUR REPLACEMENT HAS BEEN SENT IN TO CLEAN UP THE MESS.
REALLY. WHO'S THE NEW MEAT?
I DON'T KNOW.
COOP-- C'MON.
NOBODY KNOWS WHO THE GUY IS. IT'S A NEW PROTOCOL.
SURE-- AFTER I QUIT--
FIRED. YOU GOT YOURSELF FIRED, JOHN...AND FOR NOTHING. ALL YOU HAD TO DO...

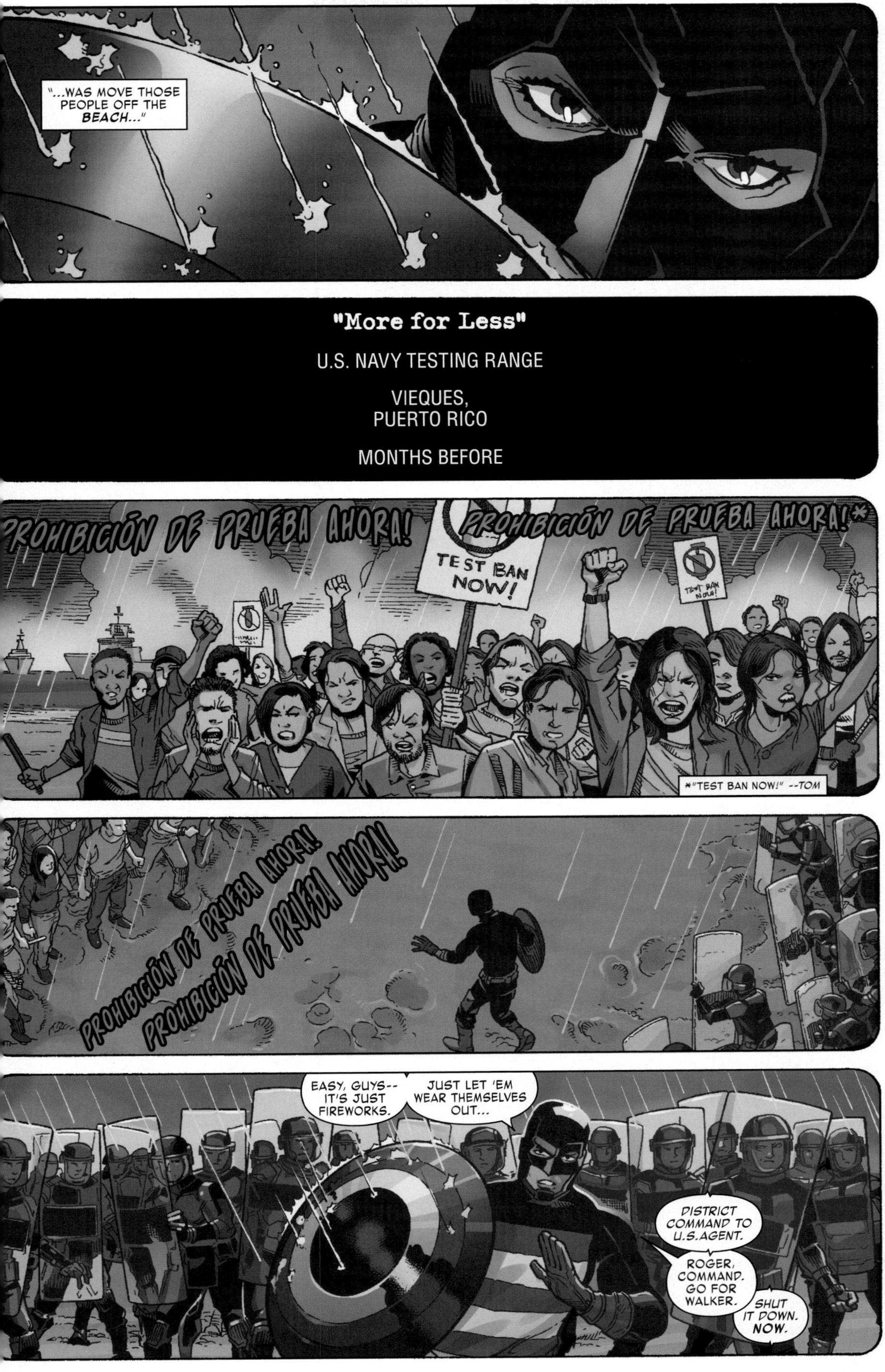
"...WAS MOVE THOSE PEOPLE OFF THE BEACH..."
"More for Less"
U.S. NAVY TESTING RANGE
VIEQUES, PUERTO RICO
MONTHS BEFORE
PROHIBICIÓN DE PRUEBA AHORA!
PROHIBICIÓN DE PRUEBA AHORA!*
TEST BAN NOW!
*"TEST BAN NOW!" --TOM
PROHIBICIÓN DE PRUEBA AHORA!
PROHIBICIÓN DE PRUEBA AHORA!
EASY, GUYS-- IT'S JUST FIREWORKS.
JUST LET 'EM WEAR THEMSELVES OUT...
DISTRICT COMMAND TO U.S.AGENT.
ROGER, COMMAND. GO FOR WALKER.
SHUT IT DOWN. NOW.

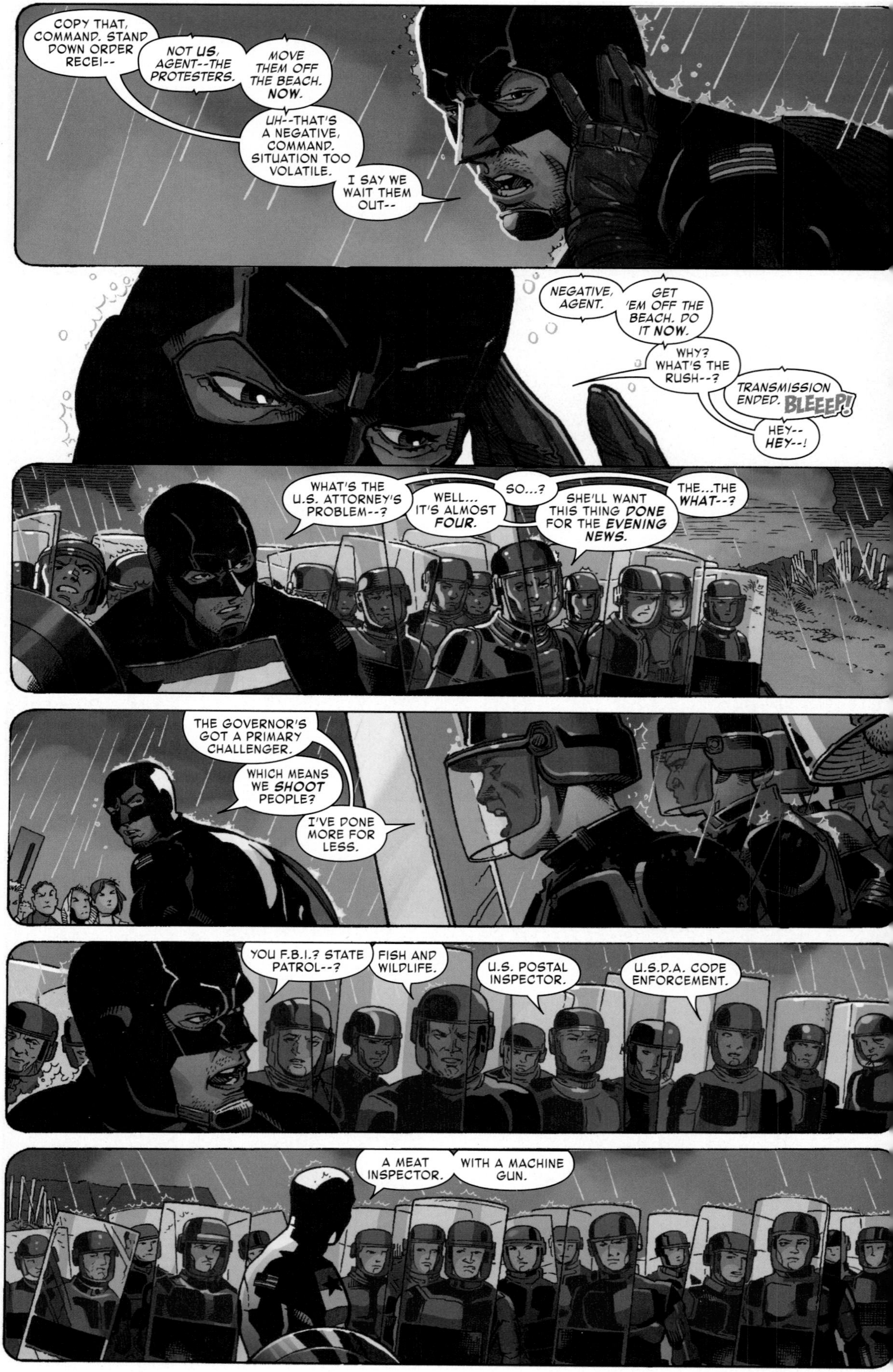
COPY THAT, COMMAND. STAND DOWN ORDER RECEI--
NOT US, AGENT--THE PROTESTERS.
MOVE THEM OFF THE BEACH. NOW.
UH--THAT'S A NEGATIVE, COMMAND. SITUATION TOO VOLATILE.
I SAY WE WAIT THEM OUT--
NEGATIVE, AGENT.
GET 'EM OFF THE BEACH. DO IT NOW.
WHY? WHAT'S THE RUSH--?
TRANSMISSION ENDED. BLEEEP!
HEY-- HEY--!
WHAT'S THE U.S. ATTORNEY'S PROBLEM--?
WELL... IT'S ALMOST FOUR.
SO...?
SHE'LL WANT THIS THING DONE FOR THE EVENING NEWS.
THE...THE WHAT--?
THE GOVERNOR'S GOT A PRIMARY CHALLENGER.
WHICH MEANS WE SHOOT PEOPLE?
I'VE DONE MORE FOR LESS.
YOU F.B.I.? STATE PATROL--?
FISH AND WILDLIFE.
U.S. POSTAL INSPECTOR.
U.S.D.A. CODE ENFORCEMENT.
A MEAT INSPECTOR.
WITH A MACHINE GUN.

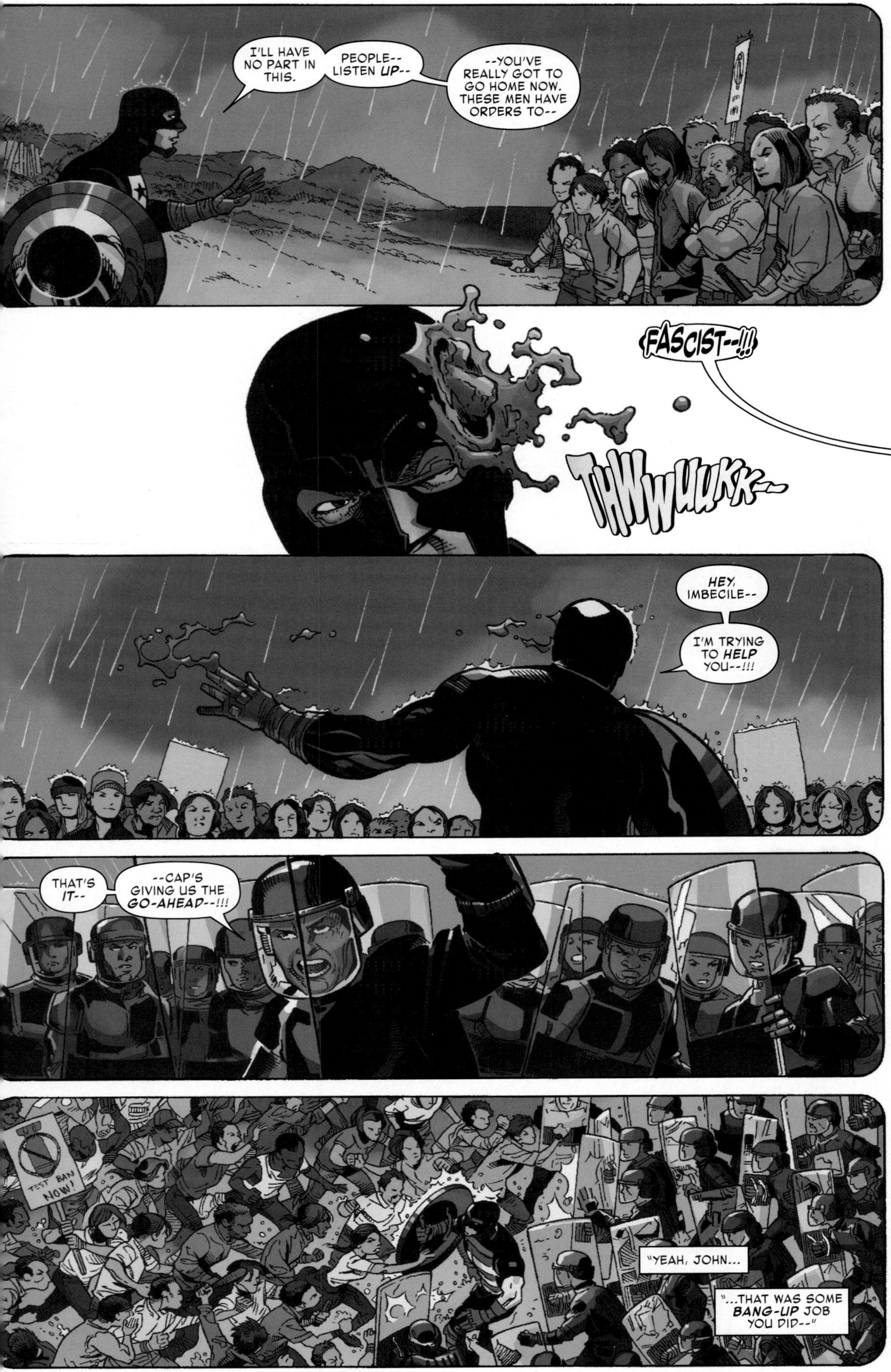
I'LL HAVE NO PART IN THIS.
PEOPLE-- LISTEN UP--
--YOU'VE REALLY GOT TO GO HOME NOW. THESE MEN HAVE ORDERS TO--
FASCIST--!!!
THWWUUKK--
HEY, IMBECILE--
I'M TRYING TO HELP YOU--!!!
THAT'S IT--
--CAP'S GIVING US THE GO-AHEAD--!!!
TEST BAN NOW!
"YEAH, JOHN...
"...THAT WAS SOME BANG-UP JOB YOU DID--"

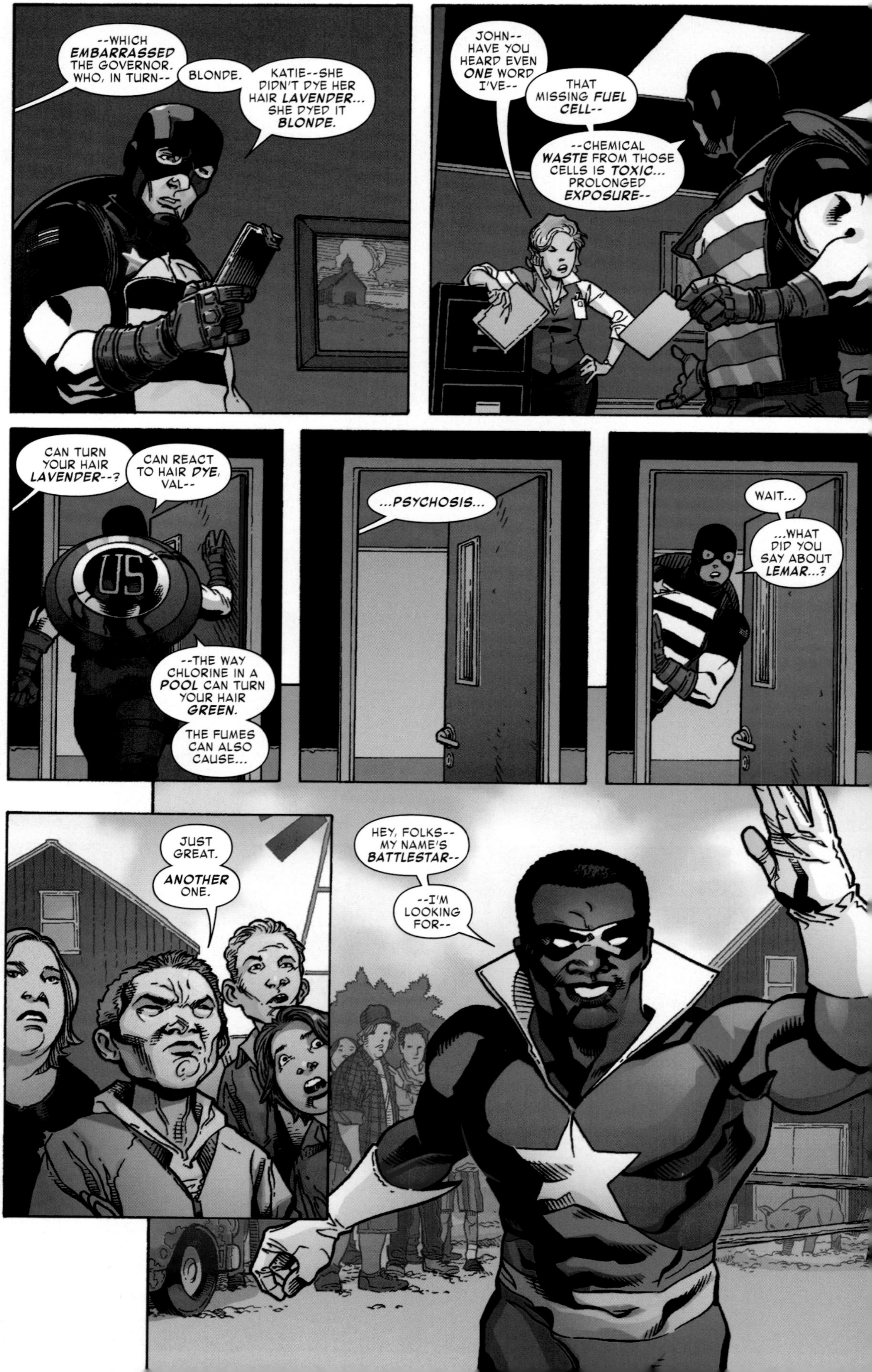
--WHICH EMBARRASSED THE GOVERNOR. WHO, IN TURN--
BLONDE.
KATIE--SHE DIDN'T DYE HER HAIR LAVENDER... SHE DYED IT BLONDE.
JOHN-- HAVE YOU HEARD EVEN ONE WORD I'VE--
THAT MISSING FUEL CELL--
--CHEMICAL WASTE FROM THOSE CELLS IS TOXIC... PROLONGED EXPOSURE--
CAN TURN YOUR HAIR LAVENDER--?
CAN REACT TO HAIR DYE, VAL--
--THE WAY CHLORINE IN A POOL CAN TURN YOUR HAIR GREEN.
THE FUMES CAN ALSO CAUSE...
...PSYCHOSIS...
WAIT...
...WHAT DID YOU SAY ABOUT LEMAR...?
JUST GREAT. ANOTHER ONE.
HEY, FOLKS-- MY NAME'S BATTLESTAR--
--I'M LOOKING FOR--

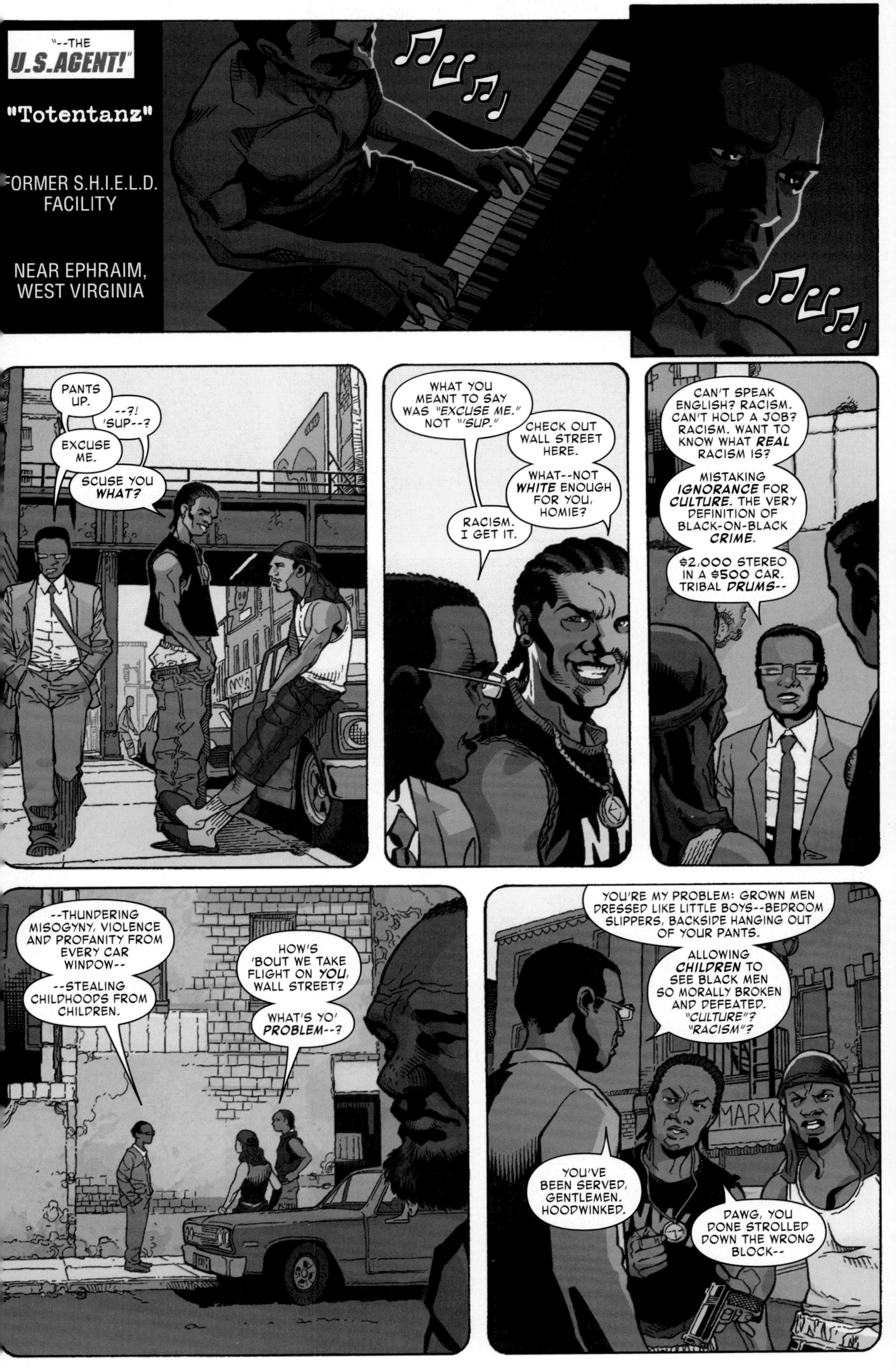
"--THE U.S.AGENT!"
"Totentanz"
FORMER S.H.I.E.L.D. FACILITY
NEAR EPHRAIM, WEST VIRGINIA
PANTS UP.
--?! 'SUP--?
EXCUSE ME.
SCUSE YOU WHAT?
WHAT YOU MEANT TO SAY WAS "EXCUSE ME." NOT "'SUP."
CHECK OUT WALL STREET HERE.
WHAT--NOT WHITE ENOUGH FOR YOU, HOMIE?
RACISM. I GET IT.
CAN'T SPEAK ENGLISH? RACISM. CAN'T HOLD A JOB? RACISM. WANT TO KNOW WHAT REAL RACISM IS?
MISTAKING IGNORANCE FOR CULTURE. THE VERY DEFINITION OF BLACK-ON-BLACK CRIME.
$2,000 STEREO IN A $500 CAR. TRIBAL DRUMS--
--THUNDERING MISOGYNY, VIOLENCE AND PROFANITY FROM EVERY CAR WINDOW--
--STEALING CHILDHOODS FROM CHILDREN.
HOW'S 'BOUT WE TAKE FLIGHT ON YOU, WALL STREET?
WHAT'S YO' PROBLEM--?
YOU'RE MY PROBLEM: GROWN MEN DRESSED LIKE LITTLE BOYS--BEDROOM SLIPPERS, BACKSIDE HANGING OUT OF YOUR PANTS.
ALLOWING CHILDREN TO SEE BLACK MEN SO MORALLY BROKEN AND DEFEATED. "CULTURE"? "RACISM"?
YOU'VE BEEN SERVED, GENTLEMEN. HOODWINKED.
DAWG, YOU DONE STROLLED DOWN THE WRONG BLOCK--

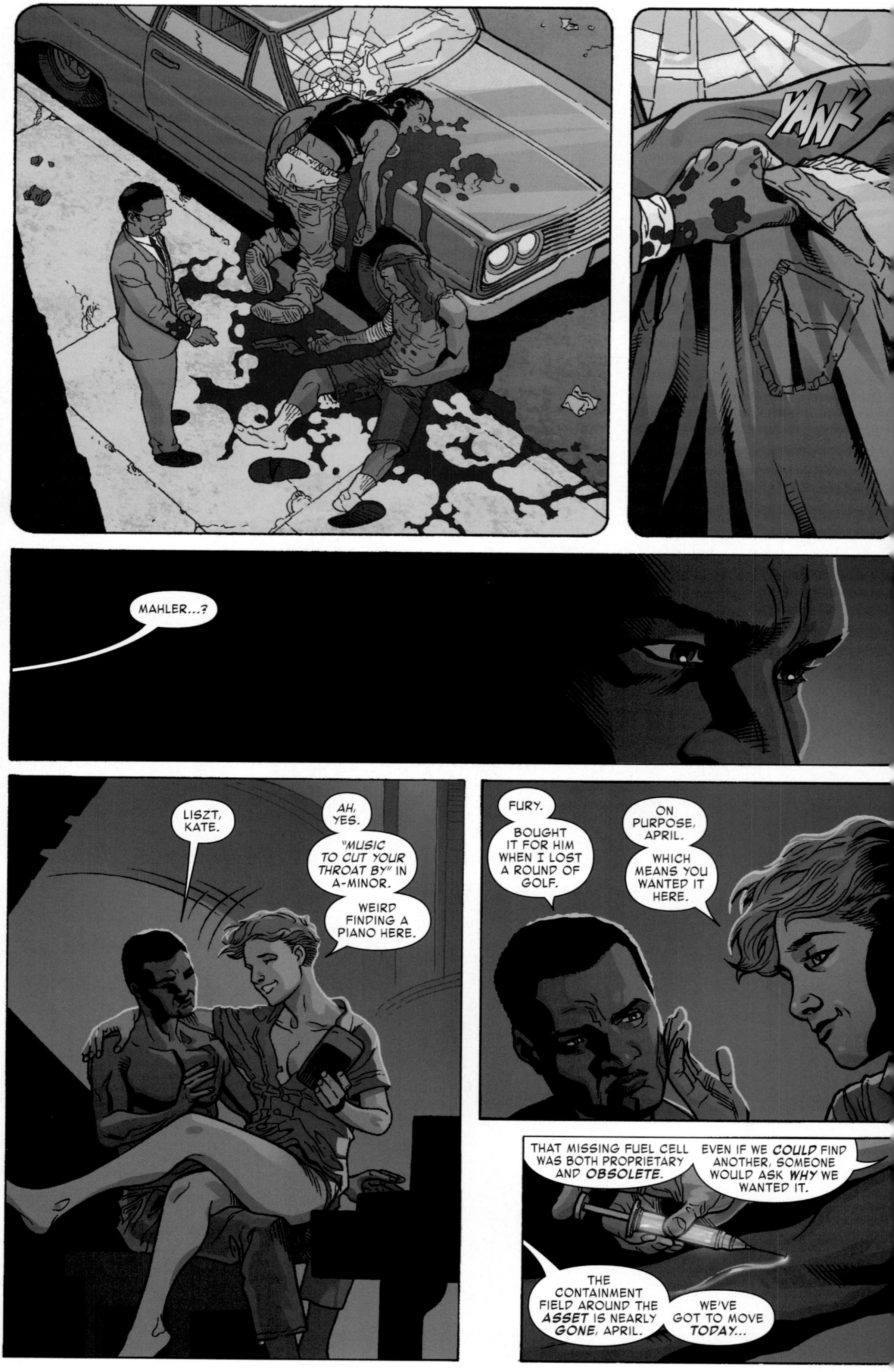
YANK
MAHLER...?
LISZT, KATE.
AH, YES.
"MUSIC TO CUT YOUR THROAT BY" IN A-MINOR.
WEIRD FINDING A PIANO HERE.
FURY.
BOUGHT IT FOR HIM WHEN I LOST A ROUND OF GOLF.
ON PURPOSE, APRIL.
WHICH MEANS YOU WANTED IT HERE.
THAT MISSING FUEL CELL WAS BOTH PROPRIETARY AND OBSOLETE.
EVEN IF WE COULD FIND ANOTHER, SOMEONE WOULD ASK WHY WE WANTED IT.
THE CONTAINMENT FIELD AROUND THE ASSET IS NEARLY GONE, APRIL.
WE'VE GOT TO MOVE TODAY...

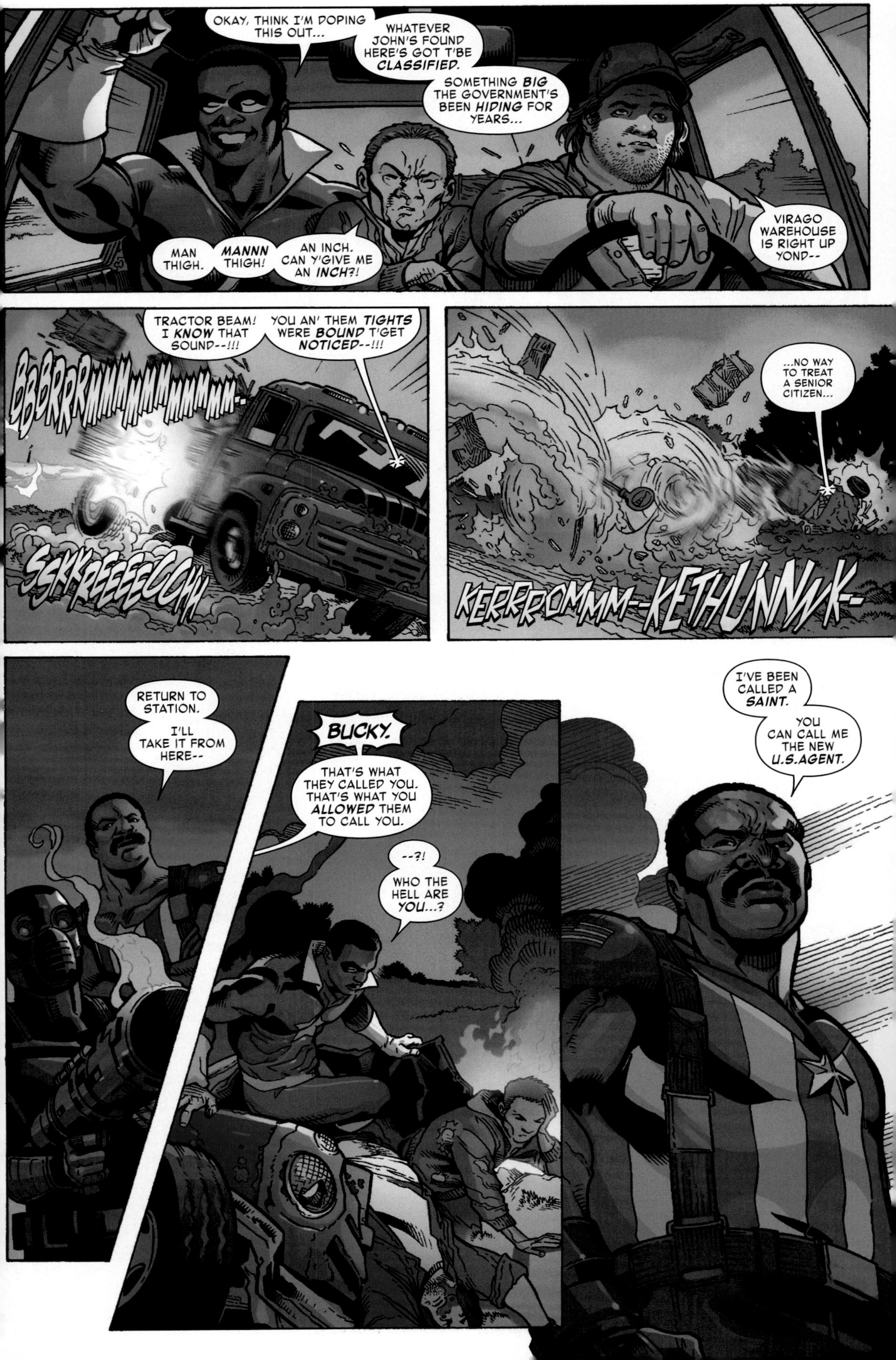
OKAY, THINK I'M DOPING THIS OUT...
WHATEVER JOHN'S FOUND HERE'S GOT T'BE CLASSIFIED.
SOMETHING BIG THE GOVERNMENT'S BEEN HIDING FOR YEARS...
MAN THIGH.
MANNN THIGH!
AN INCH. CAN Y'GIVE ME AN INCH?!
VIRAGO WAREHOUSE IS RIGHT UP YOND--
TRACTOR BEAM! I KNOW THAT SOUND--!!!
YOU AN' THEM TIGHTS WERE BOUND T'GET NOTICED--!!!
BBBRRRMMMMMMMMMMMM-
SSKKREEEEECCHH
...NO WAY TO TREAT A SENIOR CITIZEN...
KERRROMMM--KETHUNNNK-
RETURN TO STATION.
I'LL TAKE IT FROM HERE--
BUCKY.
THAT'S WHAT THEY CALLED YOU. THAT'S WHAT YOU ALLOWED THEM TO CALL YOU.
--?!
WHO THE HELL ARE YOU...?
I'VE BEEN CALLED A SAINT.
YOU CAN CALL ME THE NEW U.S.AGENT.

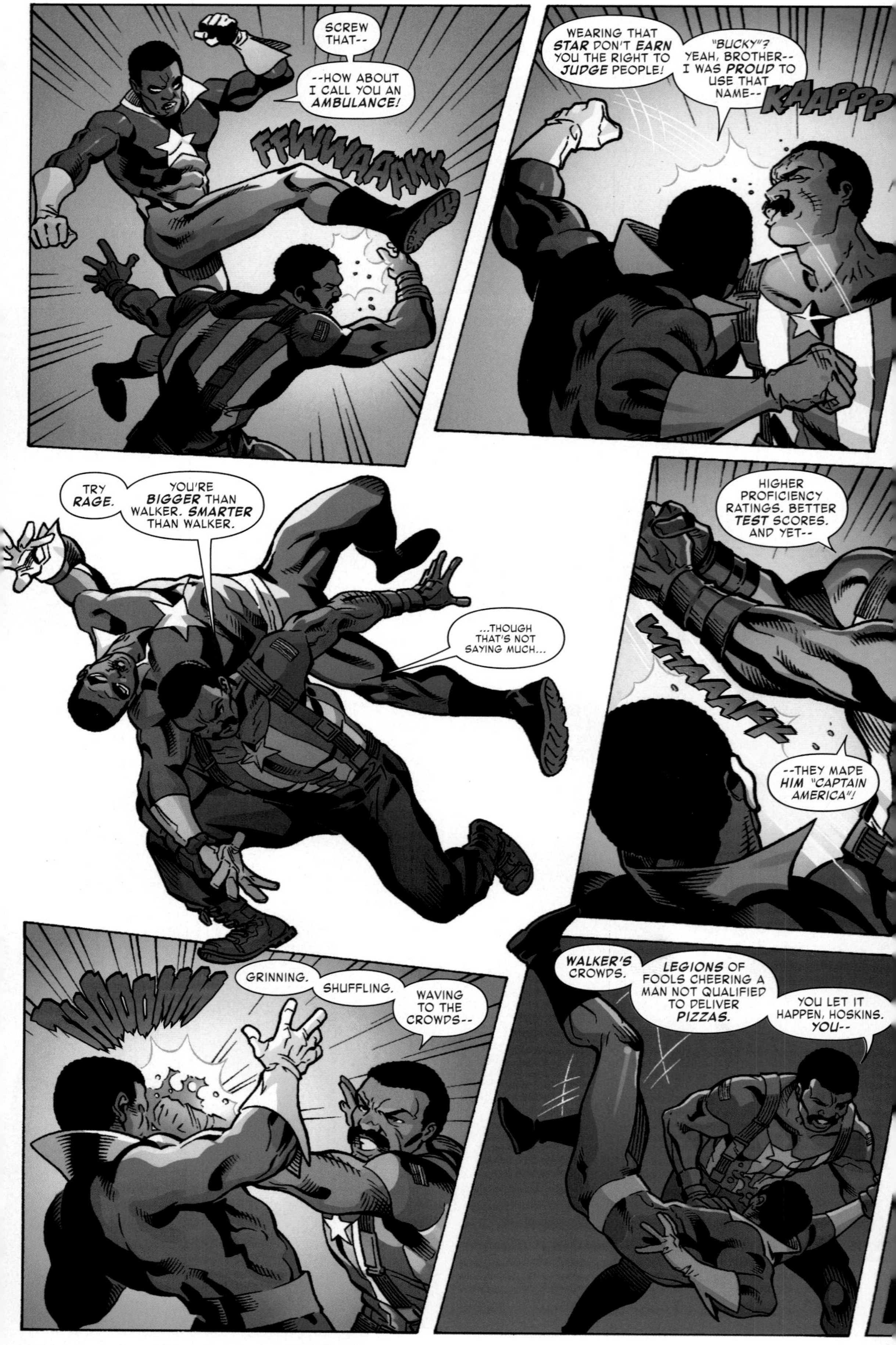
SCREW THAT--
--HOW ABOUT I CALL YOU AN AMBULANCE!
FFWWAAAKK
WEARING THAT STAR DON'T EARN YOU THE RIGHT TO JUDGE PEOPLE!
"BUCKY"? YEAH, BROTHER-- I WAS PROUD TO USE THAT NAME--
KAAPPP
TRY RAGE.
YOU'RE BIGGER THAN WALKER. SMARTER THAN WALKER.
...THOUGH THAT'S NOT SAYING MUCH...
HIGHER PROFICIENCY RATINGS. BETTER TEST SCORES. AND YET--
WHAAAAFK
--THEY MADE HIM "CAPTAIN AMERICA"!
GRINNING.
SHUFFLING.
WAVING TO THE CROWDS--
WALKER'S CROWDS.
LEGIONS OF FOOLS CHEERING A MAN NOT QUALIFIED TO DELIVER PIZZAS.
YOU LET IT HAPPEN, HOSKINS. YOU--

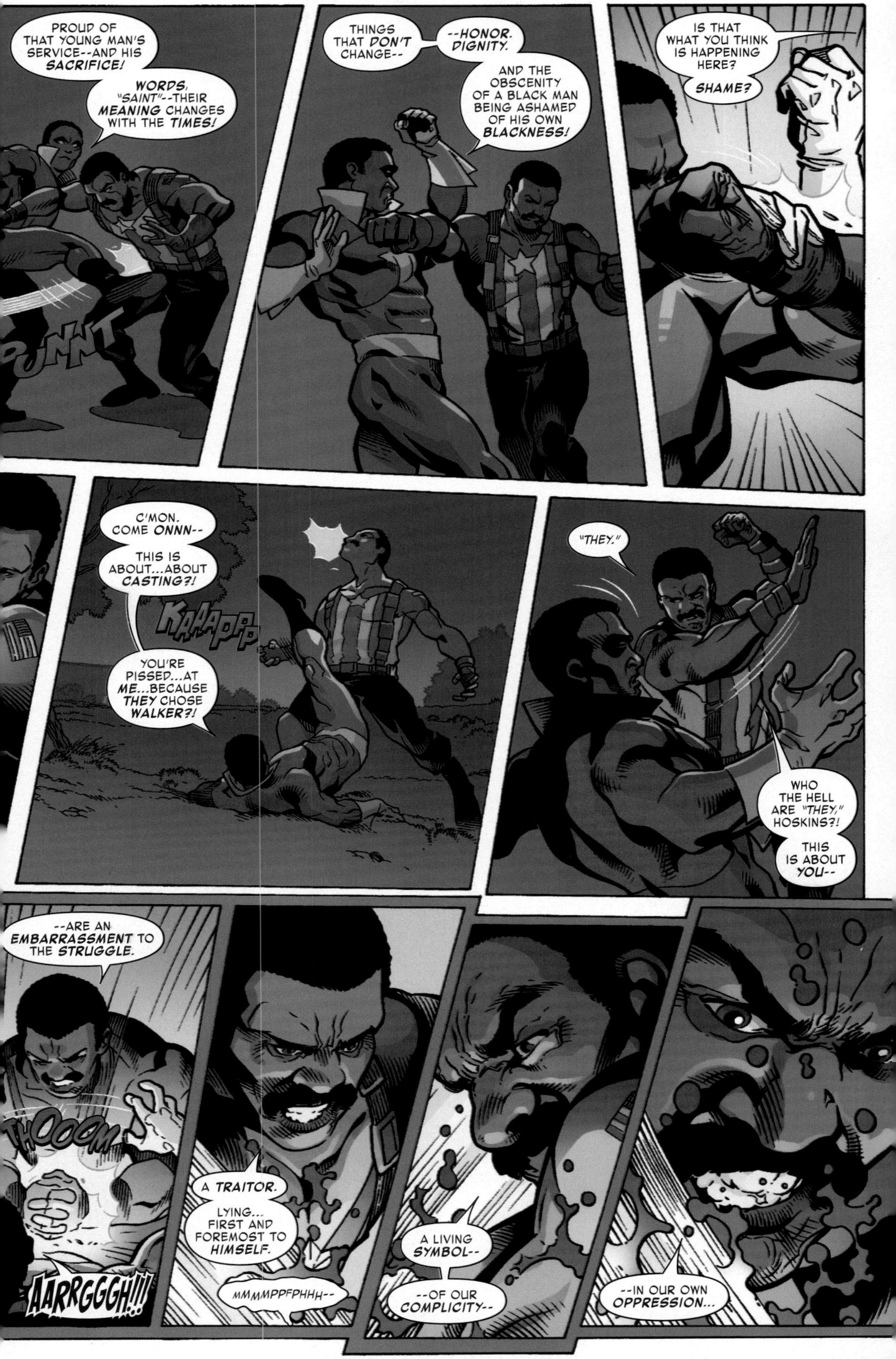
PROUD OF THAT YOUNG MAN'S SERVICE--AND HIS SACRIFICE!
WORDS, "SAINT"--THEIR MEANING CHANGES WITH THE TIMES!
PUNNT
THINGS THAT DON'T CHANGE--
--HONOR. DIGNITY.
AND THE OBSCENITY OF A BLACK MAN BEING ASHAMED OF HIS OWN BLACKNESS!
IS THAT WHAT YOU THINK IS HAPPENING HERE?
SHAME?
C'MON. COME ONNN--
THIS IS ABOUT...ABOUT CASTING?!
KAAAPPP
YOU'RE PISSED...AT ME...BECAUSE THEY CHOSE WALKER?!
"THEY."
WHO THE HELL ARE "THEY," HOSKINS?!
THIS IS ABOUT YOU--
--ARE AN EMBARRASSMENT TO THE STRUGGLE.
THOOOM
AARRGGGH!!!
A TRAITOR.
LYING... FIRST AND FOREMOST TO HIMSELF.
MMMMPPFPHHH--
A LIVING SYMBOL--
--OF OUR COMPLICITY--
--IN OUR OWN OPPRESSION...

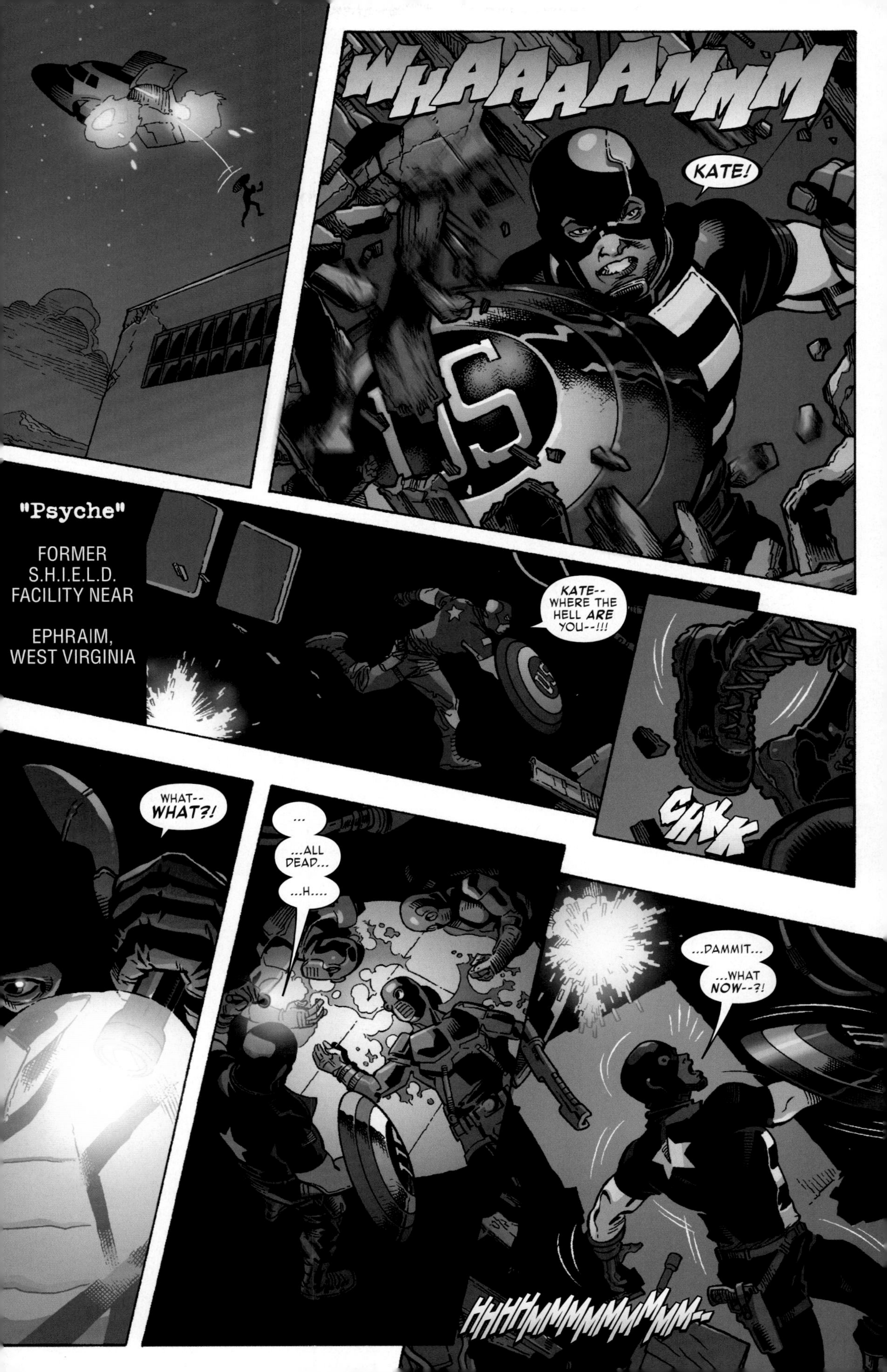
WHAAAAAMMM
KATE!
"Psyche"
FORMER S.H.I.E.L.D. FACILITY NEAR
EPHRAIM, WEST VIRGINIA
KATE-- WHERE THE HELL ARE YOU--!!!
CHKK
WHAT-- WHAT?!
...
...ALL DEAD...
...H....
...DAMMIT...
...WHAT NOW--?!
HHHHMMMMMMMMMM-

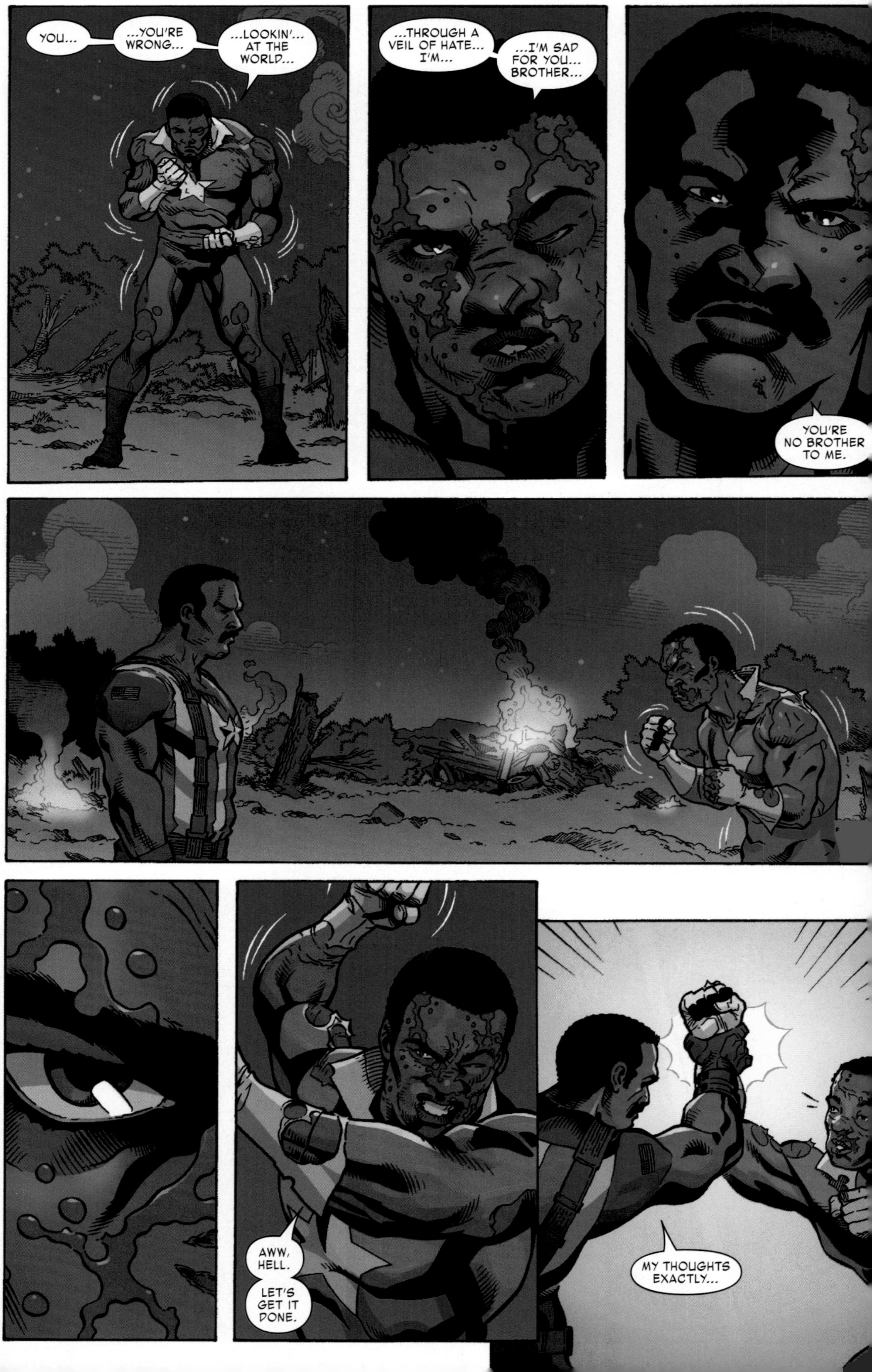
YOU...
...YOU'RE WRONG...
...LOOKIN'... AT THE WORLD...
...THROUGH A VEIL OF HATE... I'M...
...I'M SAD FOR YOU... BROTHER...
YOU'RE NO BROTHER TO ME.
AWW, HELL.
LET'S GET IT DONE.
MY THOUGHTS EXACTLY...

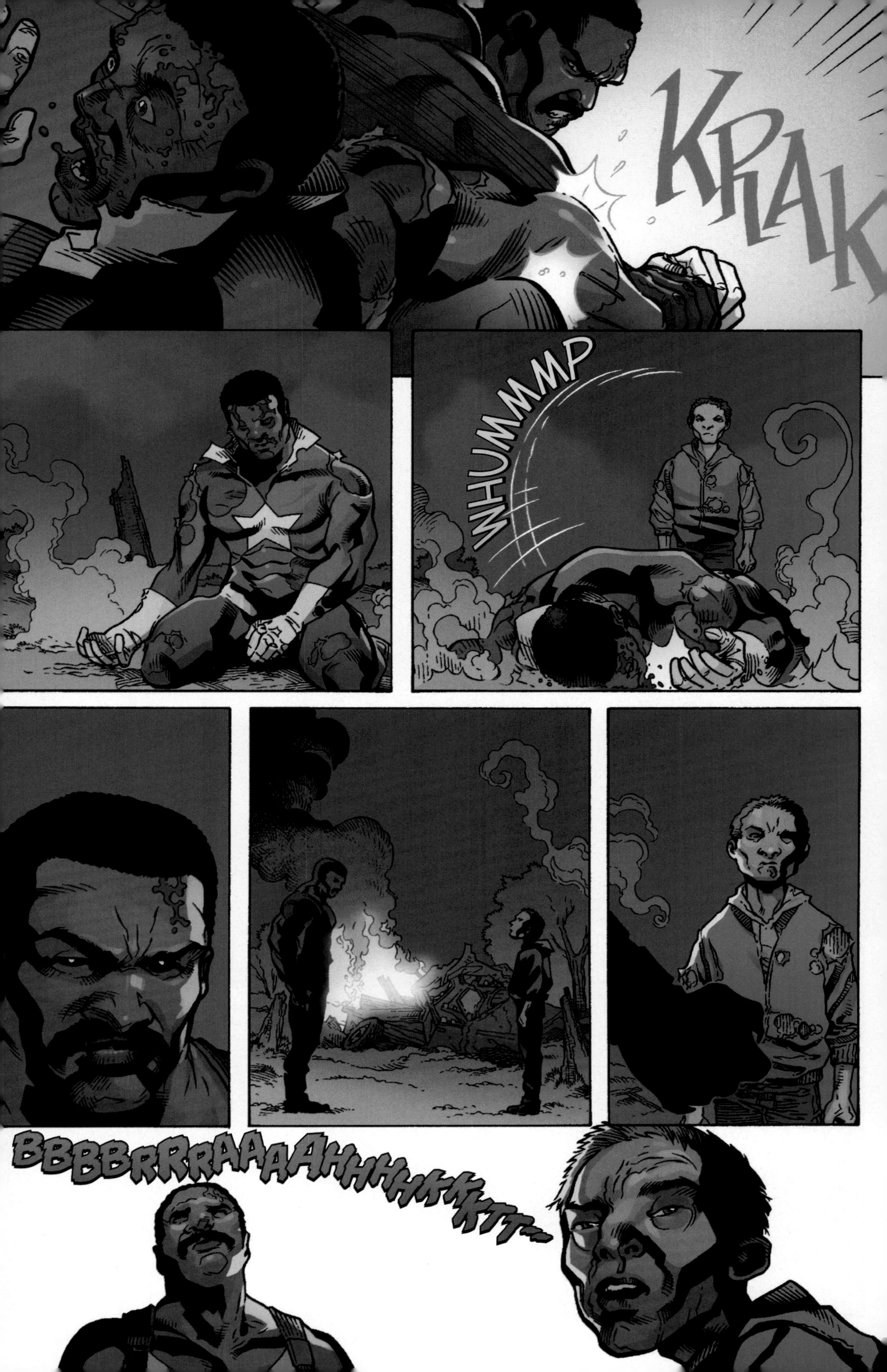
KRAK
WHUMMMP
BBBBRRRAAAAHHHHKKKTT--

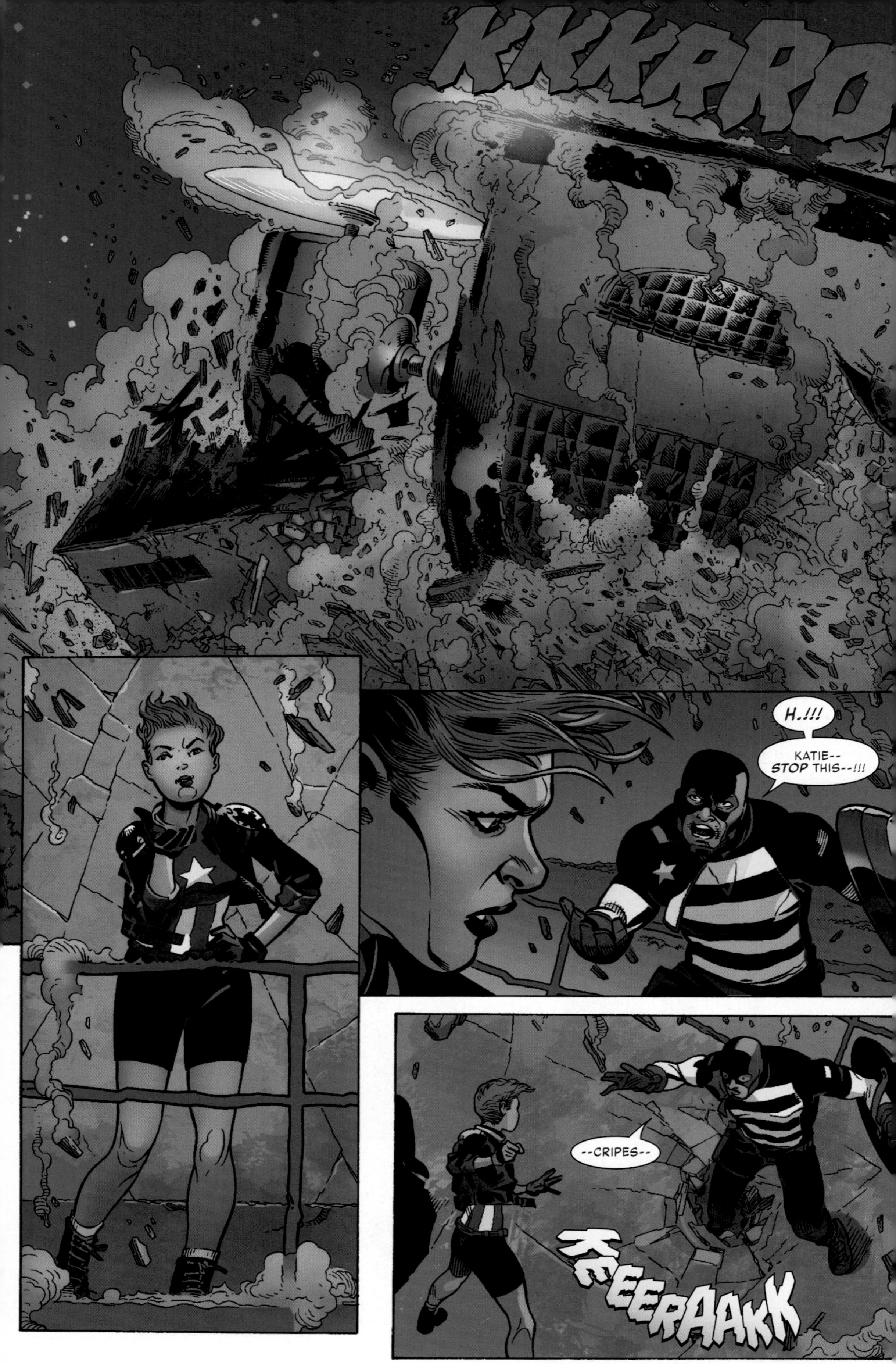
KKKRRO
H..!!!
KATIE--
STOP THIS--!!!
--CRIPES--
KEEERAAKK

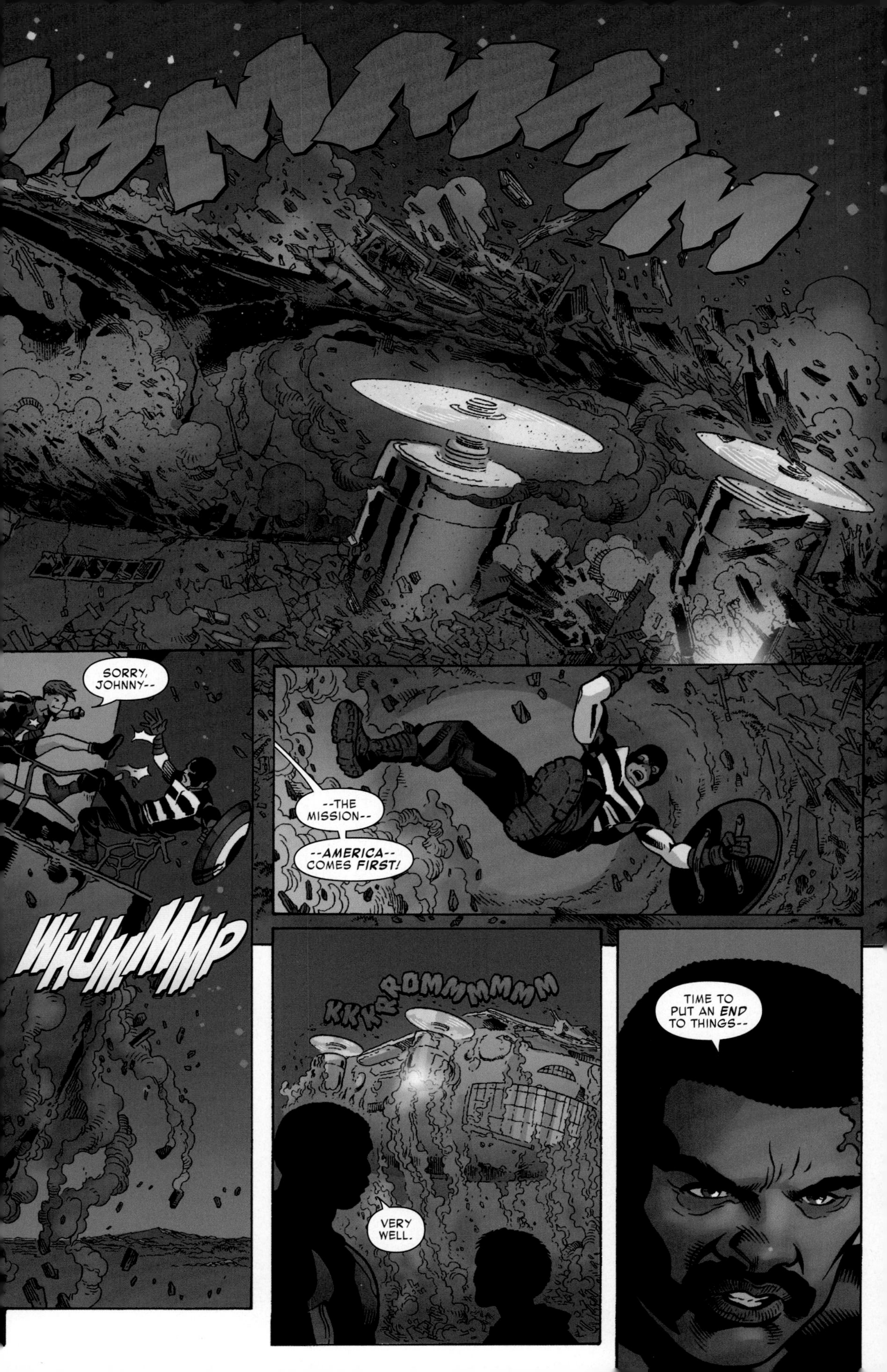
MMMMMMMM
SORRY, JOHNNY--
--THE MISSION--
--AMERICA-- COMES FIRST!
WHUMMMMP
KKKRROMMMMMMM
VERY WELL.
TIME TO PUT AN END TO THINGS--

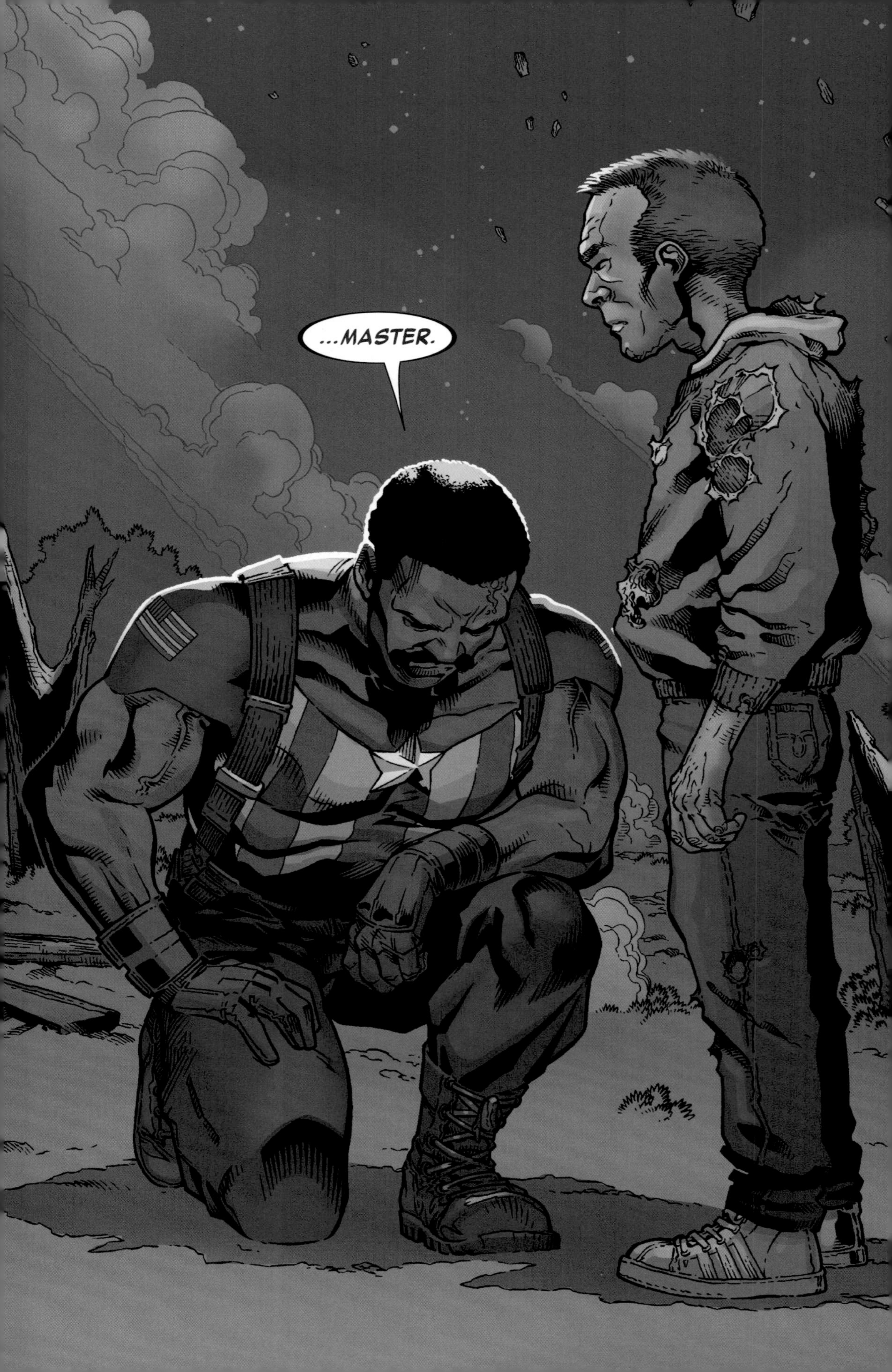
...MASTER.

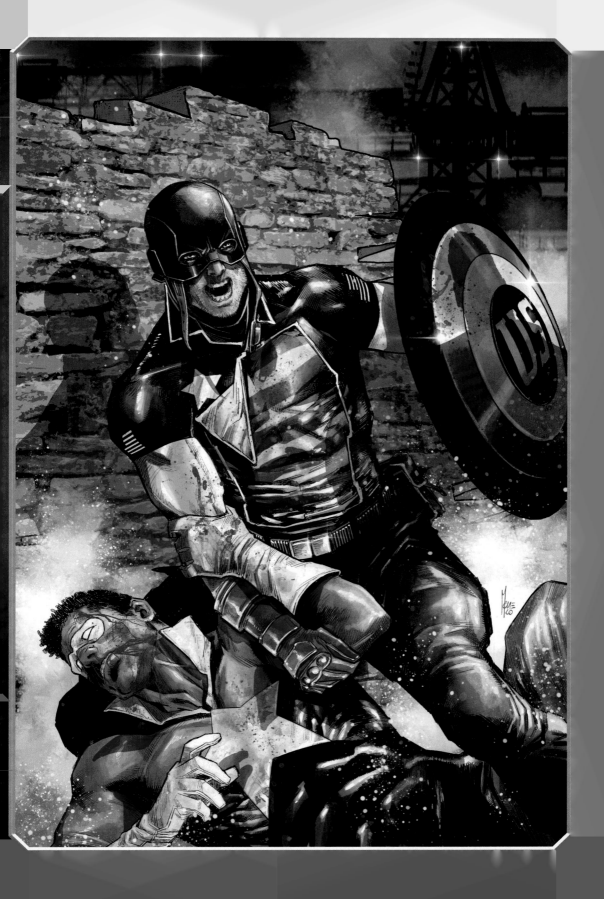

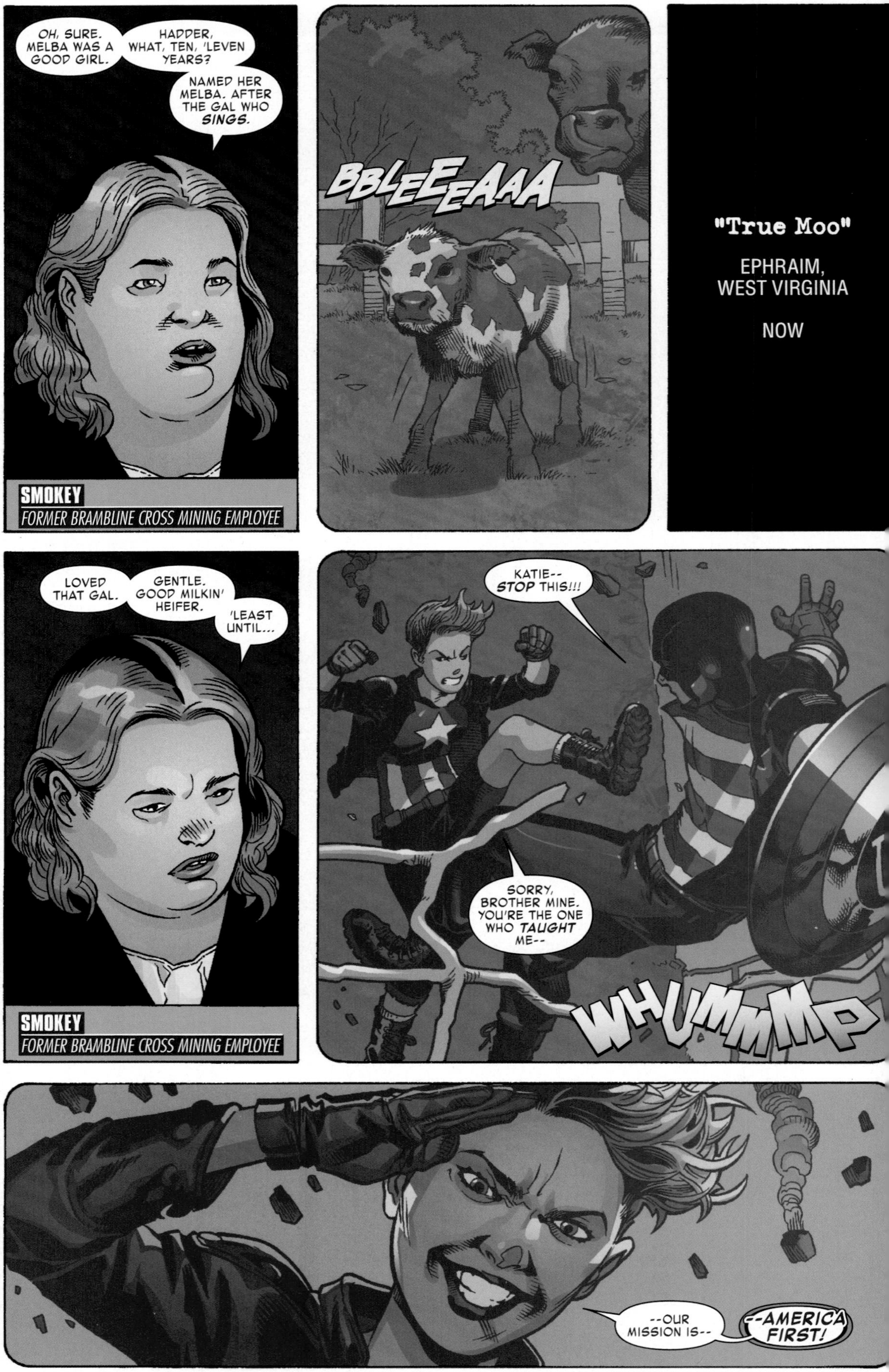
OH, SURE. MELBA WAS A GOOD GIRL.
HADDER, WHAT, TEN, 'LEVEN YEARS?
NAMED HER MELBA. AFTER THE GAL WHO SINGS.
SMOKEY
FORMER BRAMBLINE CROSS MINING EMPLOYEE
BBLEEEAAA
"True Moo"
EPHRAIM, WEST VIRGINIA
NOW
LOVED THAT GAL.
GENTLE. GOOD MILKIN' HEIFER.
'LEAST UNTIL...
SMOKEY
FORMER BRAMBLINE CROSS MINING EMPLOYEE
KATIE-- STOP THIS!!!
SORRY, BROTHER MINE. YOU'RE THE ONE WHO TAUGHT ME--
WHUMMMP
--OUR MISSION IS--
--AMERICA FIRST!

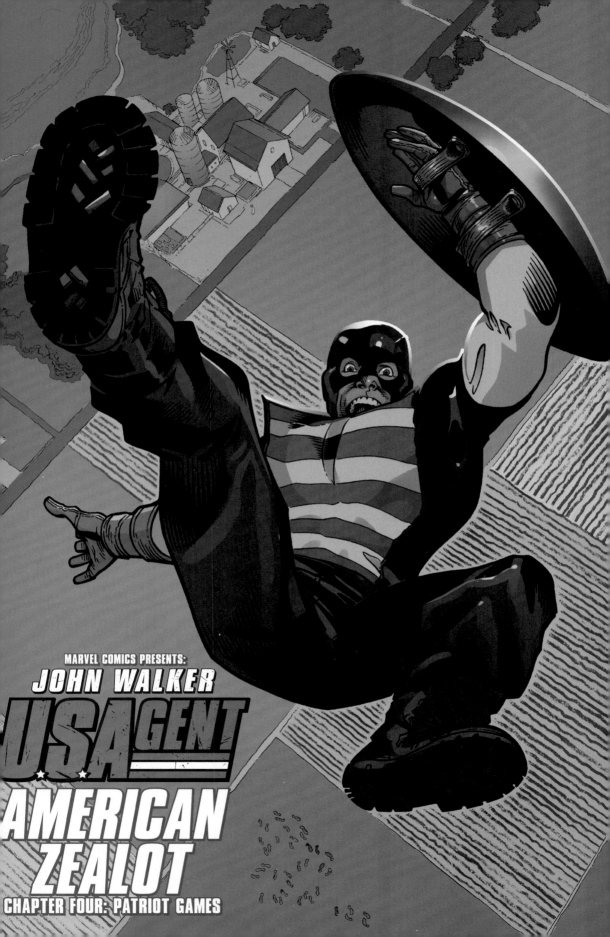

MARVEL COMICS PRESENTS:
JOHN WALKER
U.S.AGENT
AMERICAN ZEALOT
CHAPTER FOUR: PATRIOT GAMES

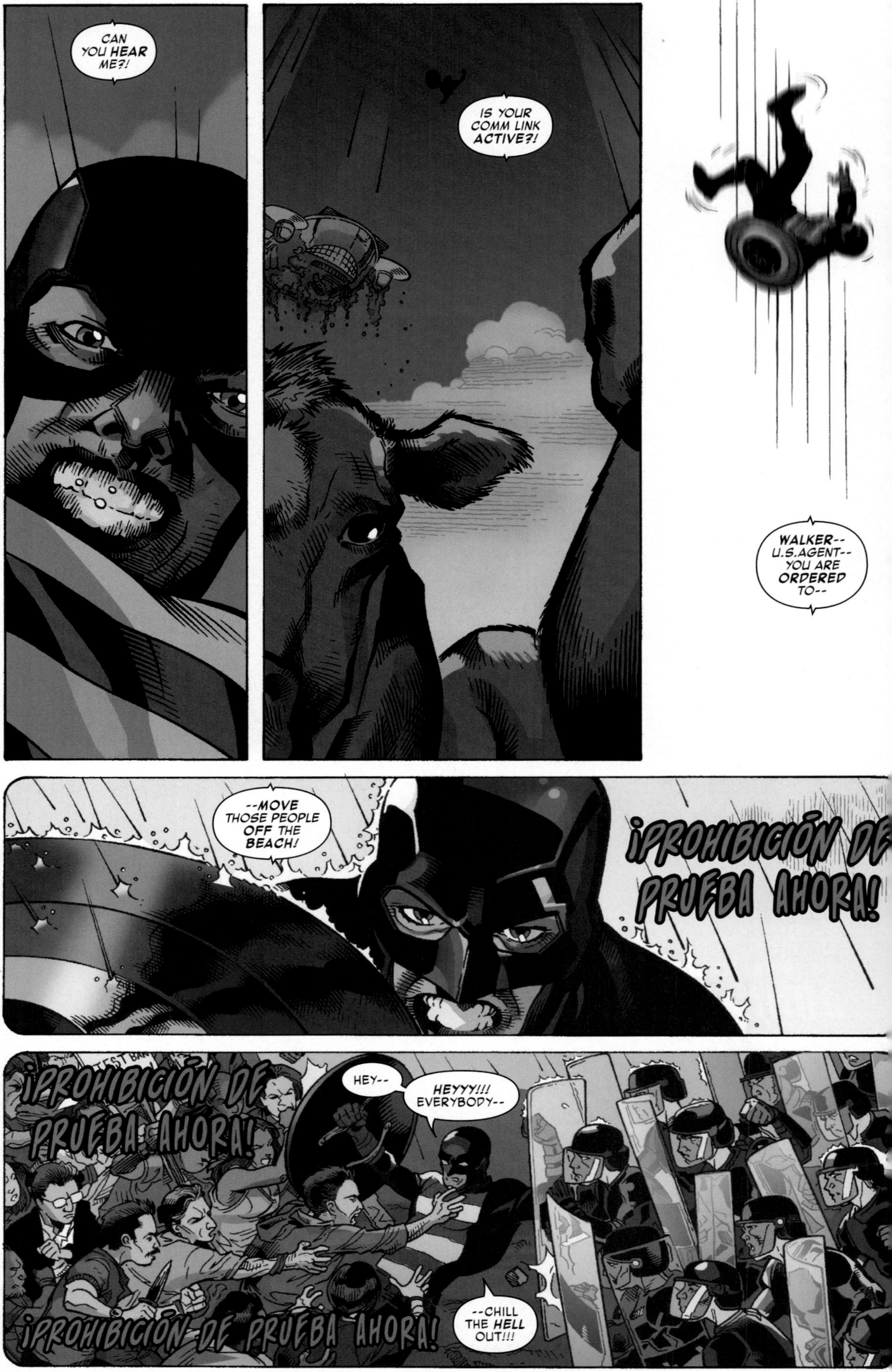
CAN YOU HEAR ME?!
IS YOUR COMM LINK ACTIVE?!
WALKER-- U.S.AGENT-- YOU ARE ORDERED TO--
--MOVE THOSE PEOPLE OFF THE BEACH!
¡PROHIBICIÓN DE PRUEBA AHORA!
¡PROHIBICIÓN DE PRUEBA AHORA!
HEY--
HEYYY!!! EVERYBODY--
--CHILL THE HELL OUT!!!
¡PROHIBICIÓN DE PRUEBA AHORA!

"Beach Blanket Protest"

U.S. NAVY TESTING RANGE

VIEQUES, PUERTO RICO

MONTHS BEFORE

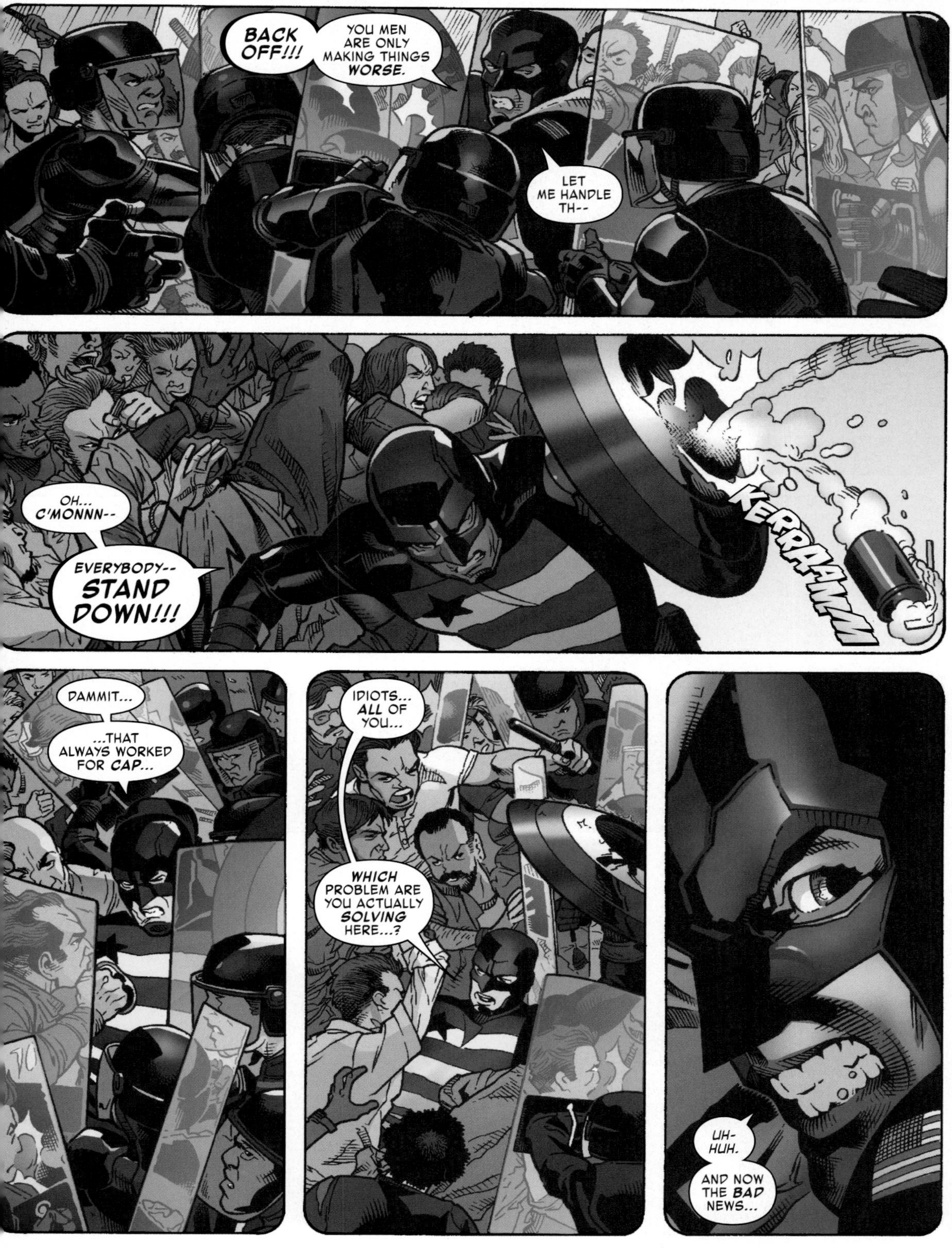
BACK OFF!!!
YOU MEN ARE ONLY MAKING THINGS WORSE.
LET ME HANDLE TH--
OH... C'MONNN--
EVERYBODY-- STAND DOWN!!!
KERRAANM
DAMMIT...
...THAT ALWAYS WORKED FOR CAP...
IDIOTS... ALL OF YOU...
WHICH PROBLEM ARE YOU ACTUALLY SOLVING HERE...?
UH-HUH.
AND NOW THE BAD NEWS...

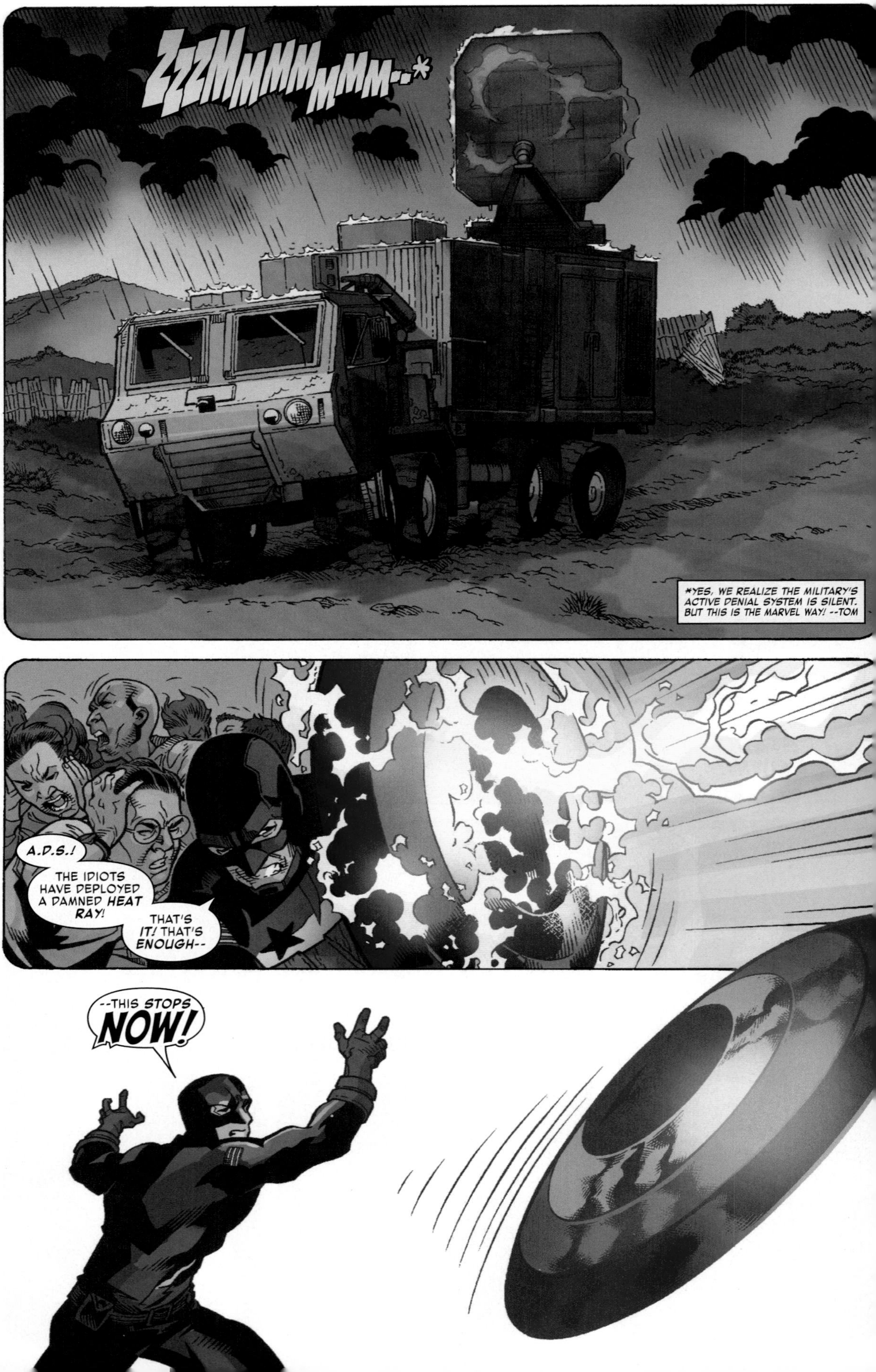
ZZZMMMMMMMM..*
*YES, WE REALIZE THE MILITARY'S ACTIVE DENIAL SYSTEM IS SILENT. BUT THIS IS THE MARVEL WAY! --TOM
A.D.S.!
THE IDIOTS HAVE DEPLOYED A DAMNED HEAT RAY!
THAT'S IT! THAT'S ENOUGH--
--THIS STOPS NOW!

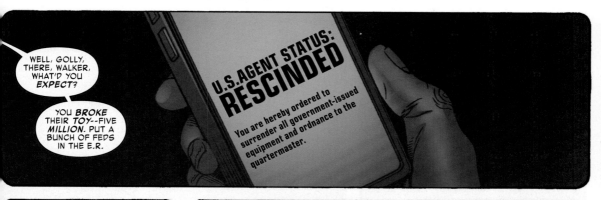

WELL, GOLLY, THERE, WALKER, WHAT'D YOU *EXPECT*?

YOU *BROKE* THEIR *TOY*--FIVE *MILLION*. PUT A BUNCH OF FEDS IN THE E.R.

U.S. AGENT STATUS:
RESCINDED
You are hereby ordered to surrender all government-issued equipment and ordnance to the quartermaster.

"Dear John"

STONE RIDGE, VIRGINIA

MONTHS BEFORE

IT WAS A PEACEFUL PROTEST.

I CAN TELL BY ALL THE BLOOD AND BONE FRACTURES.

THOSE PEOPLE HAD A RIGHT TO--

TO *WHAT*, WALKER?

HOLD UP THE MILITARY TRAINING INDEFINITELY? WALKER--

--WE WAITED *30 HOURS* BEFORE WE WERE FORCED TO SHUT IT DOWN.

FORCED BY *WHO*, COOP? AND FOR *WHAT*--

--SOME POLITICIAN'S PHOTO OP?

THOSE NAVAL FORCES NEEDED TO *DEPLOY*.

THE ELECTION HAD NOTHING TO DO WITH IT.

NOT *EVERYTHING* IS A POLITICAL SHELL GAME, WALKER.

COOP...

DON'T CALL ME "COOP."

YEAH.

MELBA WAS MY GIRL. MY GOOD GIRL...

SMOKEY
FORMER BRAMBLINE CROSS MINING EMPLOYEE

WALKER-- IT'S COOP. I DON'T THINK THAT MISSING FUEL CELL WAS STOLEN.

I THINK YOUR *SISTER* DISABLED IT INTENTIONALLY.

JUST DON'T KNOW *WHY*.

THOSE FUEL CELLS POWER A *CONTAINMENT FIELD*...

WHICH IS *"CONTAINING"* SOMETHING S.H.I.E.L.D. *BURIED* OUT HERE IN COW-LAND--

--ONLY *YOU* WON'T TELL ME *WHAT* THAT SOMETHING *IS!*

IT'S CLASSIFIED.

YOU'RE NOT OUR U.S. AGENT ANYMORE, JOHN.

KATE WANTS THE FIELD TO *COLLAPSE*... BUT *WHY...?*

BECAUSE SHE'S *CRAZY!*

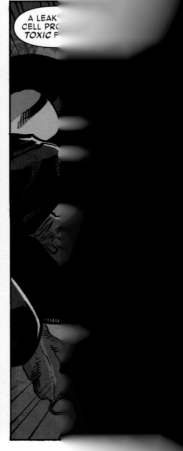

A LEAK CELL PRO TOXIC F

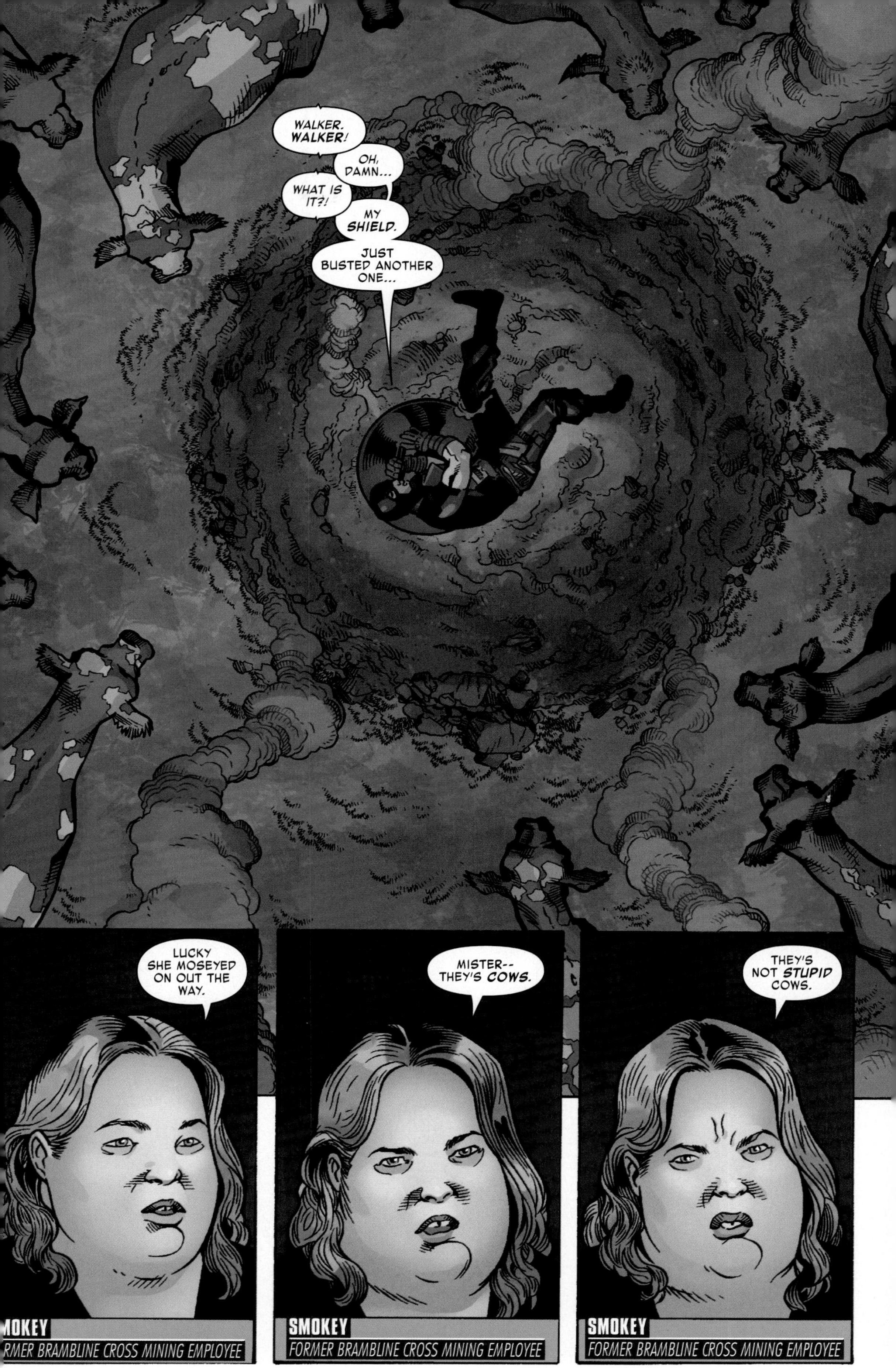
WALKER. WALKER!
OH, DAMN...
WHAT IS IT?!
MY SHIELD.
JUST BUSTED ANOTHER ONE...
LUCKY SHE MOSEYED ON OUT THE WAY.
MOKEY
RMER BRAMBLINE CROSS MINING EMPLOYEE
MISTER-- THEY'S COWS.
SMOKEY
FORMER BRAMBLINE CROSS MINING EMPLOYEE
THEY'S NOT STUPID COWS.
SMOKEY
FORMER BRAMBLINE CROSS MINING EMPLOYEE

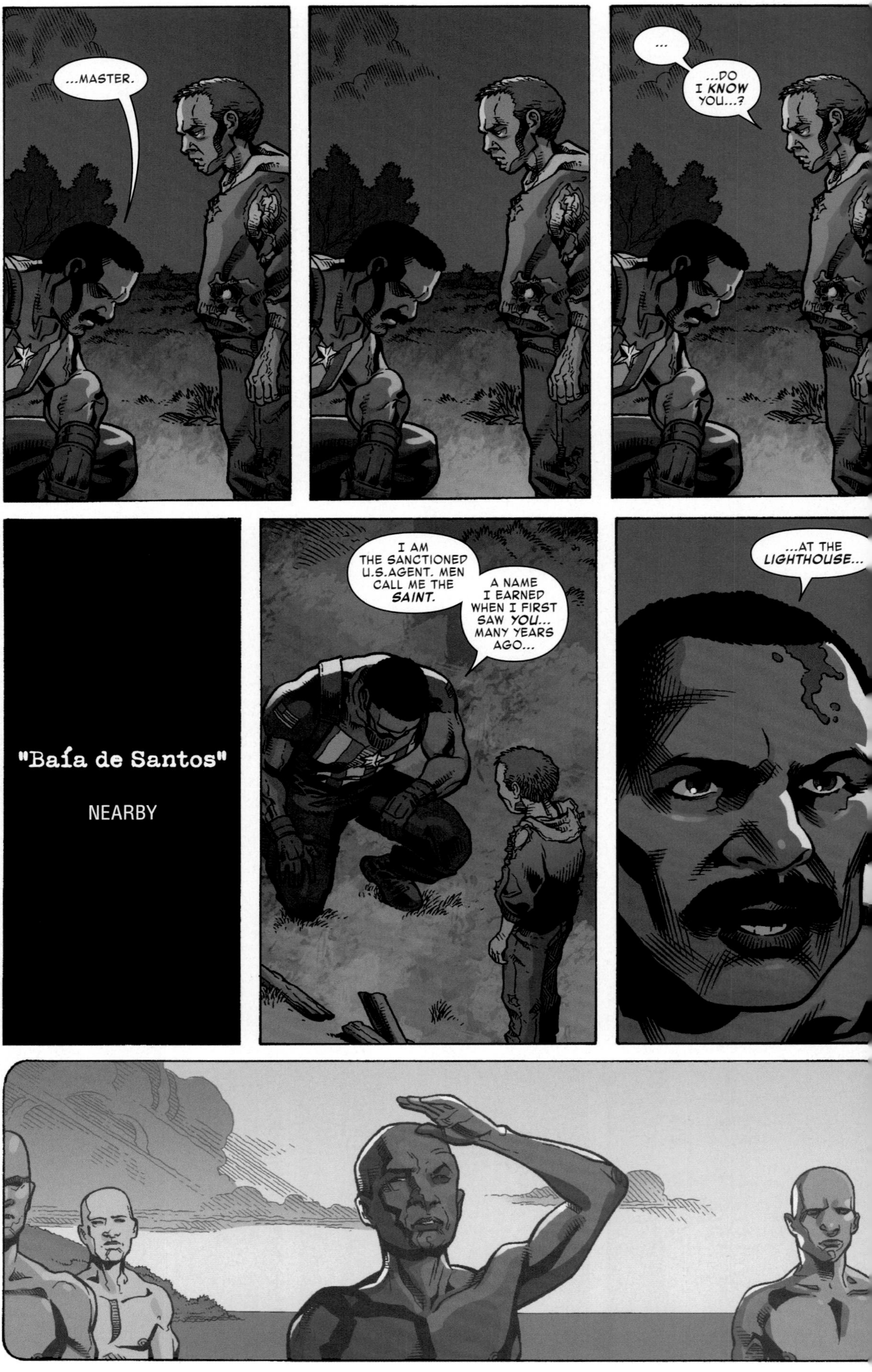
...MASTER.
...
...DO I KNOW YOU...?
"Baía de Santos"
NEARBY
I AM THE SANCTIONED U.S.AGENT. MEN CALL ME THE SAINT.
A NAME I EARNED WHEN I FIRST SAW YOU... MANY YEARS AGO...
...AT THE LIGHTHOUSE...

BEGIN.

BRRATT--

UGGGHHNNNN--

KRAAKK

BRRRATATATTATTAT--

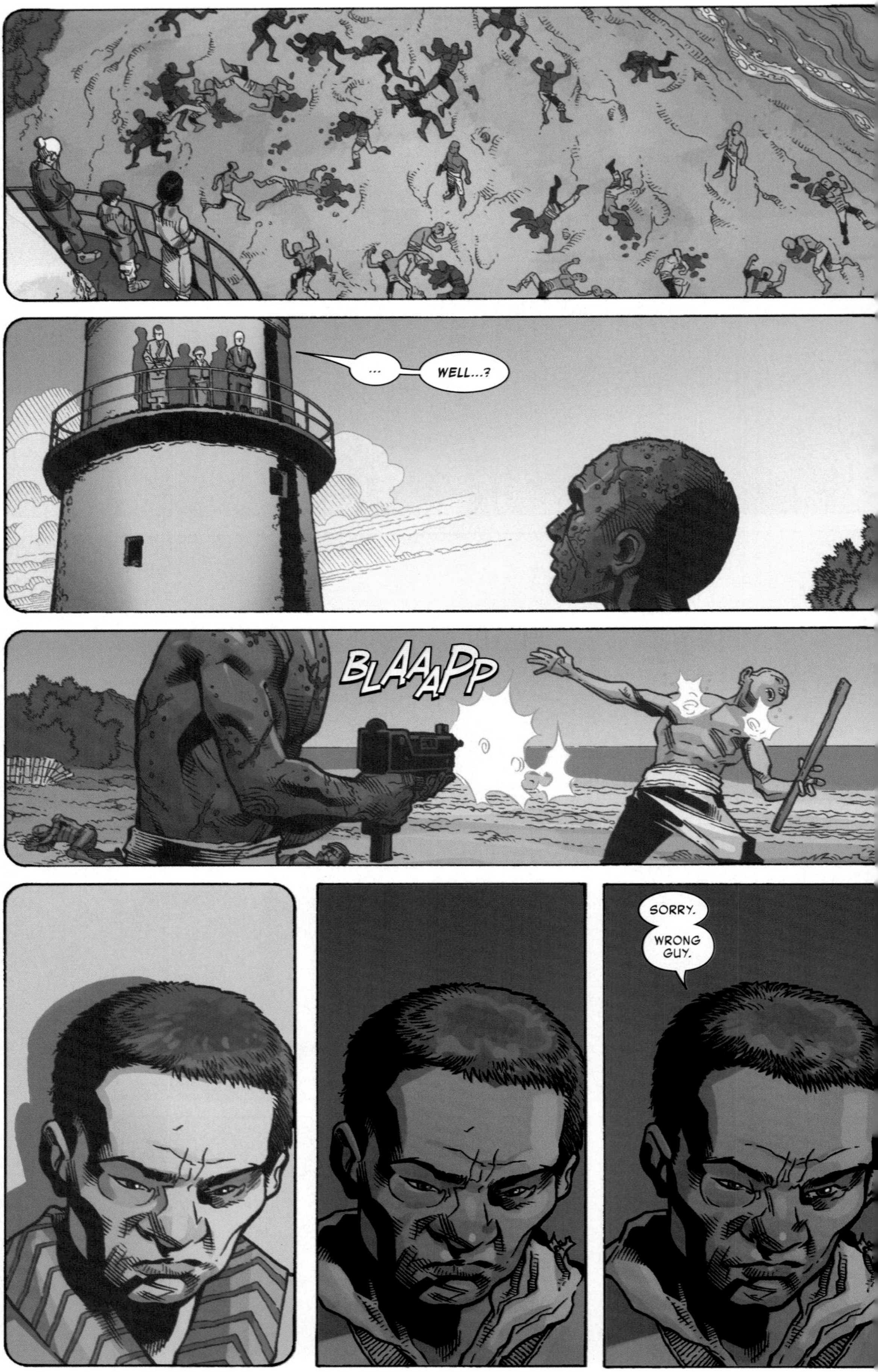
...
WELL...?
BLAAAPP
SORRY.
WRONG GUY.

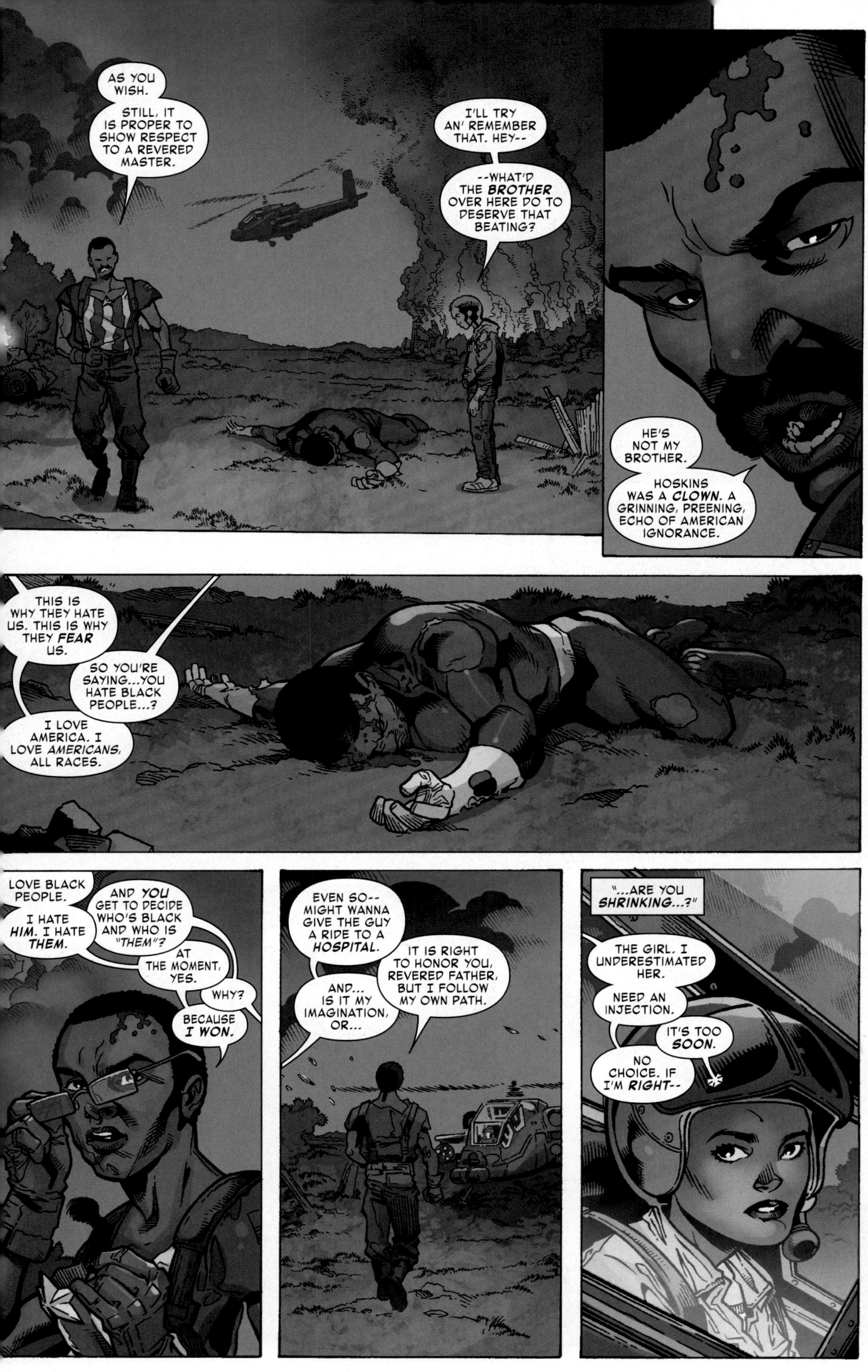
AS YOU WISH.
STILL, IT IS PROPER TO SHOW RESPECT TO A REVERED MASTER.
I'LL TRY AN' REMEMBER THAT. HEY--
--WHAT'D THE BROTHER OVER HERE DO TO DESERVE THAT BEATING?
HE'S NOT MY BROTHER.
HOSKINS WAS A CLOWN. A GRINNING, PREENING, ECHO OF AMERICAN IGNORANCE.
THIS IS WHY THEY HATE US. THIS IS WHY THEY FEAR US.
SO YOU'RE SAYING...YOU HATE BLACK PEOPLE...?
I LOVE AMERICA. I LOVE AMERICANS, ALL RACES.
LOVE BLACK PEOPLE.
I HATE HIM. I HATE THEM.
AND YOU GET TO DECIDE WHO'S BLACK AND WHO IS "THEM"?
AT THE MOMENT, YES.
WHY?
BECAUSE I WON.
EVEN SO--MIGHT WANNA GIVE THE GUY A RIDE TO A HOSPITAL.
AND... IS IT MY IMAGINATION, OR...
IT IS RIGHT TO HONOR YOU, REVERED FATHER, BUT I FOLLOW MY OWN PATH.
"...ARE YOU SHRINKING...?"
THE GIRL. I UNDERESTIMATED HER.
NEED AN INJECTION.
IT'S TOO SOON.
NO CHOICE. IF I'M RIGHT--

YOU'RE RIGHT, JOHN--

--EXPOSURE TO A LEAKY FUEL CELL *COULD* CAUSE PSYCHOSIS. BUT...

...WOULD IT CAUSE *SUPER-STRENGTH?* JOHN? WALKER--DID YOU CUT YOUR COMM CHANNEL?!

COOPER

NO.

YOU GAINED SUPER-STRENGTH AND NEAR-INVULNERABILITY...

...FROM AN INSANE PRO WRESTLING DOCTOR*--

*THE POWER BROKE SEE CAP #333. --

NEAR-INVULNERABILITY... OUCH...

KATE IS 110 POUNDS ON A GOOD DAY. WHERE'D SHE GET THE STRENGTH TO TOSS YOU OVERBOARD?

...I'D IMAGINE IT WAS YOUR NEW GUY...

HE'S NOT "MY" GUY, WALKER...

...I DON'T RUN THE PROGRAM ANYMORE.

I DON'T EVEN KNOW WHO THAT GUY IS--NOBODY DOES. THE RUMOR IS...

...SOME FAT-CAT POLITICAL DONOR *BOUGHT* THE U.S. AGENT GIG...

...*PAID* SOMEBODY OFF TO GIVE HIS GUY THE SHIELD.

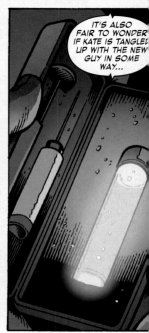

IT'S ALSO FAIR TO WONDER IF KATE IS TANGLED UP WITH THE NEW GUY IN SOME WAY...

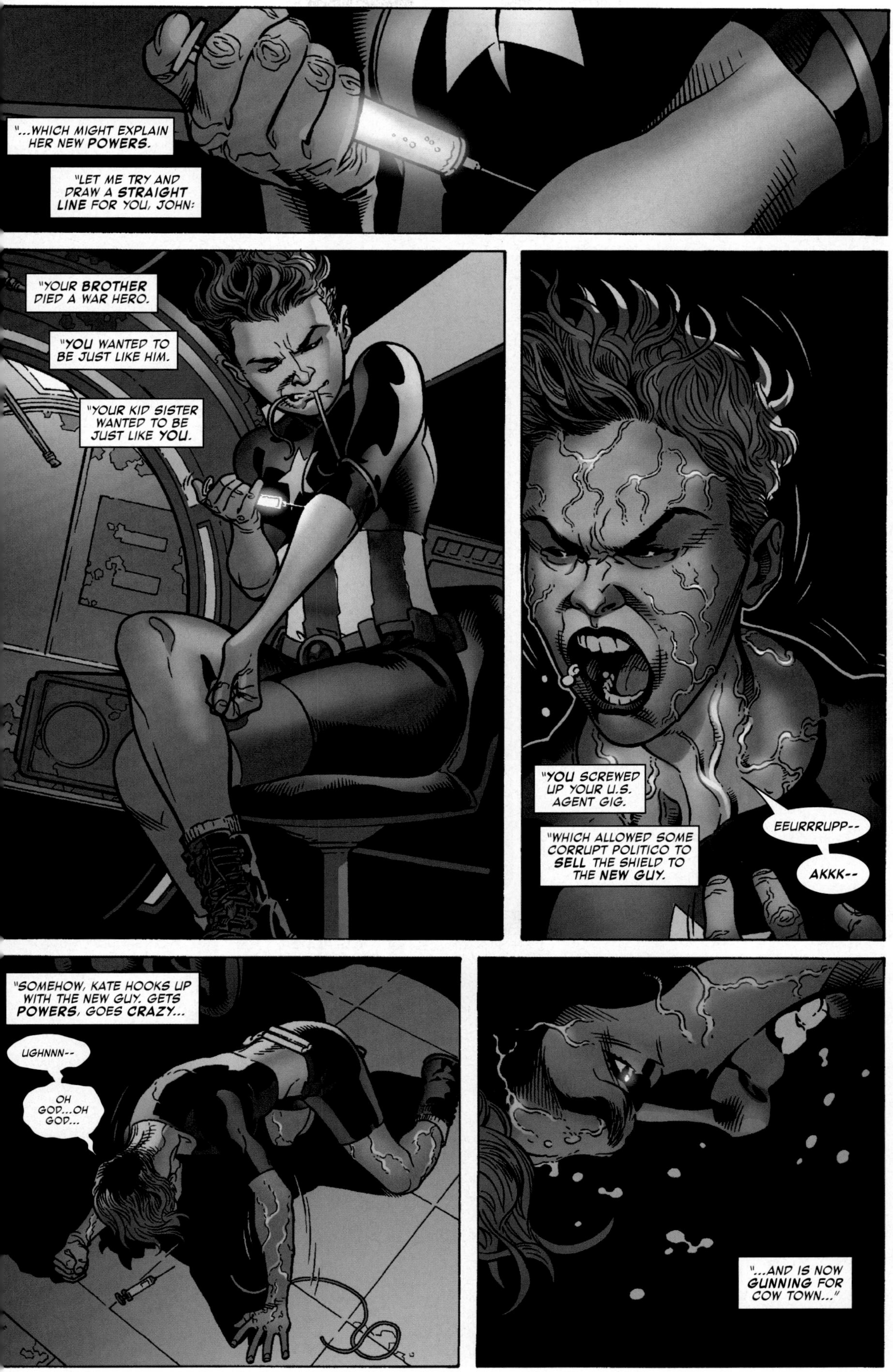
"...WHICH MIGHT EXPLAIN HER NEW POWERS.
"LET ME TRY AND DRAW A STRAIGHT LINE FOR YOU, JOHN:
"YOUR BROTHER DIED A WAR HERO.
"YOU WANTED TO BE JUST LIKE HIM.
"YOUR KID SISTER WANTED TO BE JUST LIKE YOU.
"YOU SCREWED UP YOUR U.S. AGENT GIG.
"WHICH ALLOWED SOME CORRUPT POLITICO TO SELL THE SHIELD TO THE NEW GUY.
EEURRRUPP--
AKKK--
"SOMEHOW, KATE HOOKS UP WITH THE NEW GUY. GETS POWERS, GOES CRAZY...
UGHNNN--
OH GOD...OH GOD...
"...AND IS NOW GUNNING FOR COW TOWN..."

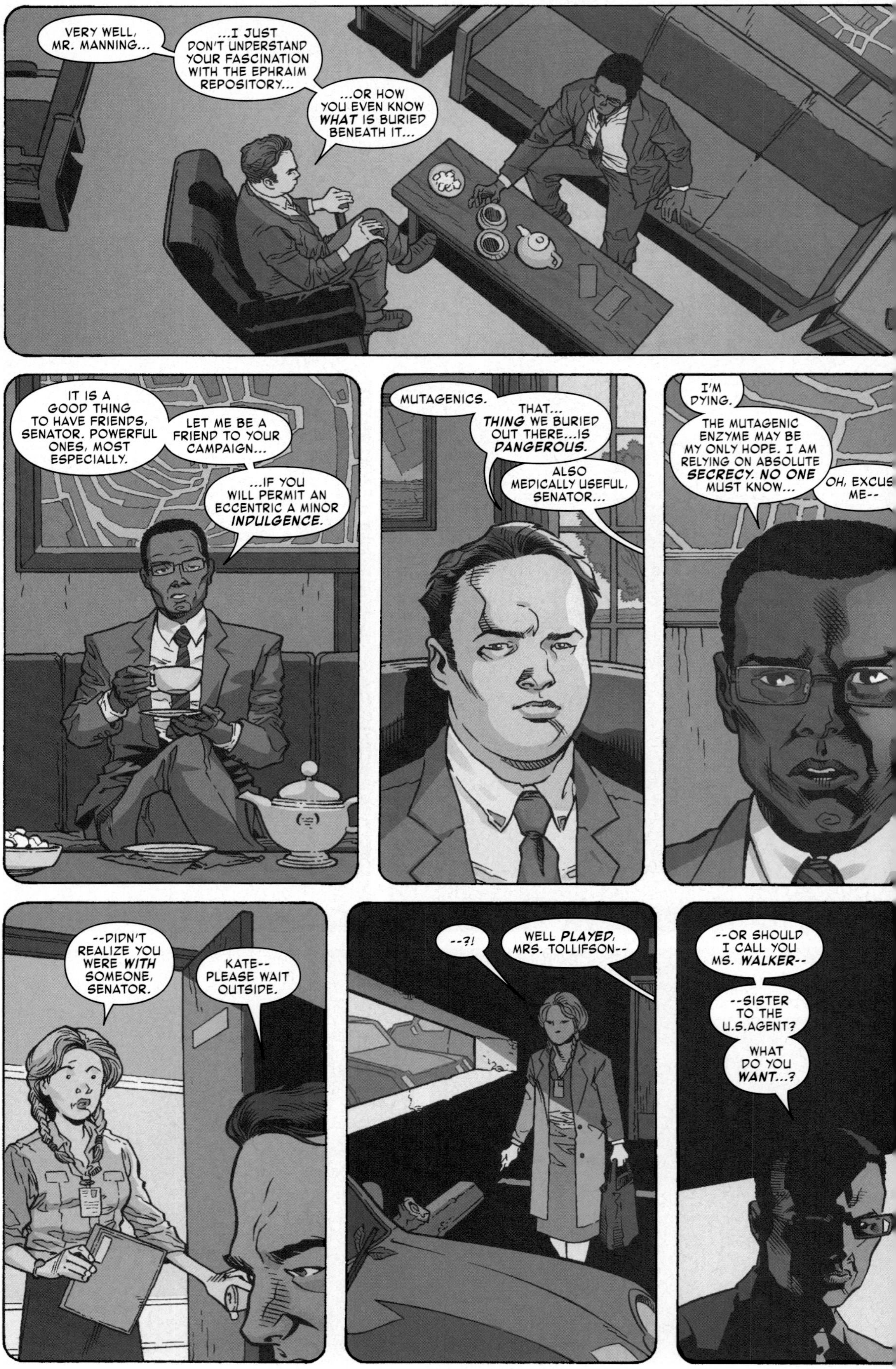
VERY WELL, MR. MANNING...
...I JUST DON'T UNDERSTAND YOUR FASCINATION WITH THE EPHRAIM REPOSITORY...
...OR HOW YOU EVEN KNOW WHAT IS BURIED BENEATH IT...
IT IS A GOOD THING TO HAVE FRIENDS, SENATOR. POWERFUL ONES, MOST ESPECIALLY.
LET ME BE A FRIEND TO YOUR CAMPAIGN...
...IF YOU WILL PERMIT AN ECCENTRIC A MINOR INDULGENCE.
MUTAGENICS.
THAT... THING WE BURIED OUT THERE...IS DANGEROUS.
ALSO MEDICALLY USEFUL, SENATOR...
I'M DYING.
THE MUTAGENIC ENZYME MAY BE MY ONLY HOPE. I AM RELYING ON ABSOLUTE SECRECY. NO ONE MUST KNOW...
OH, EXCUS ME--
--DIDN'T REALIZE YOU WERE WITH SOMEONE, SENATOR.
KATE-- PLEASE WAIT OUTSIDE.
--?!
WELL PLAYED, MRS. TOLLIFSON--
--OR SHOULD I CALL YOU MS. WALKER--
--SISTER TO THE U.S.AGENT?
WHAT DO YOU WANT...?

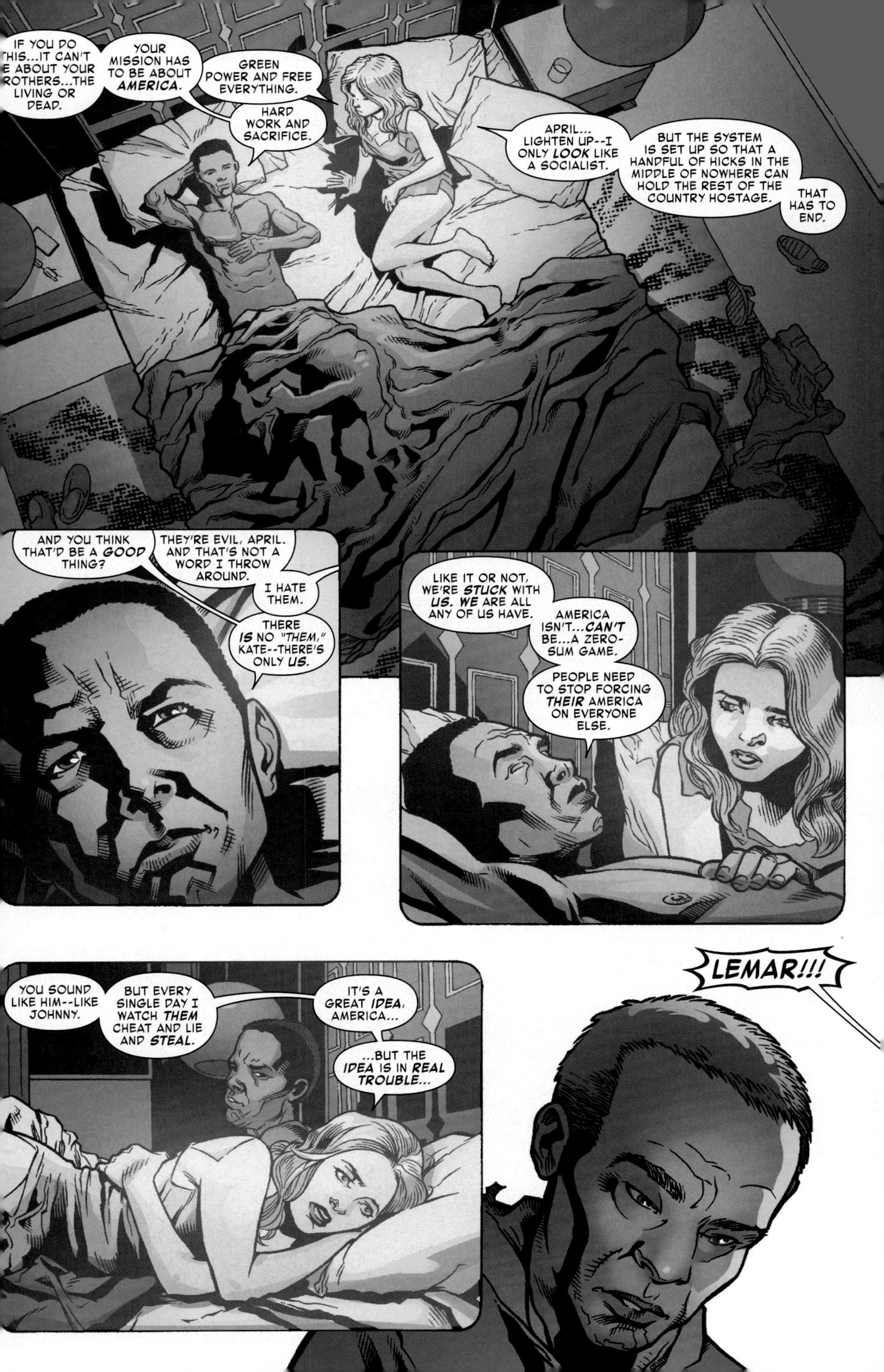
IF YOU DO THIS...IT CAN'T E ABOUT YOUR ROTHERS...THE LIVING OR DEAD.
YOUR MISSION HAS TO BE ABOUT AMERICA.
GREEN POWER AND FREE EVERYTHING.
HARD WORK AND SACRIFICE.
APRIL... LIGHTEN UP--I ONLY LOOK LIKE A SOCIALIST.
BUT THE SYSTEM IS SET UP SO THAT A HANDFUL OF HICKS IN THE MIDDLE OF NOWHERE CAN HOLD THE REST OF THE COUNTRY HOSTAGE.
THAT HAS TO END.
AND YOU THINK THAT'D BE A GOOD THING?
THEY'RE EVIL, APRIL. AND THAT'S NOT A WORD I THROW AROUND.
I HATE THEM.
THERE IS NO "THEM," KATE--THERE'S ONLY US.
LIKE IT OR NOT, WE'RE STUCK WITH US. WE ARE ALL ANY OF US HAVE.
AMERICA ISN'T...CAN'T BE...A ZERO-SUM GAME.
PEOPLE NEED TO STOP FORCING THEIR AMERICA ON EVERYONE ELSE.
YOU SOUND LIKE HIM--LIKE JOHNNY.
BUT EVERY SINGLE DAY I WATCH THEM CHEAT AND LIE AND STEAL.
IT'S A GREAT IDEA, AMERICA...
...BUT THE IDEA IS IN REAL TROUBLE...
LEMAR!!!

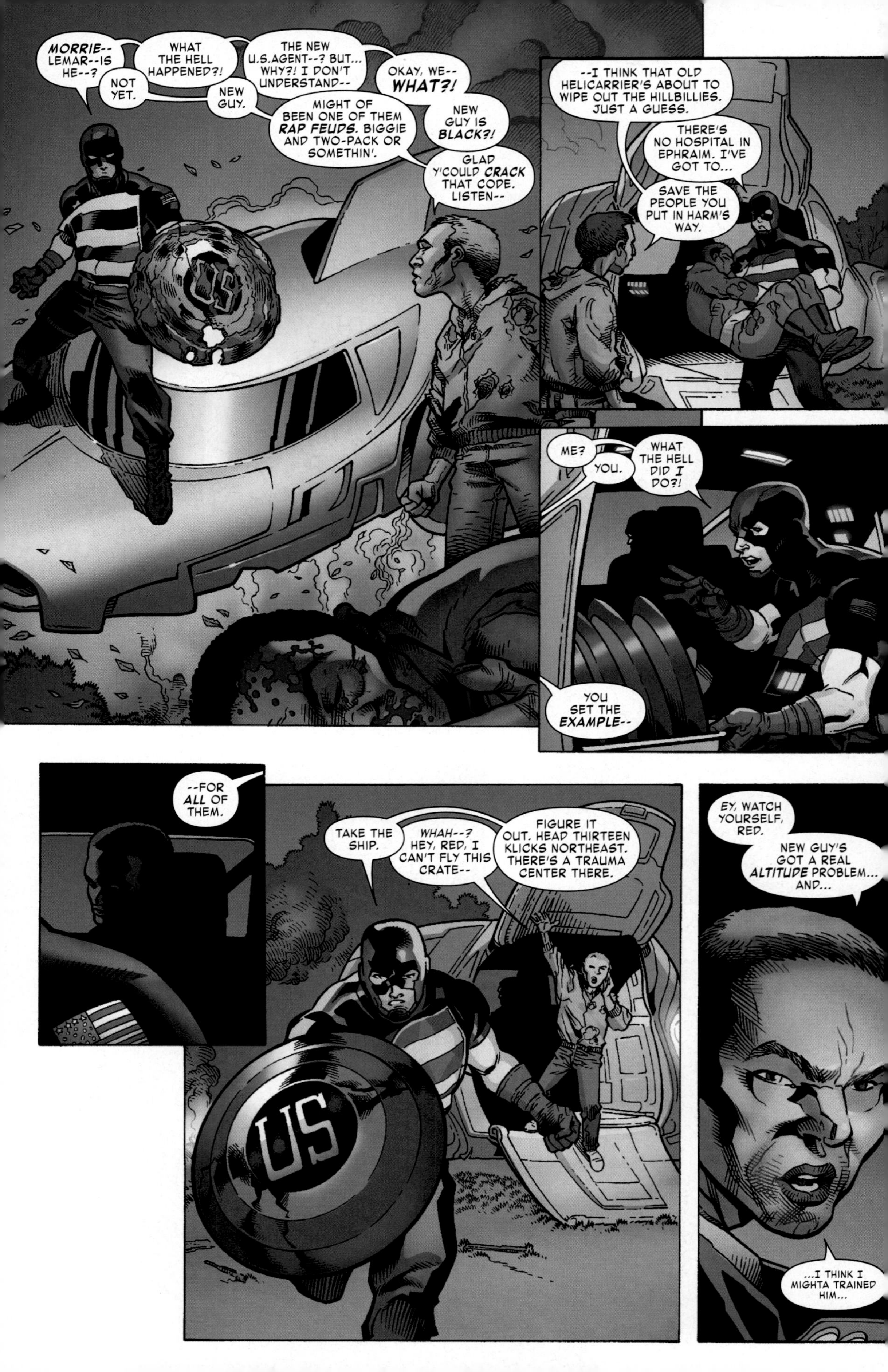
MORRIE-- LEMAR--IS HE--?
NOT YET.
WHAT THE HELL HAPPENED?!
NEW GUY.
THE NEW U.S.AGENT--? BUT... WHY?! I DON'T UNDERSTAND--
MIGHT OF BEEN ONE OF THEM RAP FEUDS. BIGGIE AND TWO-PACK OR SOMETHIN'.
OKAY, WE-- WHAT?!
NEW GUY IS BLACK?!
GLAD Y'COULD CRACK THAT CODE. LISTEN--
--I THINK THAT OLD HELICARRIER'S ABOUT TO WIPE OUT THE HILLBILLIES. JUST A GUESS.
THERE'S NO HOSPITAL IN EPHRAIM. I'VE GOT TO...
SAVE THE PEOPLE YOU PUT IN HARM'S WAY.
ME?
YOU.
WHAT THE HELL DID I DO?!
YOU SET THE EXAMPLE--
--FOR ALL OF THEM.
TAKE THE SHIP.
WHAH--? HEY, RED, I CAN'T FLY THIS CRATE--
FIGURE IT OUT. HEAD THIRTEEN KLICKS NORTHEAST. THERE'S A TRAUMA CENTER THERE.
EY, WATCH YOURSELF, RED.
NEW GUY'S GOT A REAL ALTITUDE PROBLEM... AND...
...I THINK I MIGHTA TRAINED HIM...

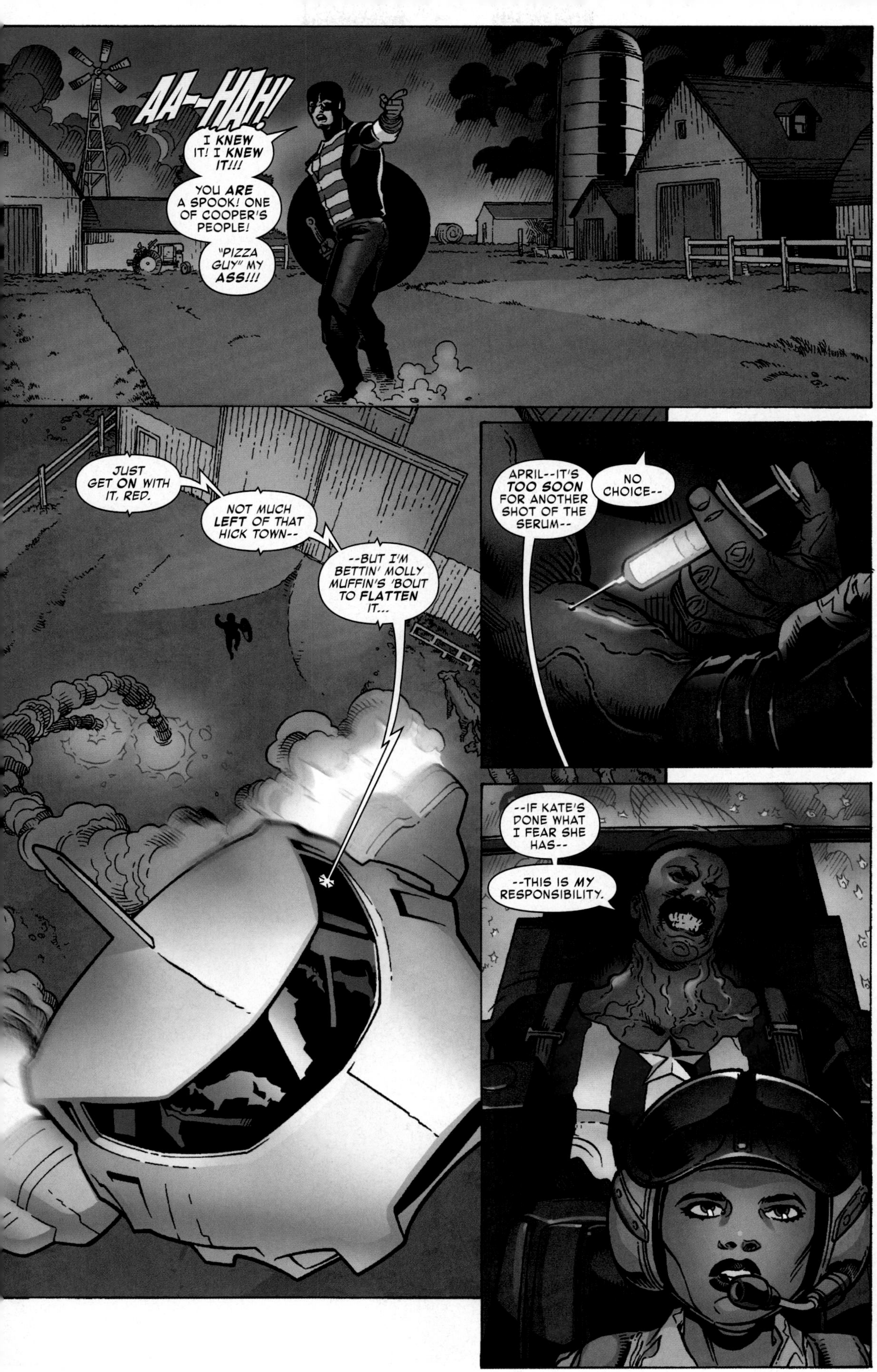
AA--HAH!
I KNEW IT! I KNEW IT!!!
YOU ARE A SPOOK! ONE OF COOPER'S PEOPLE!
"PIZZA GUY" MY ASS!!!
JUST GET ON WITH IT, RED.
NOT MUCH LEFT OF THAT HICK TOWN--
--BUT I'M BETTIN' MOLLY MUFFIN'S 'BOUT TO FLATTEN IT...
APRIL--IT'S TOO SOON FOR ANOTHER SHOT OF THE SERUM--
NO CHOICE--
--IF KATE'S DONE WHAT I FEAR SHE HAS--
--THIS IS MY RESPONSIBILITY.

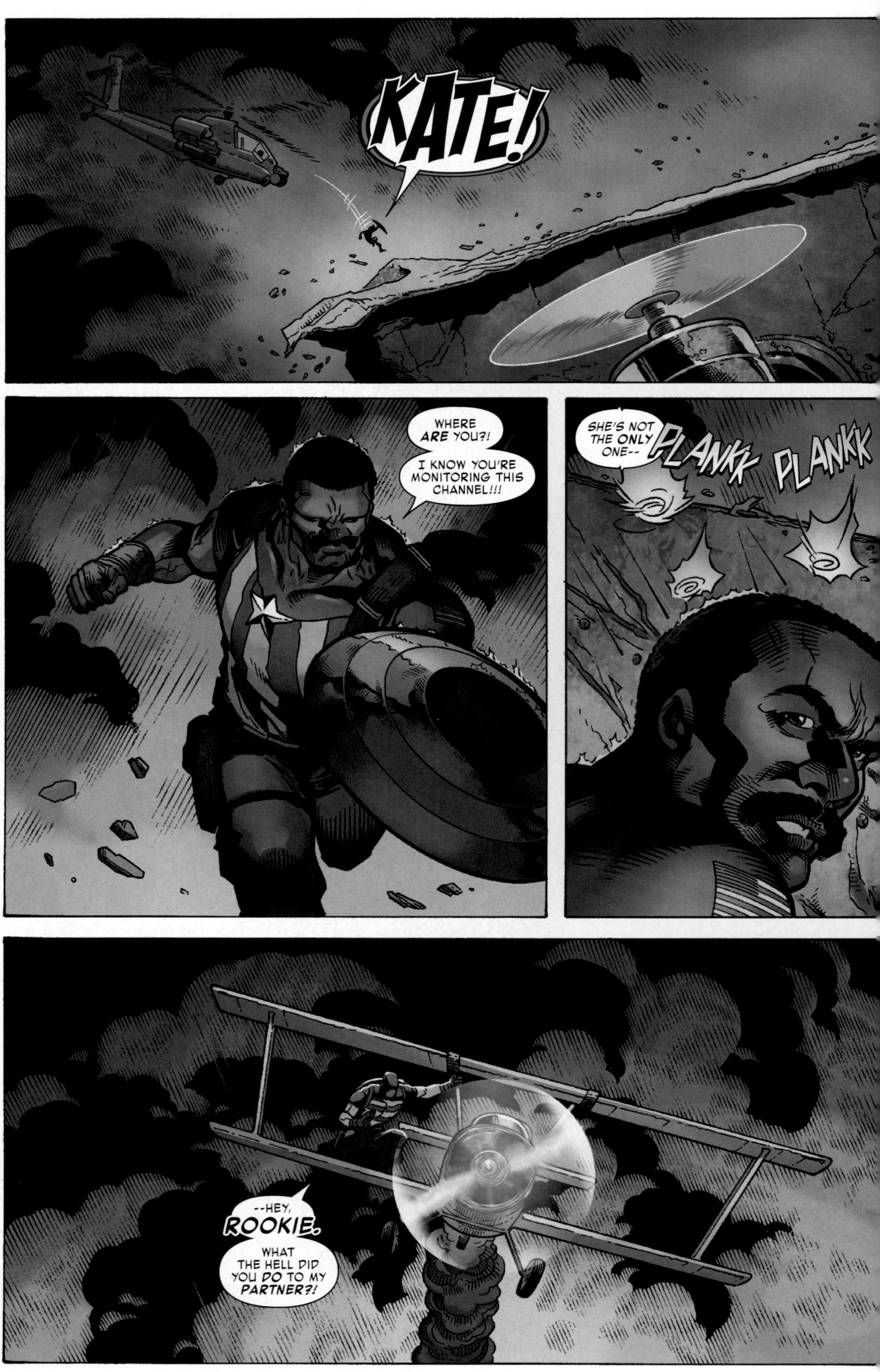
KATE!
WHERE ARE YOU?!
I KNOW YOU'RE MONITORING THIS CHANNEL!!!
SHE'S NOT THE ONLY ONE--
PLANKK
PLANKK
--HEY, ROOKIE.
WHAT THE HELL DID YOU DO TO MY PARTNER?!

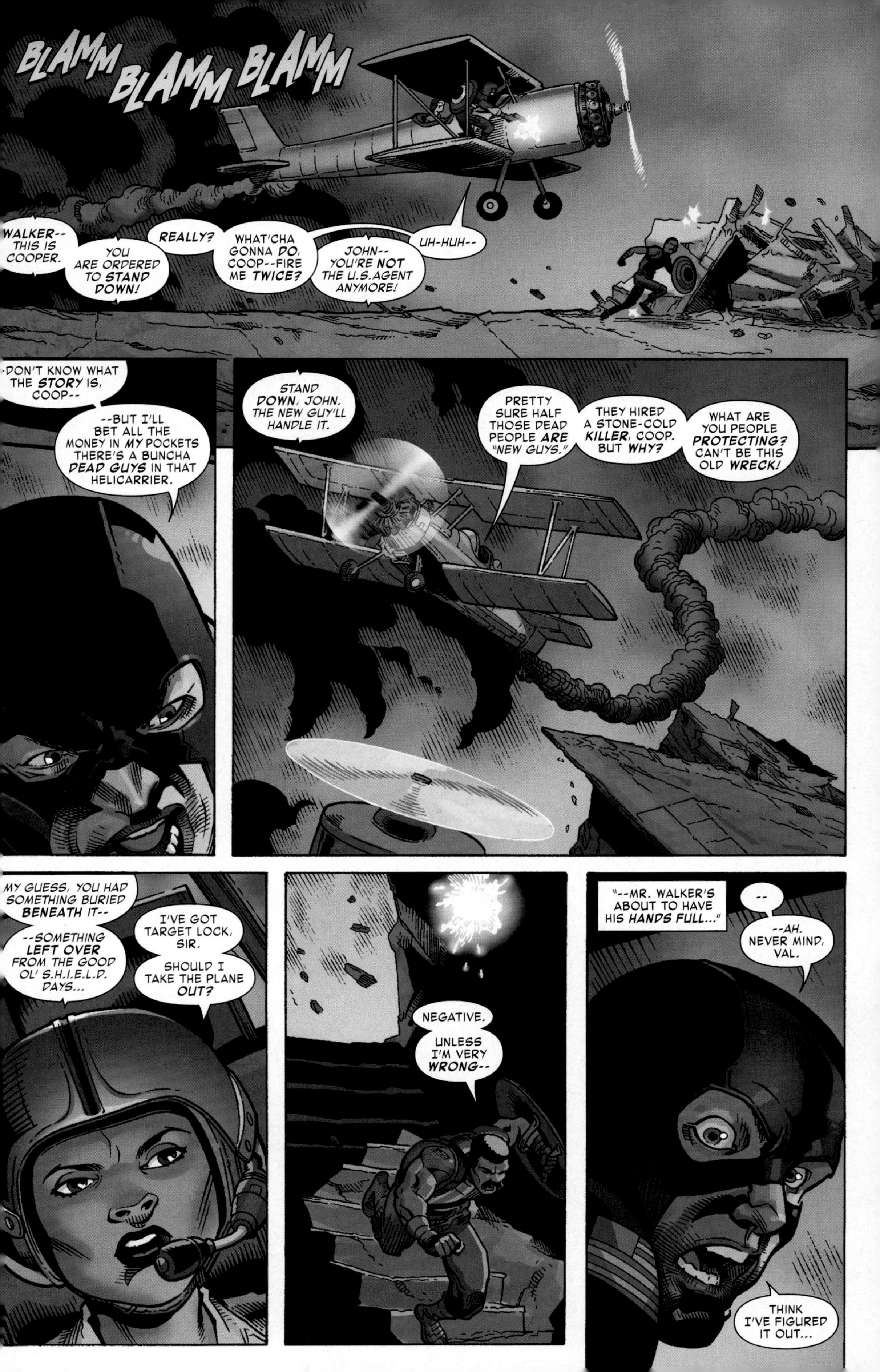
BLAMM BLAMM BLAMM
WALKER-- THIS IS COOPER.
YOU ARE ORDERED TO STAND DOWN!
REALLY?
WHAT'CHA GONNA DO, COOP--FIRE ME TWICE?
JOHN-- YOU'RE NOT THE U.S.AGENT ANYMORE!
UH-HUH--
-DON'T KNOW WHAT THE STORY IS, COOP--
--BUT I'LL BET ALL THE MONEY IN MY POCKETS THERE'S A BUNCHA DEAD GUYS IN THAT HELICARRIER.
STAND DOWN, JOHN. THE NEW GUY'LL HANDLE IT.
PRETTY SURE HALF THOSE DEAD PEOPLE ARE "NEW GUYS."
THEY HIRED A STONE-COLD KILLER, COOP. BUT WHY?
WHAT ARE YOU PEOPLE PROTECTING? CAN'T BE THIS OLD WRECK!
MY GUESS, YOU HAD SOMETHING BURIED BENEATH IT--
--SOMETHING LEFT OVER FROM THE GOOD OL' S.H.I.E.L.D. DAYS...
I'VE GOT TARGET LOCK, SIR.
SHOULD I TAKE THE PLANE OUT?
NEGATIVE.
UNLESS I'M VERY WRONG--
"--MR. WALKER'S ABOUT TO HAVE HIS HANDS FULL..."
--
--AH. NEVER MIND, VAL.
THINK I'VE FIGURED IT OUT...

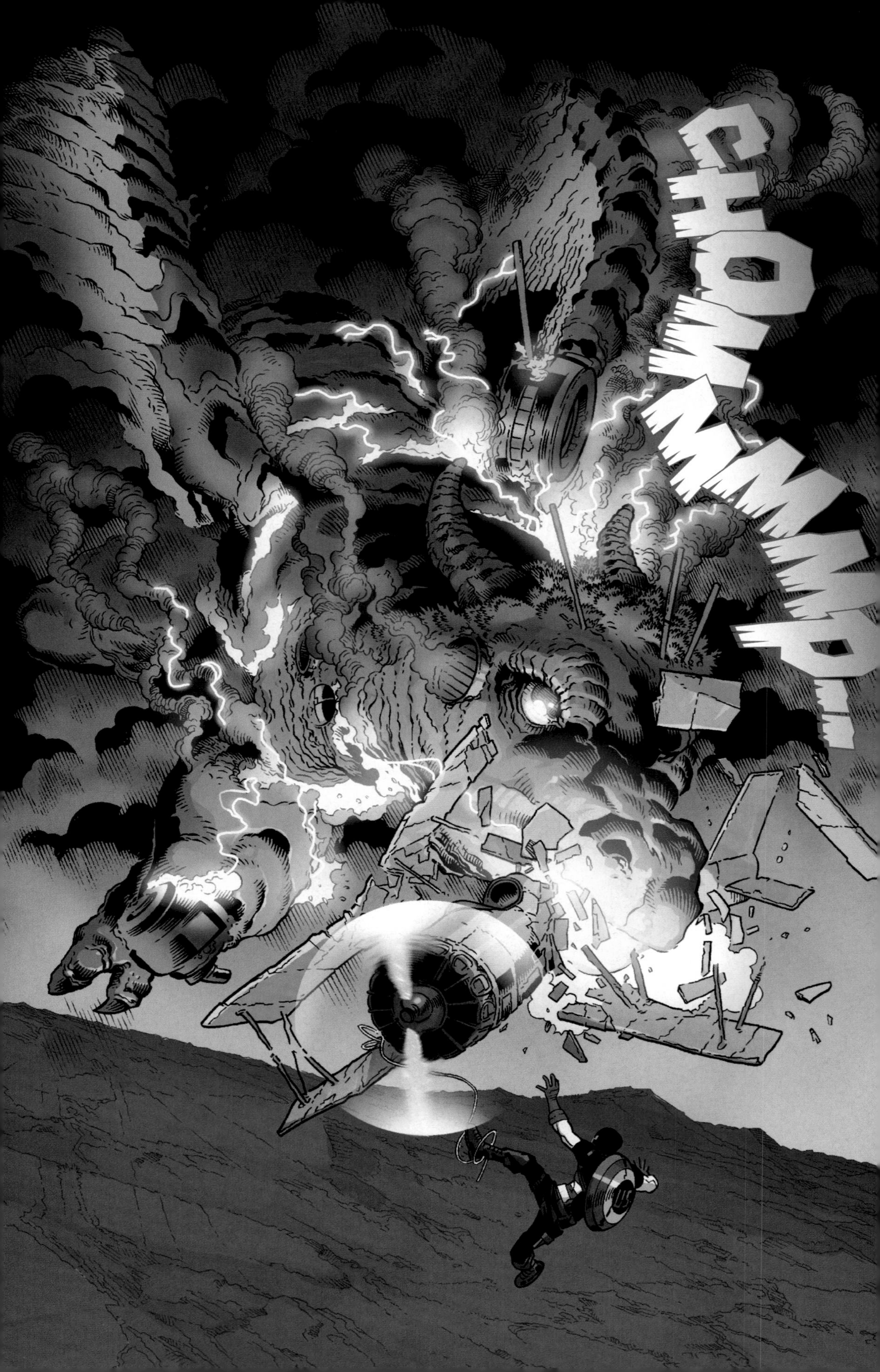
CHOMMMMP!!

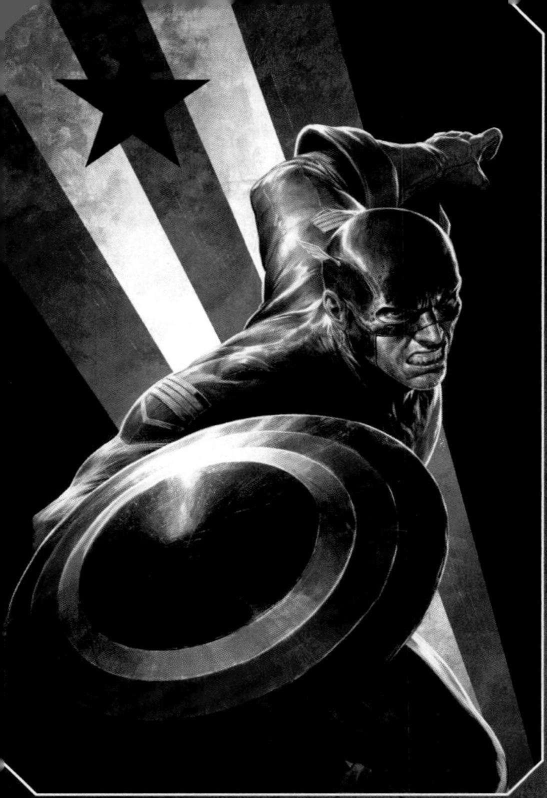

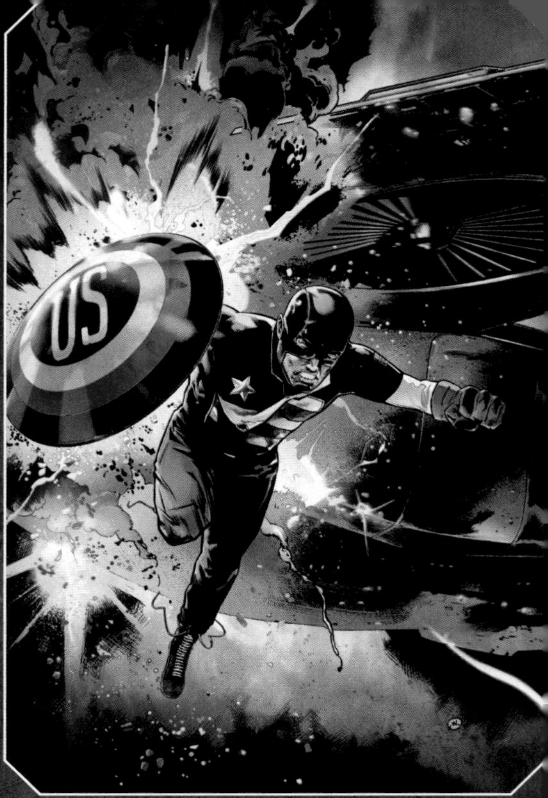
US

#2 VARIANT BY
DAVE RAPOZA

#3 VARIANT BY
WELL-BEE

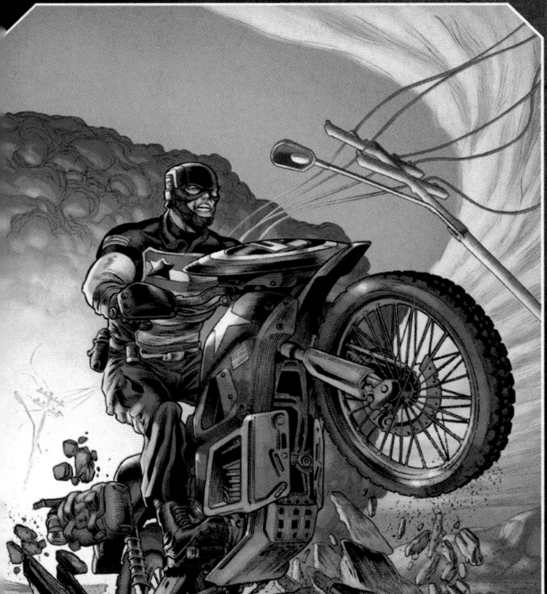

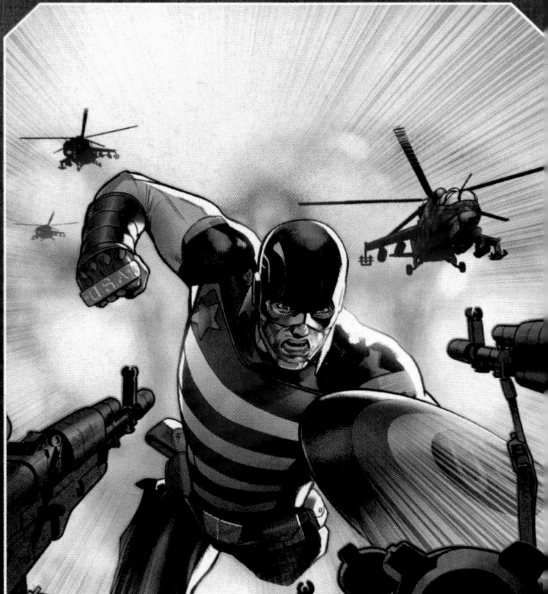

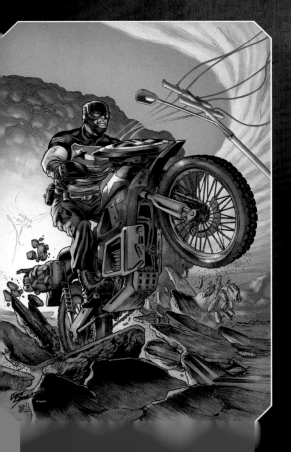

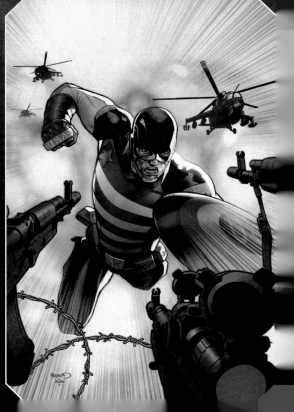

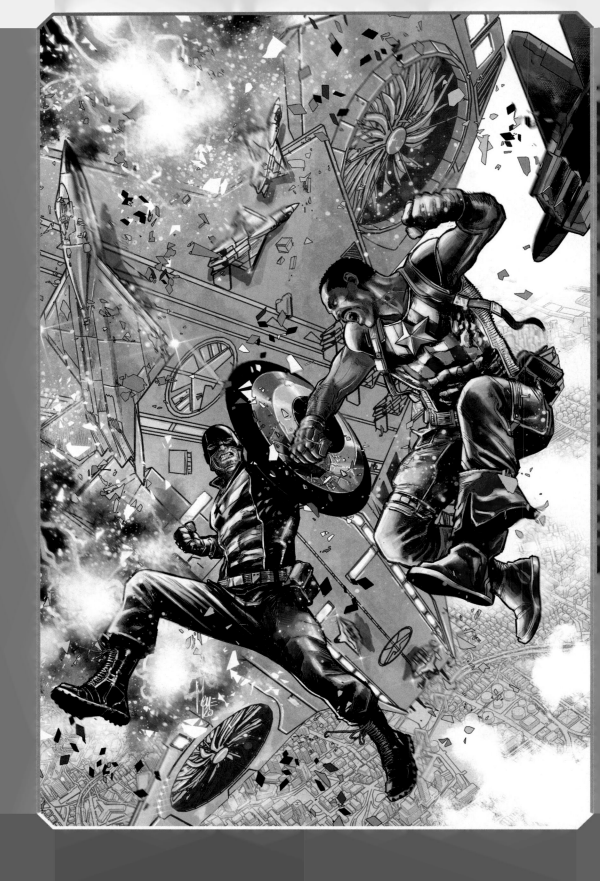

WHAT DOES AMERICA MEAN? HMMM, WELL.

THAT'S A BIG QUESTION.

MEANS A LOT...

STUBBS TATE
FORMER BRAMBLINE CROSS MINING EMPLOYEE

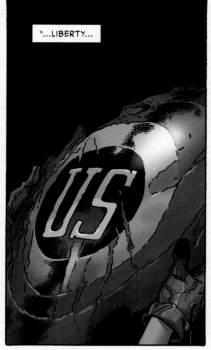

"...LIBERTY...

"Just Us"

EPHRAIM,
WEST VIRGINIA

EARLIER

"...A PLACE WHERE ER'BODY'S GOT A FAIR SHOT...

VRRRRRRRR

"...WHERE ER'BODY'S GOT AN EQUAL *SAY*...

VRRRRRRR

"...AN' WHERE GOOD FOLK *STEP UP* TO DEFEND THE AMERICAN WAY."

LAND OF THE FREE.

HOME OF THE *BRAVE*.

STUBBS TATE
FORMER BRAMBLINE CROSS MINING EMPLOYEE

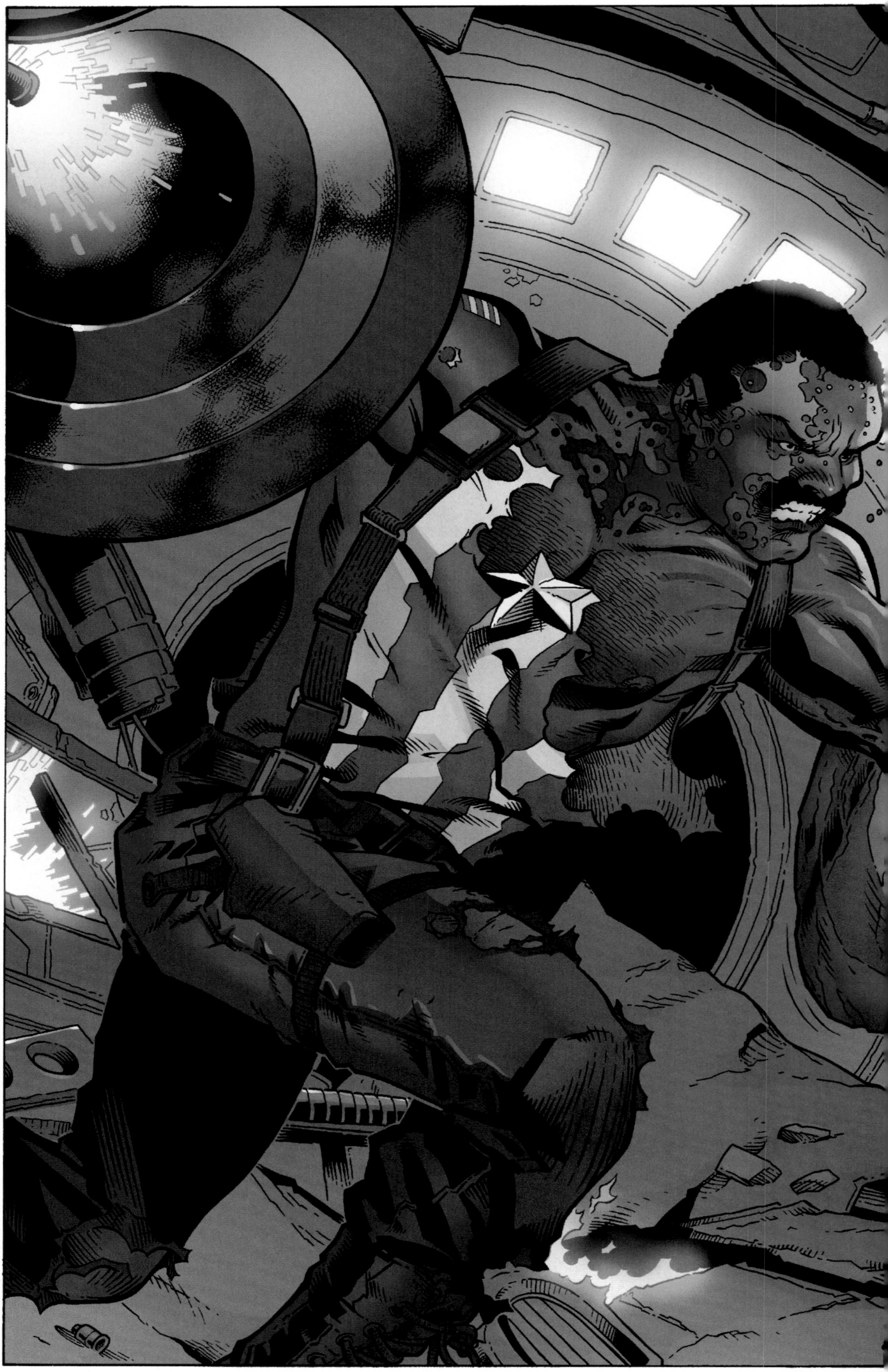

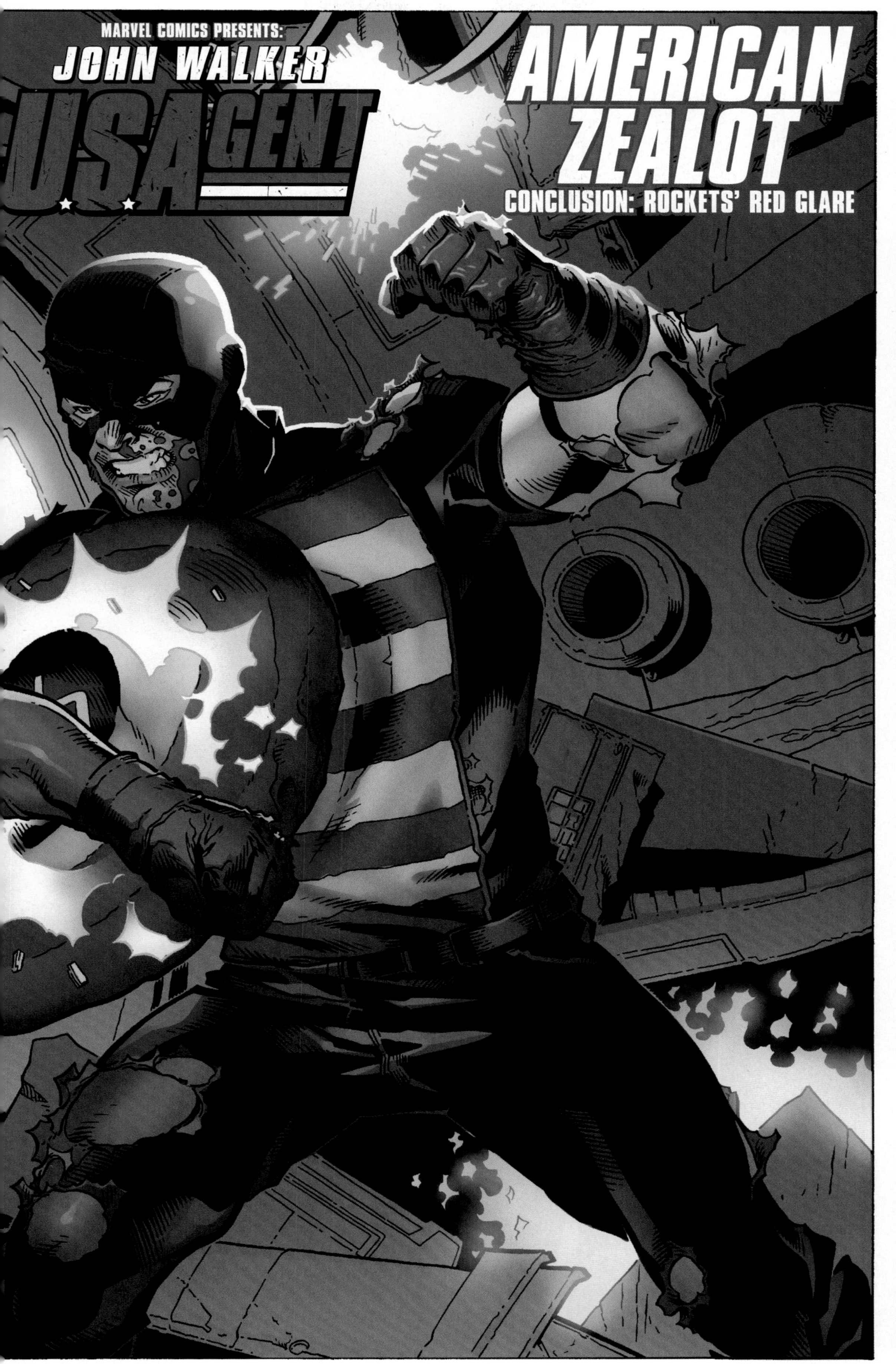
MARVEL COMICS PRESENTS:
JOHN WALKER
U.S.AGENT
AMERICAN ZEALOT
CONCLUSION: ROCKETS' RED GLARE

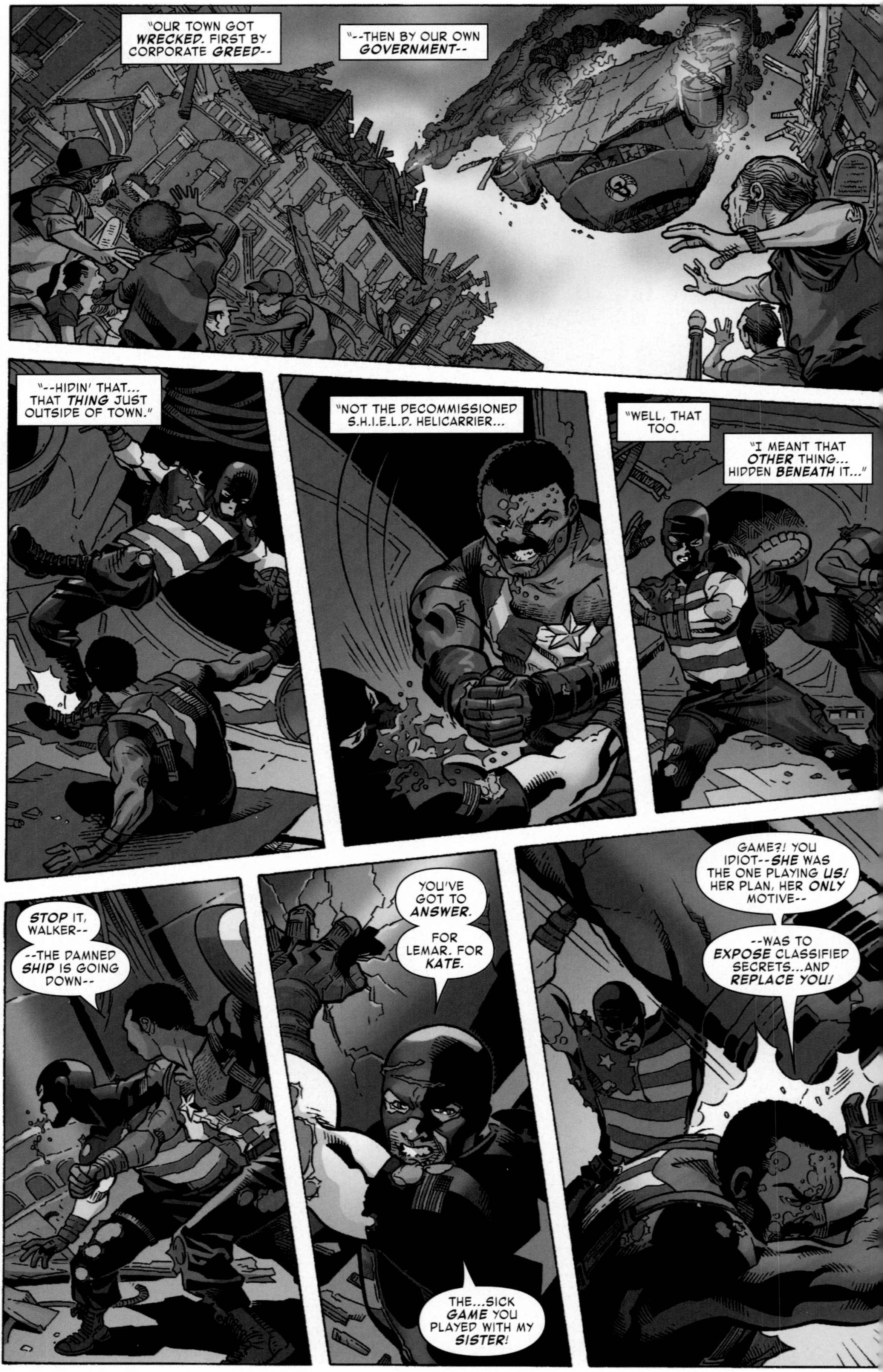
"OUR TOWN GOT WRECKED. FIRST BY CORPORATE GREED--
"--THEN BY OUR OWN GOVERNMENT--
"--HIDIN' THAT... THAT THING JUST OUTSIDE OF TOWN."
"NOT THE DECOMMISSIONED S.H.I.E.L.D. HELICARRIER...
"WELL, THAT TOO.
"I MEANT THAT OTHER THING... HIDDEN BENEATH IT..."
STOP IT, WALKER--
--THE DAMNED SHIP IS GOING DOWN--
YOU'VE GOT TO ANSWER.
FOR LEMAR. FOR KATE.
THE...SICK GAME YOU PLAYED WITH MY SISTER!
GAME?! YOU IDIOT--SHE WAS THE ONE PLAYING US! HER PLAN, HER ONLY MOTIVE--
--WAS TO EXPOSE CLASSIFIED SECRETS...AND REPLACE YOU!

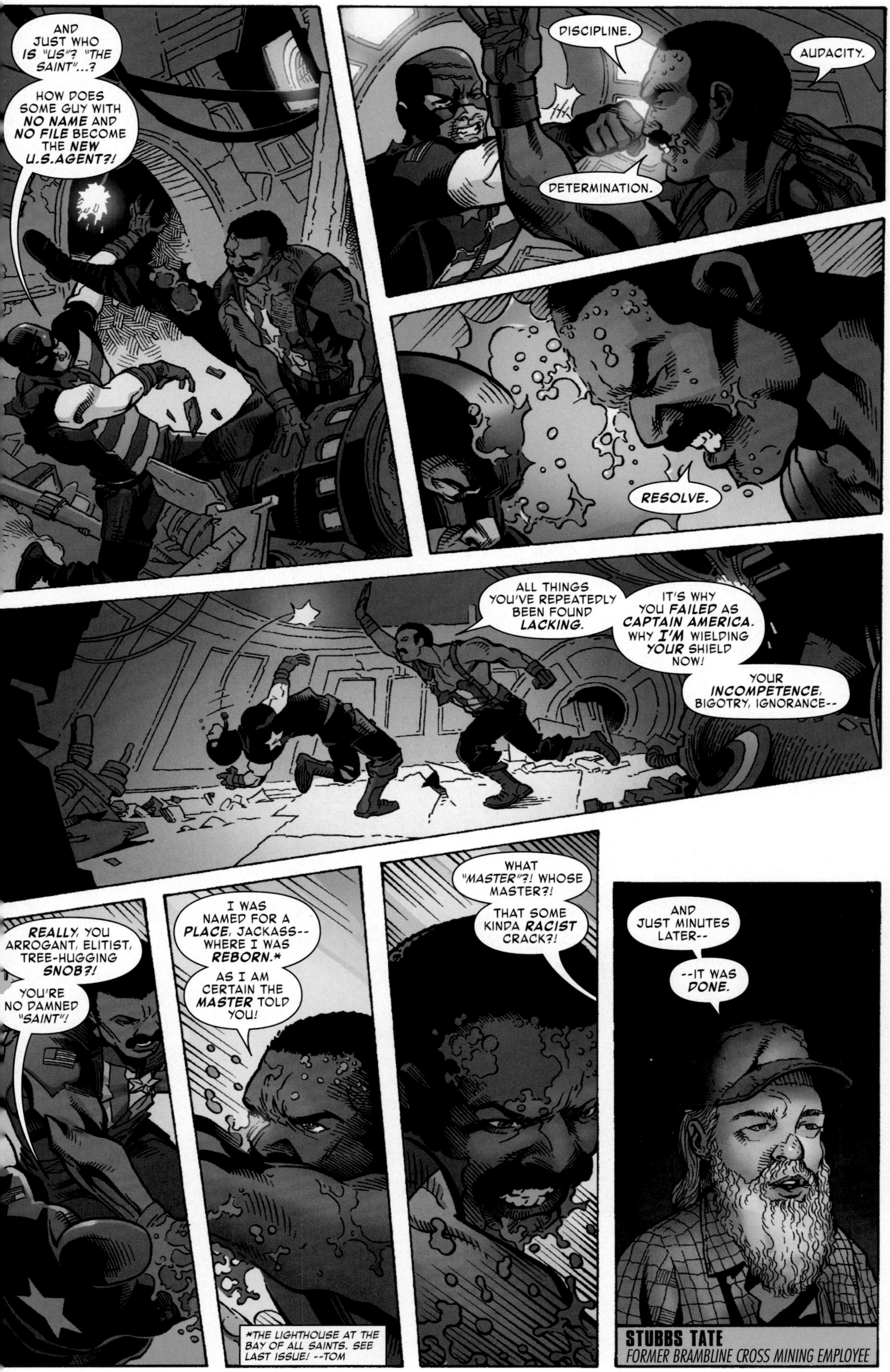
AND JUST WHO IS "US"? "THE SAINT"...?
HOW DOES SOME GUY WITH NO NAME AND NO FILE BECOME THE NEW U.S.AGENT?!
DISCIPLINE.
AUDACITY.
DETERMINATION.
RESOLVE.
ALL THINGS YOU'VE REPEATEDLY BEEN FOUND LACKING.
IT'S WHY YOU FAILED AS CAPTAIN AMERICA. WHY I'M WIELDING YOUR SHIELD NOW!
YOUR INCOMPETENCE, BIGOTRY, IGNORANCE--
REALLY, YOU ARROGANT, ELITIST, TREE-HUGGING SNOB?!
YOU'RE NO DAMNED "SAINT"!
I WAS NAMED FOR A PLACE, JACKASS-- WHERE I WAS REBORN.*
AS I AM CERTAIN THE MASTER TOLD YOU!
*THE LIGHTHOUSE AT THE BAY OF ALL SAINTS. SEE LAST ISSUE! --TOM
WHAT "MASTER"?! WHOSE MASTER?!
THAT SOME KINDA RACIST CRACK?!
AND JUST MINUTES LATER--
--IT WAS DONE.
STUBBS TATE
FORMER BRAMBLINE CROSS MINING EMPLOYEE

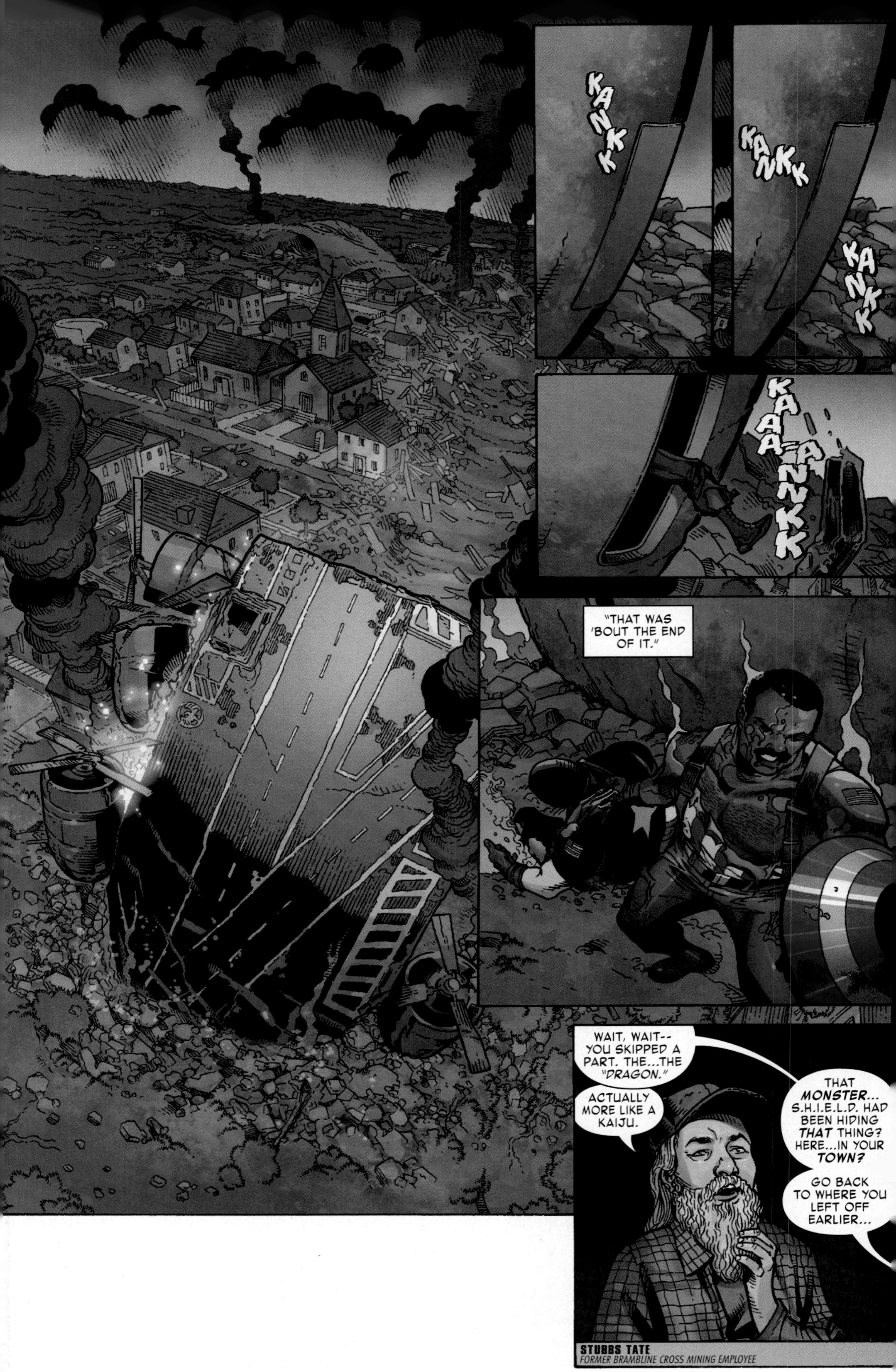
KANKK
KANKK
KANKK
KAAA-ANNKK
"THAT WAS 'BOUT THE END OF IT."
WAIT, WAIT-- YOU SKIPPED A PART. THE...THE "DRAGON."
ACTUALLY MORE LIKE A KAIJU.
THAT MONSTER... S.H.I.E.L.D. HAD BEEN HIDING THAT THING? HERE...IN YOUR TOWN?
GO BACK TO WHERE YOU LEFT OFF EARLIER...
STUBBS TATE
FORMER BRAMBLINE CROSS MINING EMPLOYEE

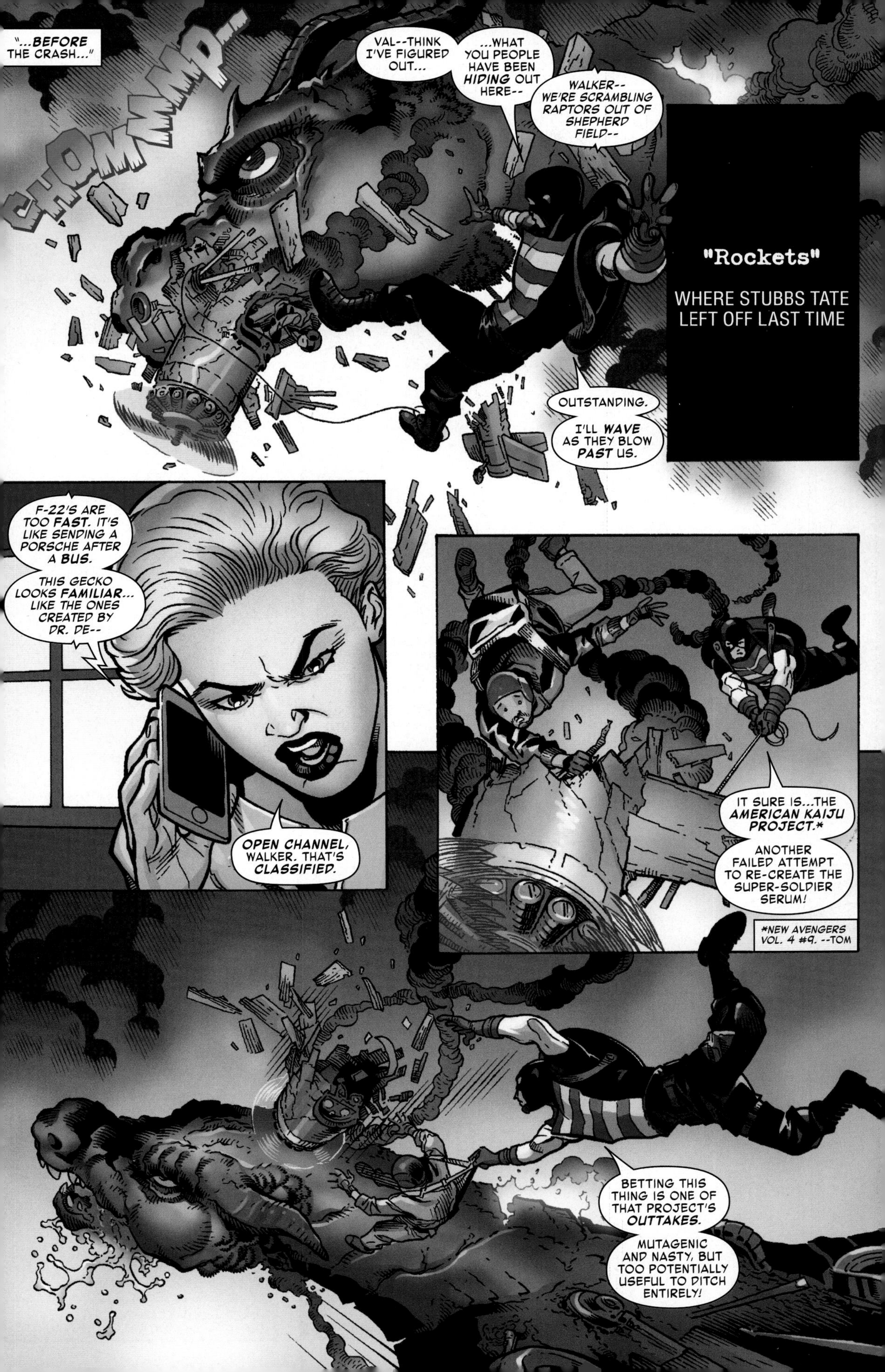
"...BEFORE THE CRASH..."
CHOMMMP
VAL--THINK I'VE FIGURED OUT...
...WHAT YOU PEOPLE HAVE BEEN HIDING OUT HERE--
WALKER-- WE'RE SCRAMBLING RAPTORS OUT OF SHEPHERD FIELD--
"Rockets"
WHERE STUBBS TATE LEFT OFF LAST TIME
OUTSTANDING.
I'LL WAVE AS THEY BLOW PAST US.
F-22'S ARE TOO FAST. IT'S LIKE SENDING A PORSCHE AFTER A BUS.
THIS GECKO LOOKS FAMILIAR... LIKE THE ONES CREATED BY DR. DE--
OPEN CHANNEL, WALKER. THAT'S CLASSIFIED.
IT SURE IS...THE AMERICAN KAIJU PROJECT.*
ANOTHER FAILED ATTEMPT TO RE-CREATE THE SUPER-SOLDIER SERUM!
*NEW AVENGERS VOL. 4 #9. --TOM
BETTING THIS THING IS ONE OF THAT PROJECT'S OUTTAKES.
MUTAGENIC AND NASTY, BUT TOO POTENTIALLY USEFUL TO DITCH ENTIRELY!

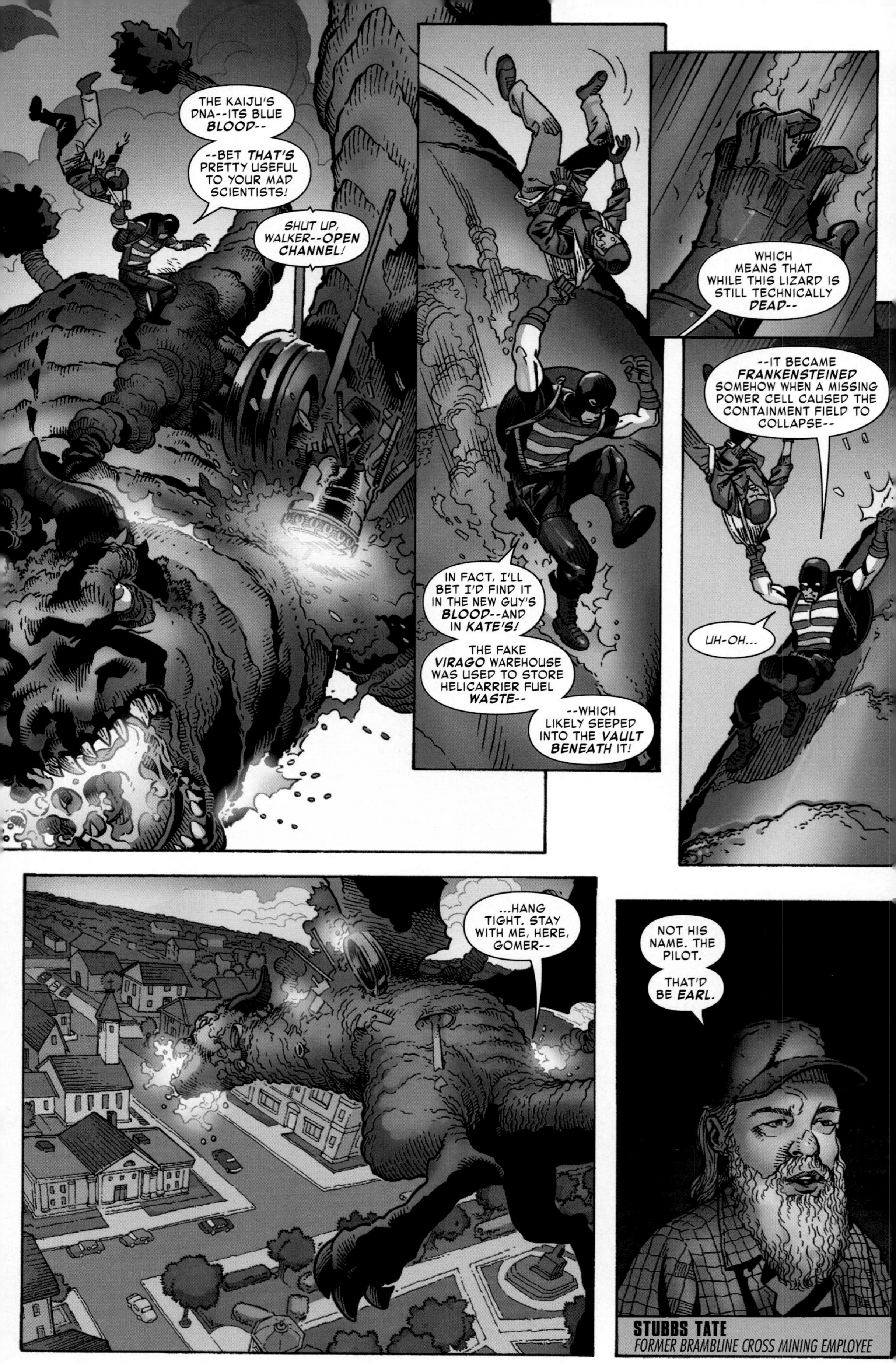
THE KAIJU'S DNA--ITS BLUE BLOOD--
--BET THAT'S PRETTY USEFUL TO YOUR MAD SCIENTISTS!
SHUT UP, WALKER--OPEN CHANNEL!
IN FACT, I'LL BET I'D FIND IT IN THE NEW GUY'S BLOOD--AND IN KATE'S!
THE FAKE VIRAGO WAREHOUSE WAS USED TO STORE HELICARRIER FUEL WASTE--
--WHICH LIKELY SEEPED INTO THE VAULT BENEATH IT!
WHICH MEANS THAT WHILE THIS LIZARD IS STILL TECHNICALLY DEAD--
--IT BECAME FRANKENSTEINED SOMEHOW WHEN A MISSING POWER CELL CAUSED THE CONTAINMENT FIELD TO COLLAPSE--
UH-OH...
...HANG TIGHT. STAY WITH ME, HERE, GOMER--
NOT HIS NAME. THE PILOT.
THAT'D BE EARL.
STUBBS TATE
FORMER BRAMBLINE CROSS MINING EMPLOYEE

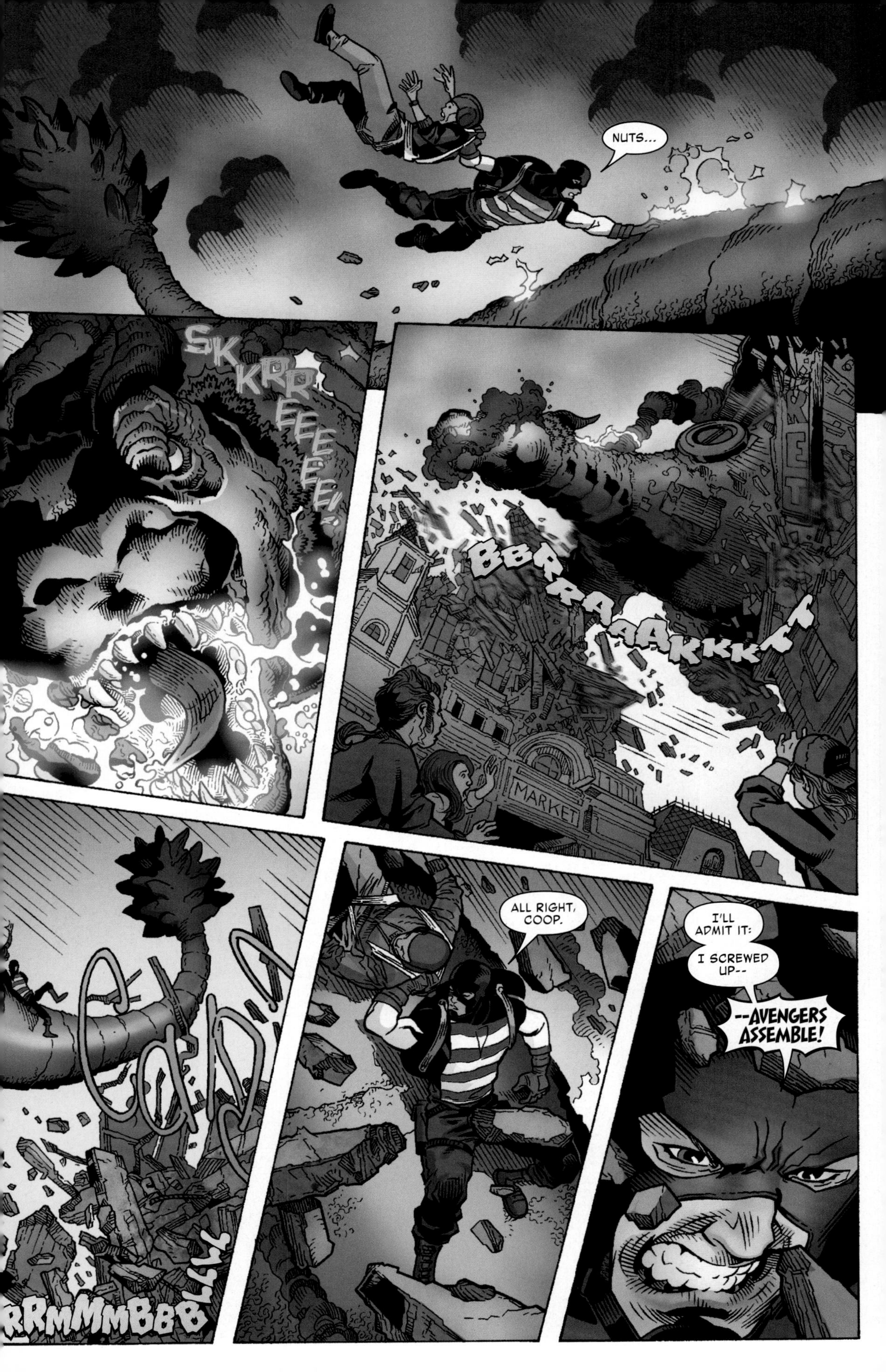
NUTS...
SKKRREEEEEE
BBRRAAAKKKT
RRMMMMBBB
ALL RIGHT, COOP.
I'LL ADMIT IT:
I SCREWED UP--
--AVENGERS ASSEMBLE!

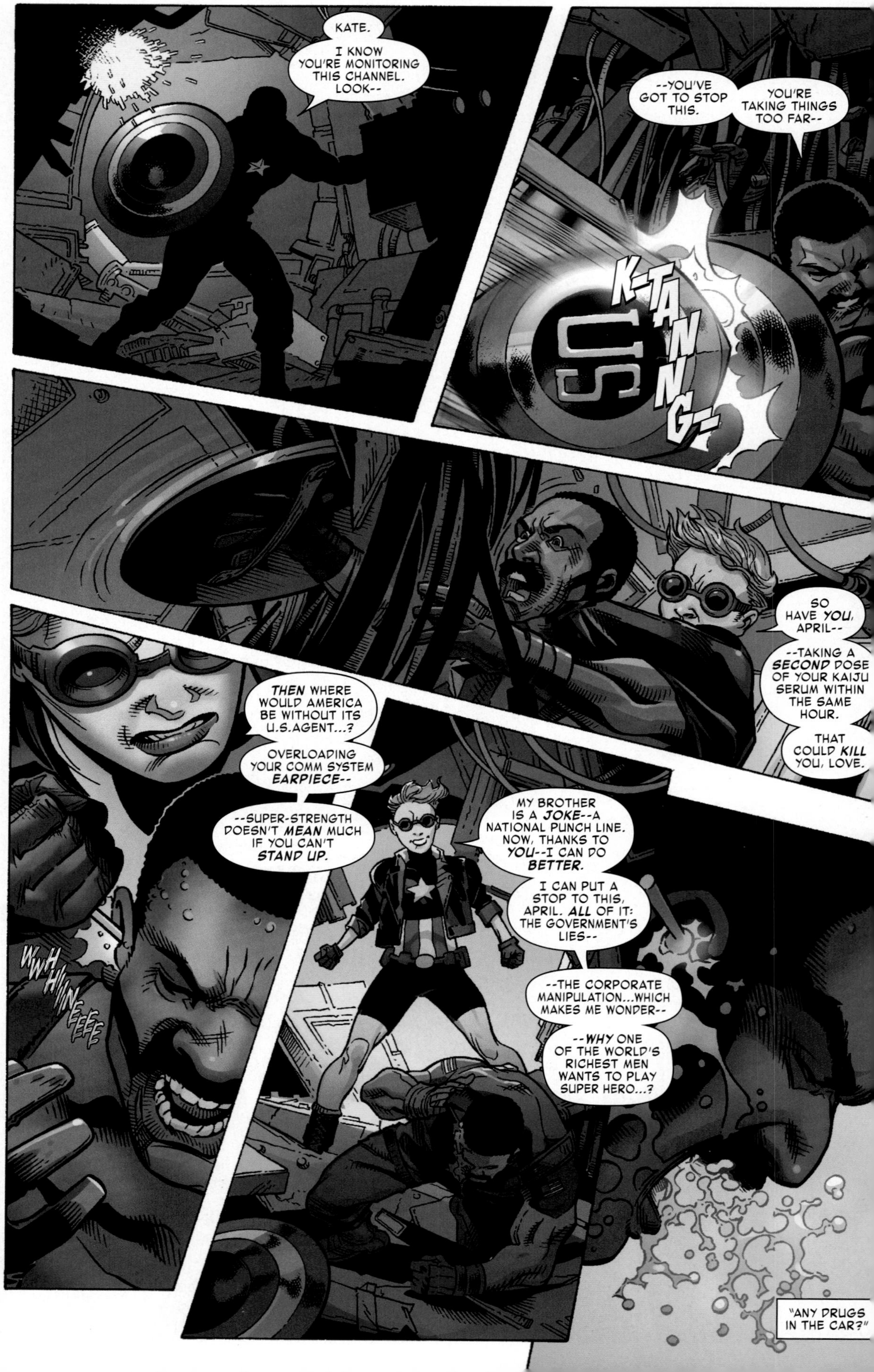
KATE.
I KNOW YOU'RE MONITORING THIS CHANNEL. LOOK--
--YOU'VE GOT TO STOP THIS.
YOU'RE TAKING THINGS TOO FAR--
K-TANNNG--
SO HAVE YOU, APRIL--
--TAKING A SECOND DOSE OF YOUR KAIJU SERUM WITHIN THE SAME HOUR.
THAT COULD KILL YOU, LOVE.
THEN WHERE WOULD AMERICA BE WITHOUT ITS U.S.AGENT...?
OVERLOADING YOUR COMM SYSTEM EARPIECE--
--SUPER-STRENGTH DOESN'T MEAN MUCH IF YOU CAN'T STAND UP.
WWHHIINEEEE
MY BROTHER IS A JOKE--A NATIONAL PUNCH LINE. NOW, THANKS TO YOU--I CAN DO BETTER.
I CAN PUT A STOP TO THIS, APRIL. ALL OF IT: THE GOVERNMENT'S LIES--
--THE CORPORATE MANIPULATION...WHICH MAKES ME WONDER--
--WHY ONE OF THE WORLD'S RICHEST MEN WANTS TO PLAY SUPER HERO...?
"ANY DRUGS IN THE CAR?"

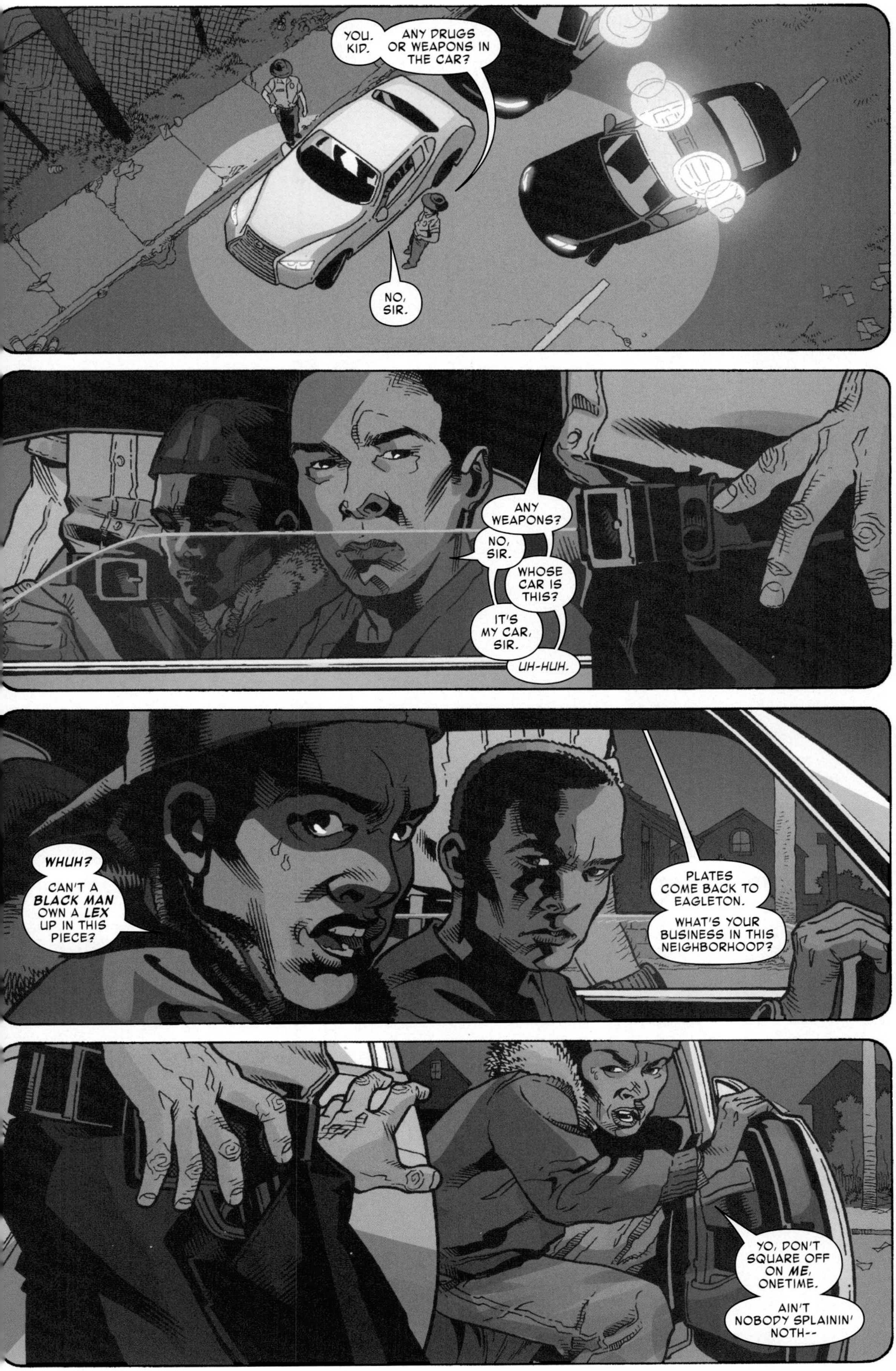
YOU. KID.
ANY DRUGS OR WEAPONS IN THE CAR?
NO, SIR.
ANY WEAPONS?
NO, SIR.
WHOSE CAR IS THIS?
IT'S MY CAR, SIR.
UH-HUH.
WHUH?
CAN'T A BLACK MAN OWN A LEX UP IN THIS PIECE?
PLATES COME BACK TO EAGLETON.
WHAT'S YOUR BUSINESS IN THIS NEIGHBORHOOD?
YO, DON'T SQUARE OFF ON ME, ONETIME.
AIN'T NOBODY SPLAININ' NOTH--

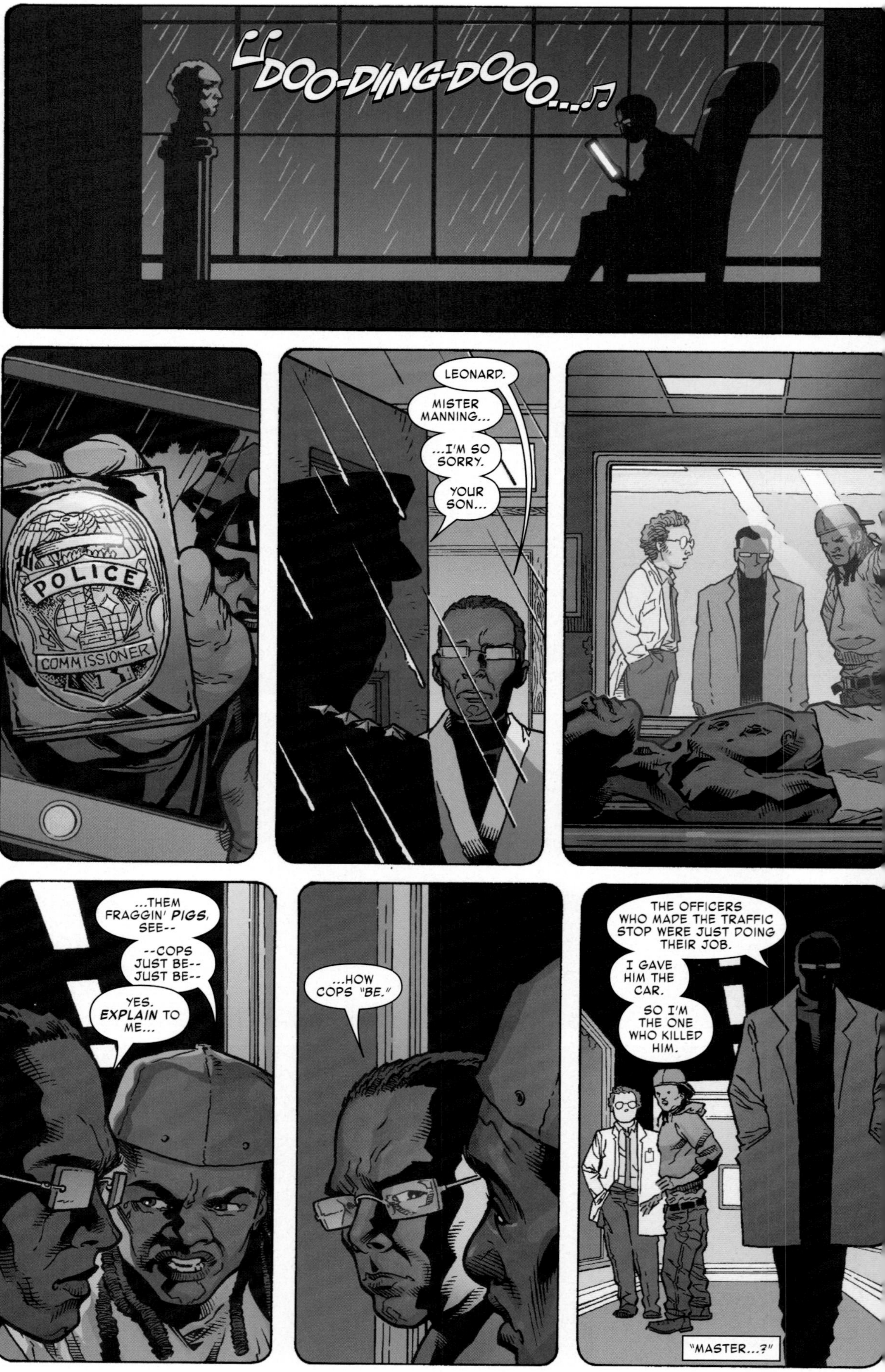
♫DOO-DIING-DOOO...♫
LEONARD.
MISTER MANNING...
...I'M SO SORRY.
YOUR SON...
POLICE
COMMISSIONER
...THEM FRAGGIN' *PIGS*, SEE--
--COPS JUST BE-- JUST BE--
YES. *EXPLAIN* TO ME...
...HOW COPS "*BE*."
THE OFFICERS WHO MADE THE TRAFFIC STOP WERE JUST DOING THEIR JOB.
I GAVE HIM THE CAR.
SO I'M THE ONE WHO KILLED HIM.
"MASTER...?"

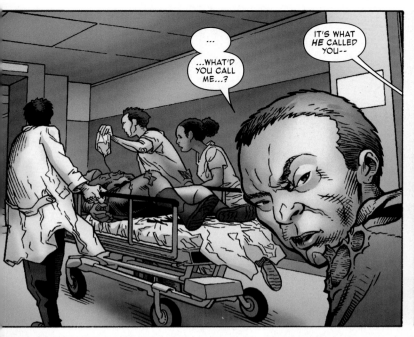
...

...WHAT'D YOU CALL ME...?

IT'S WHAT *HE* CALLED YOU--

--"MASTER."

YOU'RE WITH *HIM*--"ANGARR THE SELF-LOATHING"?

THE AUTO-BIGOT *SENT* FOR ME?

NO--

--I'M JUST HOPING YOU CAN *SAVE* HIM.

WHY WOULD I WANT TO DO THAT?!

IF I'M EVEN INDIRECTLY RESPONSIBLE FOR THAT CRACKPOT...

I SEE HE LEFT HIS *LAUNDRY* ON THE CHAIR.

LITTLE *SMALL* FOR HIM I'D BET...

HE AND YOUR *NEW* PUPIL ARE BOTH BEING MANIPULATED.

WELL, NEWS AT ELEVEN, LADY--WAIT--

--WAIT-- IS THAT...A *DRAGON*...?!

I'M SORRY IT WASN'T *LOVE*, APRIL.

THANKS FOR THE SERUM AND THE *ACCESS*...

...AND FOR YOUR *SERVICE* IN CREATING AMERICA'S NEWEST *SUPER-PATRIOT*--

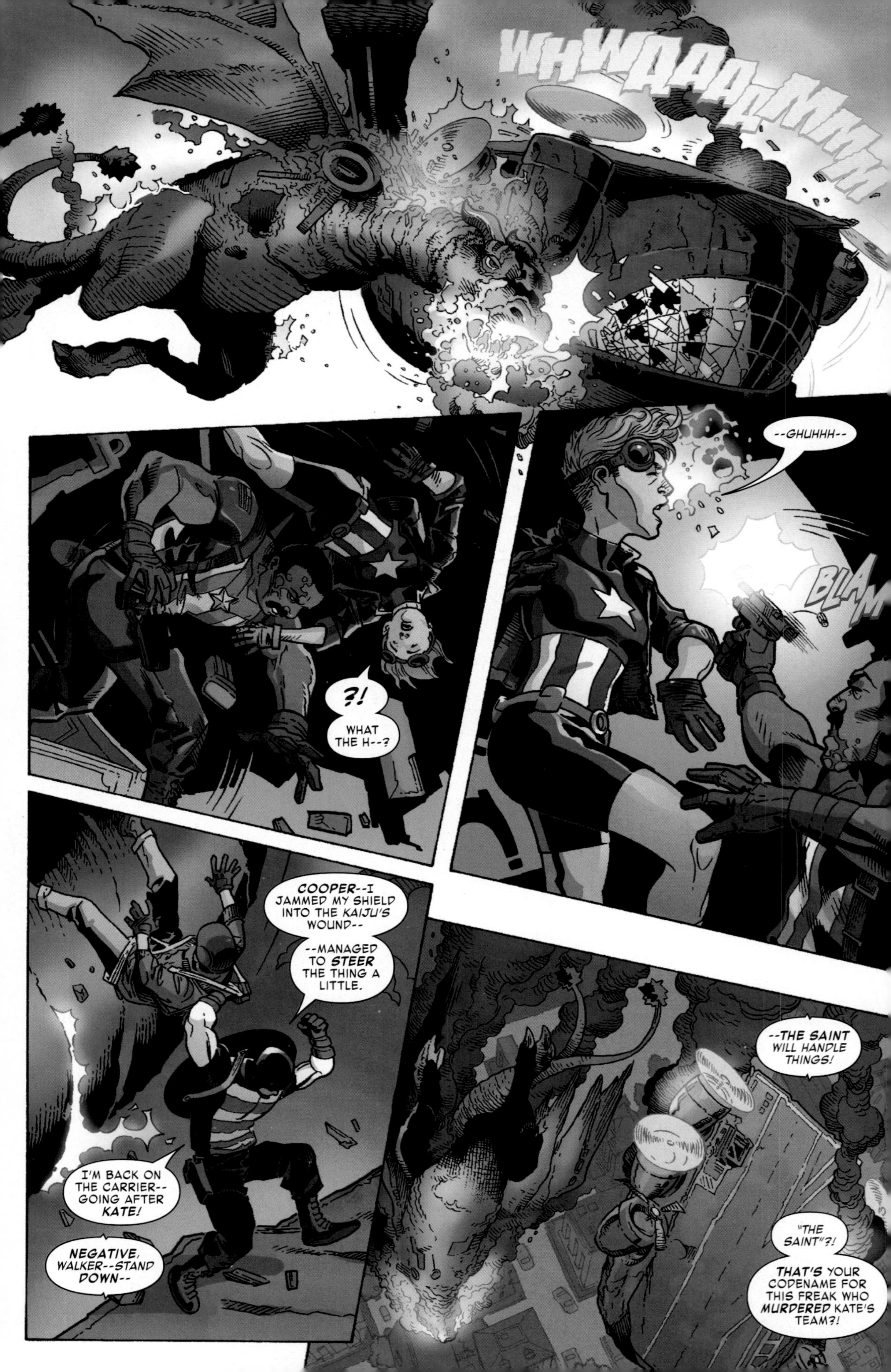
WHWAAAAMMM
?!
WHAT THE H--?
--GHUHHH--
BLAM
COOPER--I JAMMED MY SHIELD INTO THE KAIJU'S WOUND--
--MANAGED TO STEER THE THING A LITTLE.
I'M BACK ON THE CARRIER--GOING AFTER KATE!
NEGATIVE, WALKER--STAND DOWN--
--THE SAINT WILL HANDLE THINGS!
"THE SAINT"?!
THAT'S YOUR CODENAME FOR THIS FREAK WHO MURDERED KATE'S TEAM?!

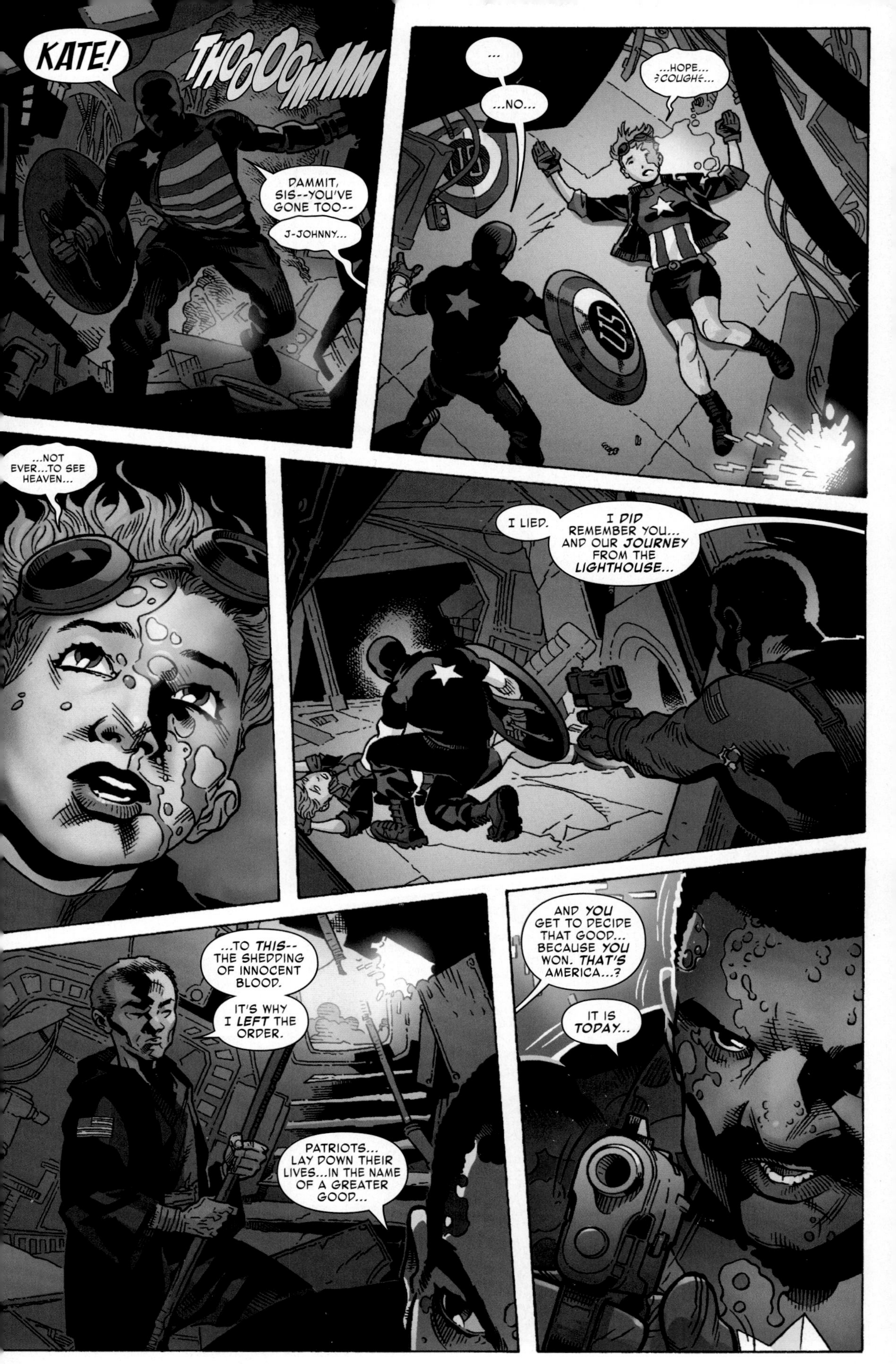

KATE!
THOOOOMMMM
DAMMIT, SIS--YOU'VE GONE TOO--
J-JOHNNY...
...
...NO...
...HOPE... COUGH...
...NOT EVER...TO SEE HEAVEN...
I LIED.
I DID REMEMBER YOU... AND OUR JOURNEY FROM THE LIGHTHOUSE...
...TO THIS-- THE SHEDDING OF INNOCENT BLOOD.
IT'S WHY I LEFT THE ORDER.
PATRIOTS... LAY DOWN THEIR LIVES...IN THE NAME OF A GREATER GOOD...
AND YOU GET TO DECIDE THAT GOOD... BECAUSE YOU WON. THAT'S AMERICA...?
IT IS TODAY...

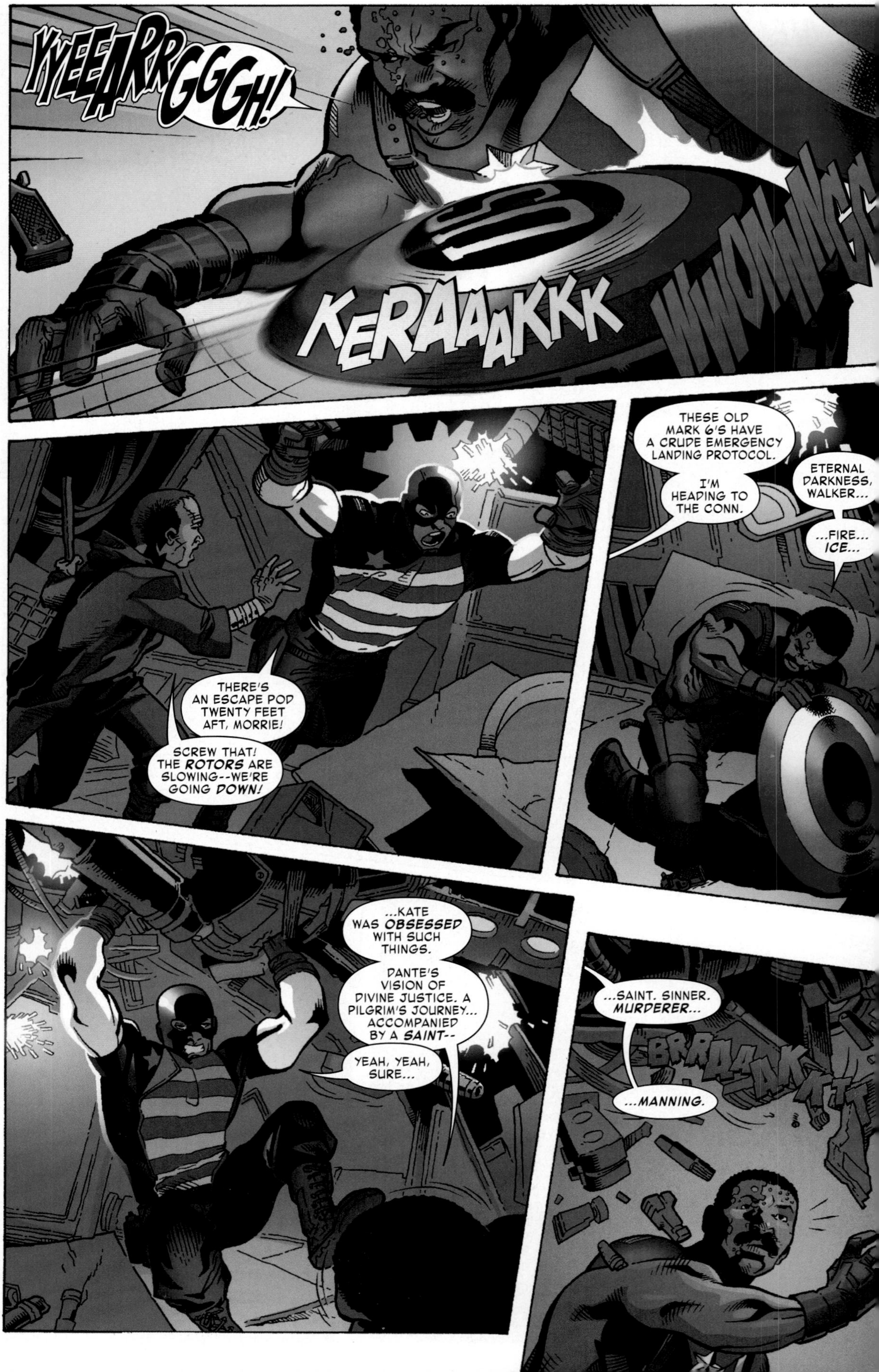
YYEEARRGGGH!
KERAAAKKK
THERE'S AN ESCAPE POD TWENTY FEET AFT, MORRIE!
SCREW THAT! THE ROTORS ARE SLOWING--WE'RE GOING DOWN!
THESE OLD MARK 6'S HAVE A CRUDE EMERGENCY LANDING PROTOCOL.
I'M HEADING TO THE CONN.
ETERNAL DARKNESS, WALKER...
...FIRE... ICE...
...KATE WAS OBSESSED WITH SUCH THINGS.
DANTE'S VISION OF DIVINE JUSTICE. A PILGRIM'S JOURNEY... ACCOMPANIED BY A SAINT--
YEAH, YEAH, SURE...
...SAINT. SINNER. MURDERER...
BRRAAAKKTT
...MANNING.

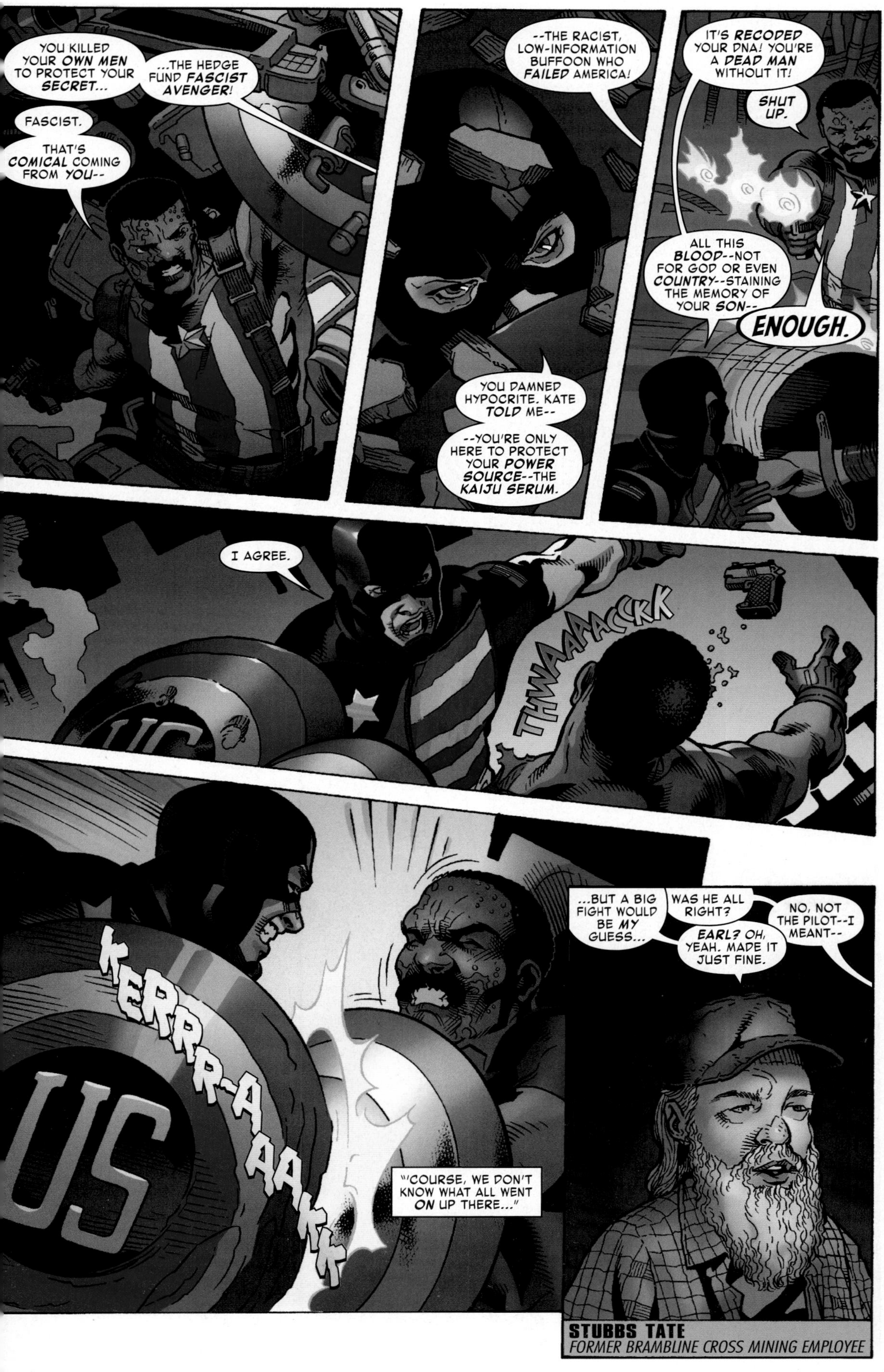
YOU KILLED YOUR OWN MEN TO PROTECT YOUR SECRET...
...THE HEDGE FUND FASCIST AVENGER!
FASCIST.
THAT'S COMICAL COMING FROM YOU--
--THE RACIST, LOW-INFORMATION BUFFOON WHO FAILED AMERICA!
YOU DAMNED HYPOCRITE. KATE TOLD ME--
--YOU'RE ONLY HERE TO PROTECT YOUR POWER SOURCE--THE KAIJU SERUM.
IT'S RECODED YOUR DNA! YOU'RE A DEAD MAN WITHOUT IT!
SHUT UP.
ALL THIS BLOOD--NOT FOR GOD OR EVEN COUNTRY--STAINING THE MEMORY OF YOUR SON--
ENOUGH.
I AGREE.
THWAAAACCKK
KERRR-AAAKKK
"'COURSE, WE DON'T KNOW WHAT ALL WENT ON UP THERE..."
...BUT A BIG FIGHT WOULD BE MY GUESS...
WAS HE ALL RIGHT?
EARL? OH, YEAH. MADE IT JUST FINE.
NO, NOT THE PILOT--I MEANT--
STUBBS TATE
FORMER BRAMBLINE CROSS MINING EMPLOYEE

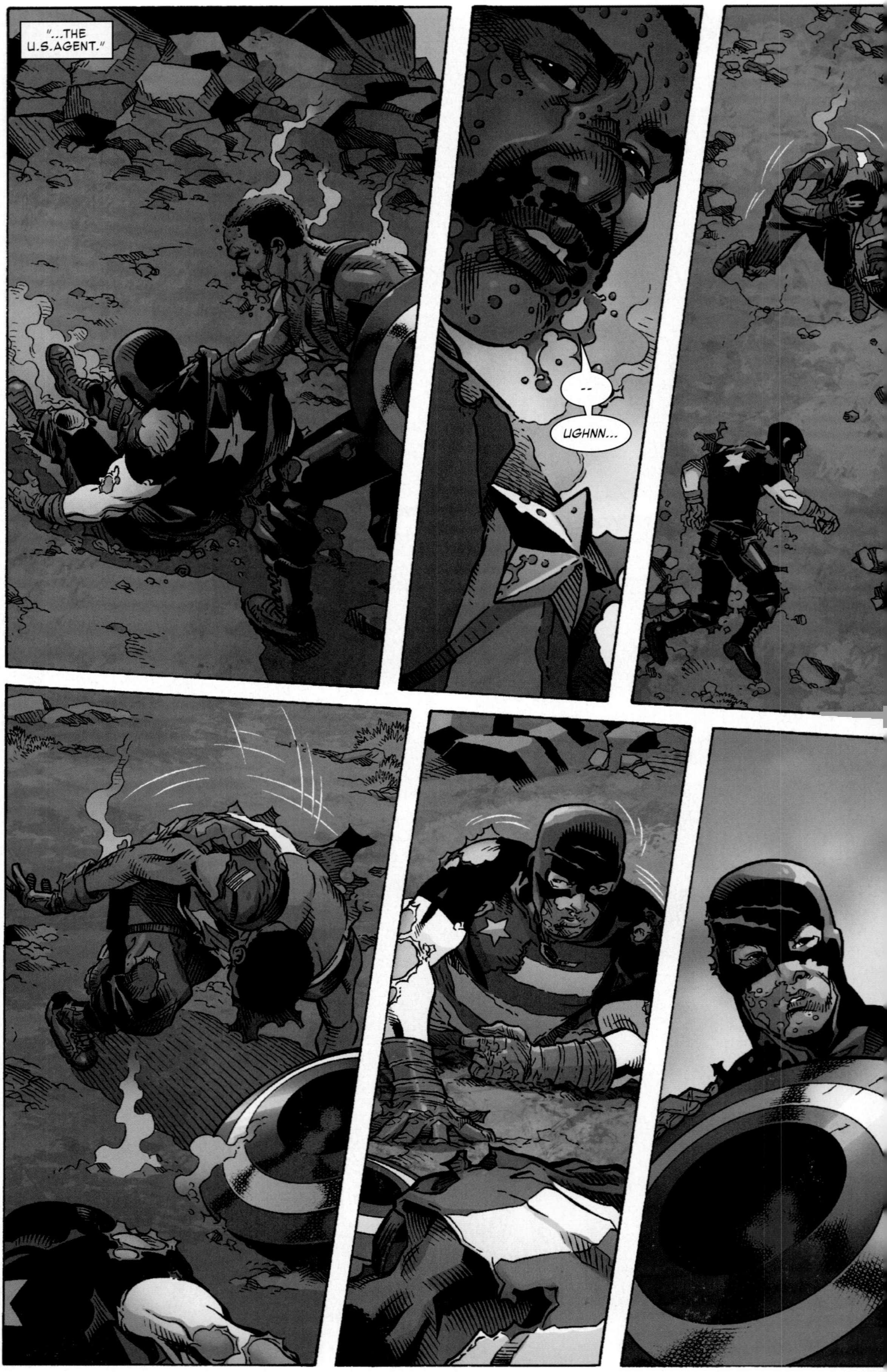
"...THE U.S.AGENT."
--
UGHNN...

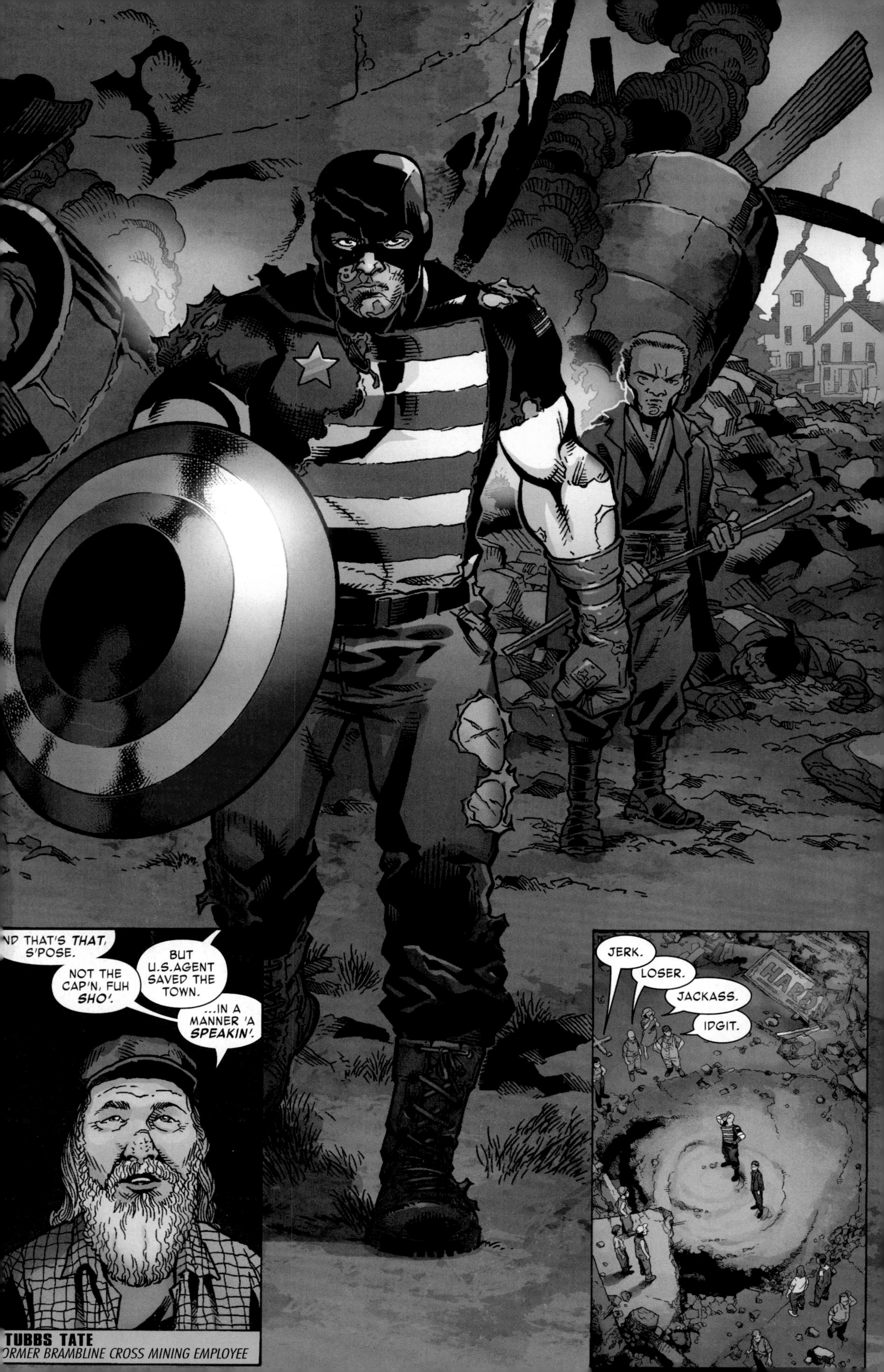

ND THAT'S THAT, S'POSE.
NOT THE CAP'N, FUH SHO'.
BUT U.S.AGENT SAVED THE TOWN.
...IN A MANNER 'A SPEAKIN'.
TUBBS TATE
ORMER BRAMBLINE CROSS MINING EMPLOYEE
JERK.
LOSER.
JACKASS.
IDGIT.

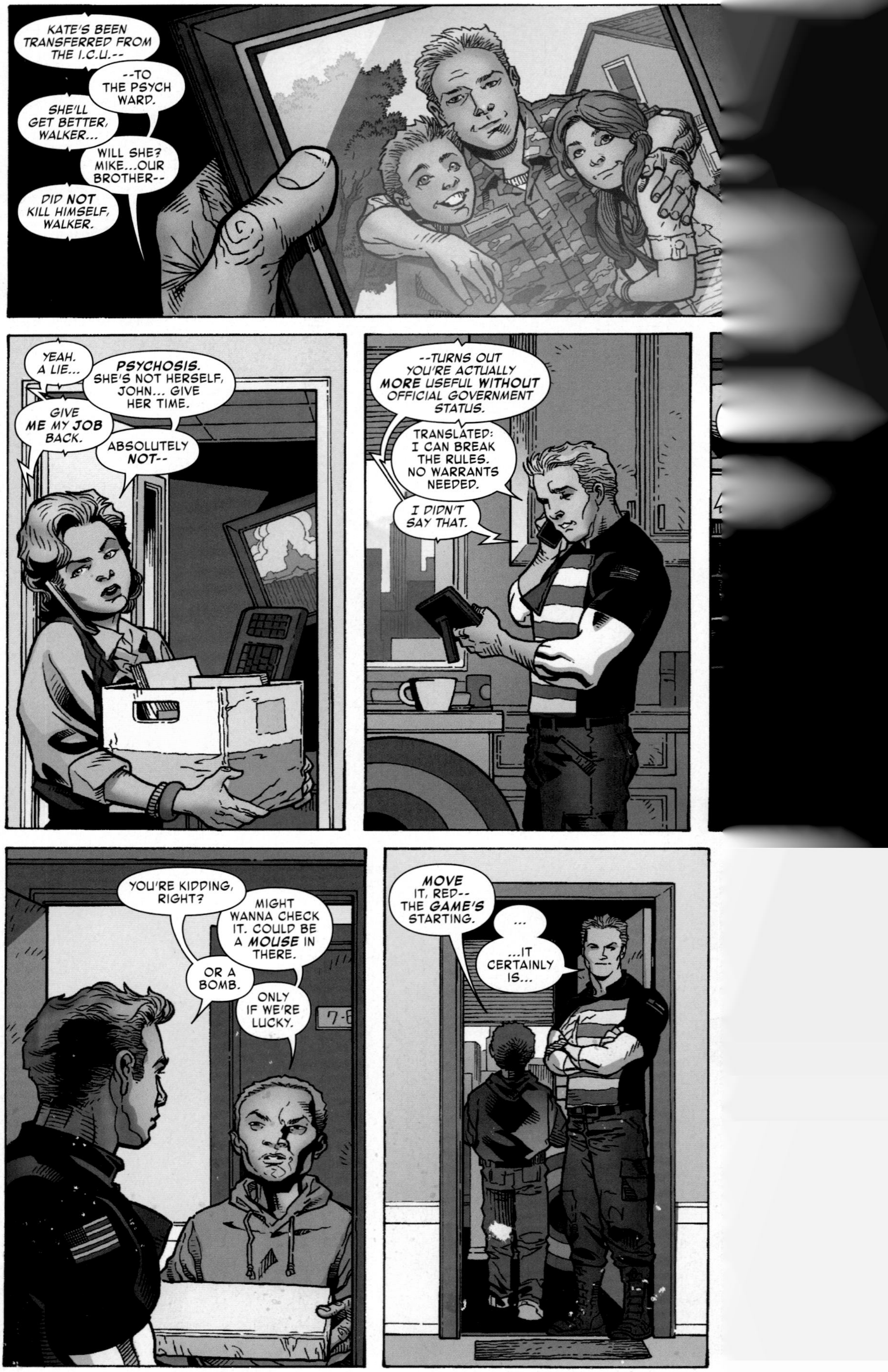
KATE'S BEEN TRANSFERRED FROM THE I.C.U.--
--TO THE PSYCH WARD.
SHE'LL GET BETTER, WALKER...
WILL SHE? MIKE...OUR BROTHER--
DID NOT KILL HIMSELF, WALKER.
YEAH. A LIE...
PSYCHOSIS. SHE'S NOT HERSELF, JOHN... GIVE HER TIME.
GIVE ME MY JOB BACK.
ABSOLUTELY NOT--
--TURNS OUT YOU'RE ACTUALLY MORE USEFUL WITHOUT OFFICIAL GOVERNMENT STATUS.
TRANSLATED: I CAN BREAK THE RULES. NO WARRANTS NEEDED.
I DIDN'T SAY THAT.
YOU'RE KIDDING, RIGHT?
MIGHT WANNA CHECK IT. COULD BE A MOUSE IN THERE.
OR A BOMB.
ONLY IF WE'RE LUCKY.
MOVE IT, RED-- THE GAME'S STARTING.
...
...IT CERTAINLY IS...